FROM RUSSIAN INTO ENGLISH

AN INTRODUCTION TO SIMULTANEOUS INTERPRETATION

Second Edition

FROM RUSSIAN INTO ENGLISH

AN INTRODUCTION TO SIMULTANEOUS INTERPRETATION

Second Edition

LYNN VISSON

Focus Publishing
R. Pullins and Company
Newburyport MA

FOCUS TEXTS IN RUSSIAN LANGUAGE STUDY

From Russian into English: An Introduction to Simultaneous Interpretation, 2e • Lynn Visson • 1999

START: An Introduction to the Sound and Writing Systems of Russian • Benjamin Rifkin • 1998

Listening to Okudzhava: Oral Comprehension Exercises in Russian • Vladmir Tumanov • 1996

Handbook of Russian Prepositions • Frank Miller • 1991

Reading and Speaking About Russian Newspapers, 3e • M. Kasper, V. Lebedeva, F. Miller • 1995

Advanced Russian Language Study Modules I -XII • Galina McLaws • 1995

An Overview of Russian Cases • Galina McLaws • 1995

Handbook of Russian Verb Morphology • Galina McLaws • 1995

Russian Fairy Tales: A Russian Language Reader • Jason Merrill • Forthcoming 1999

Copyright © 1999 Lynn Visson

ISBN 0-941051-88-9

Printed in the United States of America
10 9 8 7 6 5 4 3 2 1

Мы переводим стрелки часов, переводим поезда с одного пути на другой, переводим по почте или телеграфу деньги. Кстати, и само слово "перевод" – переводное.

С. Маршак

ACKNOWLEDGMENTS

Interpretation is a collective undertaking, a profession based on teamwork. Working together, listening to each other, helping each other and learning from each other, interpreters discuss words, idioms, sentences and syntax. A phrase may be picked up from one colleague, a translation of a proverb from another, a way of rendering an idiom from a third. Hastily scribbled down lexical items and syntactic devices find their way into the huge luggage of language which the interpreter uses every day. Since fifty professional interpreters faced with the same Russian-English interpretation problem will probably come up with no more than five or six reasonable solutions, it is extremely difficult in a work of this sort to give full credit where credit might be due. With the best will in the world most interpreters would find it hard to identify the original source of a specific expression they use over and over. Some interpreters who firmly believe that a certain way of translating a particular phrase is their unique personal discovery might be surprised to find that identical language was being utilized by their colleagues twenty or thirty years ago. The literature of interpretation reveals that, slowly but surely, we all make the same discoveries.

Several people and organizations, however, deserve special thanks. The author is most grateful to many colleagues in the English and Russian booths of the Interpretation Service of the United Nations, the Language Services of the US Department of State, and free-lance interpreters, and apologizes for the impossibility of singling out all these individuals. Particular thanks go to the Kennan Institute for Advanced Russian Studies in Washington, DC and to the International Research and Exchanges Board for research grants for work in Washington and Moscow. I also would like to thank Mr. Dmitry Zarechnak and Cyril Muromcew (retired) of the US Department of State, Maureen Cote, Dr. Frank Miller of the Department of Slavic Languages of Columbia University, Leonora Chernyakhovskaya, Director of the Moscow International School for Translation and Interpreting, Gelii Chernov, Natalya Strelkova, and Mark Slay, for their valuable advice and assistance. Ellendea Proffer and Mary Ann Szporluk of Ardis supported the original project, and Ron Pullins at Focus made this edition a reality.

CONTENTS

PART II. SELECTED PRACTICE TEXTS AND VOCABULARY

PREFACE

Interpretation has become a vitally important field in a world where Russian-American communication has become a daily fact of life. Since the collapse of the Soviet Union there has been a huge expansion of business contacts between the two countries, and with the lifting of travel restrictions hundreds of public and private organizations in all fields are sending delegations back and forth on a regular basis. Individual travel, too, is on the rise. While many American students are studying Russian, very few are receiving training as interpreters or even giving thought to interpretation as a fascinating and rewarding profession. Hardly any training materials or texts are available in the US.

The second, revised edition of this book is intended to assist students of interpretation and individuals involved in Russian-American contacts in coping with some of the lexical, syntactical and cultural problems of Russian-English interpretation. Part I deals with practical problems of vocabulary, grammar, syntax, idiom, style, delivery, and conference terminology. Part II includes short practice texts, specialized vocabulary, and common phrases useful in escorting delegations, planning schedules, making toasts, etc. These vocabulary aids are not intended as exhaustive listings; rather, they are examples of terms which pop up regularly at conferences and in work with delegations and may be unfamiliar or confusing to students of Russian.

The fall of the Soviet Union opened the linguistic floodgates. The Russian language has undergone enormous changes, for the last decade has seen the creation of a huge vocabulary required to cover the terminology of international banking, computer technology, and non-governmental organizations, especially those dealing with issues such as women or religion. There has been an enormous influence of English on Russian, especially in such international fields as finance or computer science, while the old Marxist clichés and political prose studded with sentences creaking under the burden of three of four lengthy subordinate clauses have been fading away. The Russian print media, radio and television are rediscovering and recreating the language at a dizzying pace.

Since both the Russian used by the mass media and the language spoken by delegates at international conferences is far more colloquial than the stiff, stylized jargon of the Soviet period, and since spoken Russian has undergone amazing expansion and transformation since *perestroika*, the English-language interpreter can no longer complacently rely on an array of translations of well-known clichés. Ten years ago a well-trained monkey or robot armed with a vocabulary of some 2000 words and a file of Marxist fixed expressions could have coped with most of the formal Russian statements made at international meetings. These texts were frequently so predictable that the interpreter could safely risk translating a sentence well before the speaker had ended the Russian phrase. The vastly more colorful and colloquial statements written by today's Russian speech writers and delivered by more relaxed, younger delegates have put the monkeys and robots out of business, and are making far greater demands on the interpreter. The Russian spoken in public today has truly become a spoken language, rather than the written language read out loud by speakers in the past.

The interpreter must now be prepared for the newly minted words, conversational phrases, slang expressions, names of new governmental and nongovernmental organizations, borrowings from English and terms for modern concepts which have replaced stodgy Marxist language. The cooling of cold war passions led to the replacement of a vocabulary of "battling," "struggling," and "opposing" by a lexicon of "cooperation" and "promoting and advancing." The universalism imposed by the globalization of international finance, business, the telecommunications-computer revolution and advertising have transformed languages around the world, and Russian is no exception. As new terms are created and old ones eliminated Russian roots and English borrowings are competing for the "survival of the fittest." Компьютер won the day over ЭВМ, but Russian created its own word, "автоответчик," for answering machine. The interpreter must be constantly alert for concepts which can be expressed by means of several words vying for a permanent lexical niche. While it is impossible to include exhaustive glossaries in a book of this length, selected vocabulary from the newly important fields of finance, law, computers, religion, and women's issues have been included here, as well as the new titles of Russian government organizations which have replaced the one-Party system.

The second edition of *From Russian into English* can serve as a supplement to grammars and readers and as an introduction to problems of stylistics, translation, and interpretation in third and fourth-year college Russian courses. Since the book is intended for advanced students, stress marks have been provided selectively in the vocabulary section. The student interpreter should, of course, work with tapes, which for practical reasons cannot be included in a book of this type.

More than ever, there is a need today for trained, professional interpreters, native speakers of English who can keep up with the times and cope with the rapidly developing language of post-Soviet Russia. It is to the students of today, the interpreters of tomorrow, that this book is dedicated.

INTRODUCTION

Interpreters have the dubious honor of belonging to one of the world's oldest professions, for after that brief time when "the whole earth was of one language" (Gen.11:1) the Tower of Babel abruptly launched the careers of generations of interpreters. Communication is the key to understanding among nations, for when there is literally no comprehension of what the other side is saying there can be no meaningful contact. Nowhere in today's world is communication more vital than in the relationship between the major powers.

A leading Russian expert in the field of translation and interpretation, V.N. Komissarov, has noted that

> Большую потребность в переводах и переводчиках вызовет дальнейшее распространение международных контактов, обмена в области культуры, спорта, туризма, проведение различных международных форумов, встреч и переговоров, не говоря уже о представительстве нашей страны в многочисленных международных организациях, правительственных и неправительственных.[1]

For the non-Russian-speaking American communication means interpretation, since it is through interpreters that meetings are held, business is conducted, treaties are signed and individual Russians and Americans get to know each other. Though following the end of the cold war these contacts mushroomed, surprisingly few people engaged in international contacts genuinely understand what is involved in interpretation.

"By the way, here's our translator." These are the first words many simultaneous interpreters hear on arriving at a meeting. Interpreters and translators, though, are two very different animals and an interpreter does not like being called a translator any more than a cardiologist likes being called a dermatologist. While a general definition of translation can cover the work of both groups: "the transformation of a verbal product in one language into a verbal product in another language while keeping the content invariant,"[2] there is a major difference between the work of translators and interpreters.* A translator works from written materials, putting a text written in the source language (the language *from* which he translates) into the target language (the language *into* which he translates).** His work requires the "formal, prepared and written conversion of a text into another language."[3]

While working on a text the translator can consult colleagues, dictionaries, and other reference tools. He can rewrite and edit, add and delete sentences and phrases, pause to choose a more appropriate word, strike out a comma or restructure an entire sentence. The interpreter (whom most Americans insist on calling a translator) interprets oral statements made in one language into oral statements in another output in a second language, and a third person listens."[4] The interpreter's work is essentially that of the "oral conversion of a message from one language to another."[5] He has no time to consult reference works or colleagues; he must react immediately to what he hears.[6]

The differences between the work of the translator and interpreter have been neatly summarized by a Canadian interpreter, Brian Harris:

Translating	Interpreting
1. The text was produced at some time in the past.	1. The utterance is in process here and now.
2. The text is therefore a finished product; it is static, unalterable.	2. The utterance is still being developed: it is in a dynamic state and its continuation largely unpredictable.
3. The text can be examined back and forth, put aside and reexamined.	3. The utterance undergoes "rapid fading" except insofar as the interpreter can remember it.
4. The text is virtually all verbal...nor does the translator witness the circumstances in which it was composed.	4. The verbal utterance is enriched with gesture and other forms of body language, and the interpreter is in immediate contact with the circumstances and surroundings in which it is being delivered.
5. The majority of texts are the product of a single author: the translator then 'interlocks' his thinking and his writing style with those of one author at a time.	5. The interpreter has to 'interlock' with several people in the same meeting, often with rapid switches between them.
6. Because of its author's remoteness, even an emotional text rarely has the impact of a speech on its audience or on its translator.	6. The interpreter is not merely *aware* of the tension and excitements of a meeting; he is often *subject* to them.
7. Translations can be drafted, revised, criticized and edited before publication.	7. The interpreter must get his version right the first time.
8. The translator may be as remote from his readers as from his author... He does not know as a rule who his readers are. Author and reader are not in touch with one another except through the text and its translation. The separation is in time as well as in space, and it may be a wide one.	8. The interpretation is addressed to a known group of listeners... Speaker and listener are participants in the same meeting, in the same room at the same time.[7]

Most important of all, perhaps, is the difference in fidelity to the original: "Fidelity... in current professional translation practice... means above all fidelity to the author's stated text; while in interpretation it means above all fidelity to the speaker's communicative intent."[8]

Though the professions of translator and interpreter both require an excellent knowledge of the working languages, they demand very different skills. Personality factors, too, play a role. A cautious, methodical individual who likes to edit and polish may make an excellent translator, while an interpreter who continually pauses to correct or change his product will produce a rather poor interpretation. A skilled translator may turn out six to eight pages of beautifully rendered text in a single day. An interpreter may have to rattle off the same number of pages in fifteen minutes. Given the differences in the nature of their work, it is hardly surprising, as one scholar has noted, that "a highly experienced translator only rarely succeeds in interpretation. An excellent interpreter does not necessarily make a good translator."[9] The one ponders in private; the other performs in public. In international organizations such as the United Nations a number of translators have become interpreters, preferring the lively and pressured booth work, immediate contact with delegates, and working with speeches and conversation to sitting alone in a musty cubicle translating draft resolutions and dull committee reports. Interpreters' hours at meetings and conferences are generally shorter than those of translators. Aside from individuals suddenly stricken by handicaps such as deafness or stuttering, or whose reflexes are slowing as a result of aging or illness, cases of interpreters becoming translators are fairly rare.

There are basically two types of interpretation, simultaneous and consecutive. In consecutive the interpreter takes notes while listening to the speaker. When the orator pauses after a few sentences or paragraphs the interpreter, relying on his notes and memory, reads out a translation in the target language.[10] (Unless otherwise specified, "translate" and "interpret" will both be used here to mean oral interpretation.) The simultaneous interpreter does not wait for the speaker to pause. As the word implies, he interprets simultaneously while the orator is speaking, and within a few split seconds must render the speaker's words, tone, meaning, nuances and intonation.[11]

Today consecutive interpretation is used at a limited number of conferences, disarmament negotiations, and for toasts at formal dinners. It was required at the United Nations until 1951 when the shift was made to simultaneous interpretation, and until 1970 was used in the Security Council. Because simultaneous interpretation saves an enormous amount of time and provides an immediacy of tone, intonation, and emphasis often lost in consecutive, it is now used at most international, governmental, public and private conferences.

Both types of interpretation have their advocates. Champions of consecutive feel that the note-taking process and additional time available to the interpreter make it more exact but also more difficult, since the interpreter must make a greater effort in recalling, structuring and presenting his material. Consecutive allows for closer contact with the audience, as the interpreter usually sits near the speaker rather than in a remote glass booth. It also provides more time for the speaker to ponder his next move while he is being interpreted. Yet consecutive is extremely time-consuming, and since more time elapses between the original utterance and its rendering in translation there are consequently also more possibilities for omissions and errors. Though traditionally consecutive has been used at summit meetings of heads of state, to save time simultaneous interpretation was first used at the 1985 Reagan-Gorbachev Geneva summit. The former president's son, Ron Reagan, misinterpreted this as "a victory for the Americans: the Soviets preferred to slow things down by translating only after someone had finished speaking."[12] Though certain lexical and syntactic problems confront both simultaneous and consecutive interpreters, this book will deal solely with simultaneous interpretation, as analysis of Russian-English consecutive would require a study of note-taking systems which considerations of space do not permit.

Though many interpreters who work at conferences do both simultaneous and consecutive, the term "conference interpreter" is usually applied to a simultaneous interpreter. "Escort interpreting" refers to work in informal situations: conversation around a table, shopping, dining out, etc. In Russian such interpreters are known as "линейные переводчики," while simultaneous conference interpreters are "синхронные переводчики" or "синхронисты." With the expansion of Russian-American contacts and a large number of visits by small delegations, the need for interpreters who can act both as conference interpreter and as an escort—working both into English and into Russian—is growing. The interpreter may be required to translate at negotiations and at meals and also to go shopping or sightseeing with the visitors, and in such cases his active knowledge of spoken Russian is obviously extremely important.

In Russia, translators and interpreters have always enjoyed relatively high prestige. In the closed society of the Soviet Union native speakers of foreign languages were few and far between, and a good knowledge of English or French was a passport to a good job and to possibilities for travel abroad. Knowledge of a foreign language was also a key to knowledge of the West, while knowledge of Russian did not provide similar benefits to Westerners who studied the language. People with a good knowledge of foreign languages were also needed for propaganda purposes, to spread the gospel of revolution abroad. And a language could be a good and safe escape from politically risky careers; translating medieval or eighteenth-century English or French poetry or plays was unlikely to lead to clashes with the authorities.

Yet, despite the obvious need for skilled translators and interpreters, these professions have not been taken very seriously in the US. "The rising appeal of translation has not won any new respect for translators in America," states an article in the *New York Times*. "Translation is regarded as a profession overseas and has a much higher standing than in this country."[13] One observer noted that in the US the interpreter/translator is seen as a "rather low-status individual. The image is of a middle-aged person in a shabby jacket who speaks English with a noticeable accent, and who is probably an immigrant to the United States."[14] Unlike Europe and Asia, America has never understood the critical role of the interpreter in communication among nations and their leaders. To cite only a few of hundreds of disastrous examples, former President Nixon did not take an interpreter to his first meeting with Brezhnev in 1972, leaving the American side dependent on the record of the meeting written up by the Soviet interpreter.[15] After a US interpreter garbled President Carter's remarks in Poland, making the President state that he had "abandoned" rather than "left" the US and talk of the Polish people's "lusts" rather than desires for the future,

Polish interpreters had to take over, leaving Carter's statements open to political editing.[16] During President Reagan's 1983 visit to Japan interpreters were not provided for the President's private talk with Prime Minister Nakasone. "The Prime Minister knows English. Interpreters get in the way," the White House advance team insisted, clinging to the Hollywood mentality of a film in which a US President meets with his Soviet counterpart to discuss the elimination of nuclear weapons. After exchanging greetings through interpreters, he announces, "Let's send these young people away." Exit the interpreters. "And the two leaders proceed to negotiate the future of the planet in the Russian's broken English... We are forever sending the interpreters away. In doing so we court disaster; linguistic ineptitude can cause serious diplomatic misunderstandings."[17]

Even with the rapid growth of Russian-American relations in the age of *perestroika* and *glasnost,* there is an acute shortage of American professional simultaneous interpreters and of literature on simultaneous interpretation. The United Nations, State Department, and professional freelance interpreters are in no position to service all the diplomatic, business, academic, scientific and cultural conferences, meetings, exchanges, visiting delegations and radio and television programs which require such assistance. The expansion of satellite technology and spacebridges has added to the demand, and the American judicial system badly needs interpreters. In 1988 the New York courts sought interpretation some 250 times a day, and the rising Russian emigration has led to an increase in court cases involving Russian.[18] Unfortunately, the increased demand for interpreters coupled with the lack of properly trained individuals has led to the emergence of a virtual army of unqualified amateurs, including many emigres, who proclaim themselves professional simultaneous interpreters.

In interpreter training, the US lags woefully behind the USSR. While the Moscow Linguistic University and the Moscow International School of Translation and Interpreting offer full programs of translation and interpretation courses with numerous language combinations, very few American institutions teach these skills. Georgetown University and the Monterey Institute of Translation and Interpretation offer full-time interpretation programs for a limited number of languages, but a full professional program of interpretation from Russian is taught only at Monterey. This situation is a reflection of the general American neglect of foreign language study. There are more teachers of English in the Soviet Union than there are students of Russian in the US.[19] In 1985 there were only 6,405 students of Russian in American high schools, and in 1986 only 32,365 such students in American colleges. And their proficiency level is extremely poor: the Educational Testing Service data for 1988 show that on the Russian language proficiency test fourth and fifth-year Russian-language college students scored a shockingly low median listening proficiency level of 1+ and a median reading proficiency level of 2+.[20]

Interpretation in the US is an unloved stepchild of foreign language teaching, and is occasionally written off as a branch of "translation." Very little work has been done on the methodology of teaching this crucial subject. Only at the end of the 1960s did serious research—both Western and Soviet—start on the phenomenon of interpretation. The first studies focused on it as an activity carried out in extreme conditions, of interest primarily to psycholinguists, neurologists, and physiologists.[21] The French researcher Marianne Lederer describes simultaneous interpretation as "an unnatural exercise, because it makes intelligent people repeat words which are meaningless to them, a situation found only in pathological cases."[22] Interpreters have reacted negatively and even with hostility to studies of their profession, considering these as useless or just plain wrong in their assumptions and conclusions.[23] Many Russian and Western works are highly technical physio-psychological studies analyzing the number of syllables an interpreter can utter per minute or the precise length of the time lag between speaker and interpreter. Such studies (Chernov, Shiryaev, Barik, Goldmann-Eisler—see Bibliography) are of theoretical interest but little practical value to a would-be interpreter, and do not address the specific linguistic and cultural problems of Russian-English interpretation. While in the last few years there have been a few Russian works which deal with the subject in a more practical vein (see Bibliography) there is a real need for textbooks, exercise manuals and audiovisual practice materials for Russian-English and English-Russian simultaneous interpretation. While this book does not specifically deal with English-Russian interpretation, a subject which would require a separate volume, Russian-English examples often shed light on how to cope with English-Russian difficulties.

Simultaneous interpreters usually work into their native language. For better or for worse, however, in America there has been a supply of emigre interpreters with native Russian. The generation of older Russian emigres who came to the US at a young age, mastered English in primary and secondary school, and were able to work into English with ease is thinning out; many of the younger emigres of the 1970s and 1980s have made a deliberate effort to forget their native language or have lost it over time, although a few have taken advantage of their native fluency and have become translators or interpreters. Here the emigre who arrived at a young age or an interpreter of Russian background naturally has an advantage over Americans for whom the language is acquired later. Unfortunately, a number of emigres (as well as Russians living in Russia) with insufficient English skills and a performance not up to professional standards are trying to capitalize on the new market for interpreters.

There is a fundamental difference between the background and language skills of the overwhelming majority of the older Russian and American interpreters. Since there were no waves of American emigration to Russia comparable to the Russian emigration to America, there were virtually no Russian interpreters with native English. While a few Russians had an Anglophone parent or were born, raised or educated abroad because a parent was in the Soviet diplomatic corps or trade missions, for the overwhelming majority of Russian interpreters English was an acquired language.

The fact that most Russian interpreters do not have native English makes it particularly important that American individuals, delegations and firms dealing with Russia be sure that the interpreter they employ has a native-level knowledge of English rather than relying on the Russian party's interpreter. While some Russian professional interpreters do have an excellent command of English, others have serious problems with the language. And though there are a number of Russian and

American interpreters who are bilinguals or who can work quite professionally into the acquired language, the pressures of simultaneous interpretation into a foreign language can cause even an experienced interpreter's grammar to collapse into a sea of wrong choices, incorrect grammatical endings, misused prepositions and poor lexical and stylistic choices.

Native speakers of Russian working into English are constantly faced with this problem, and an entire sub-field of such translation-interpretation arose in the Soviet Union, known as "Moscow News English," "Tassisms," or "Russian English:"

> Переводя на родной русский язык, переводчик "шлифует" текст, добиваясь, чтобы последний выглядел как работа, написанная русским автором. Переводя же на английский, русский переводчик нередко порождает некий Russian English, с трудом понимаемый (или вообще непонимаемый) носителями английского языка. Интересно, что такой Russian English не вызывает обычно сомнения у русских редакторов, поскольку в его основе лежит хорошо понятный им русский язык.[24]

The problems in such Russian-English renderings by non-native speakers of English were glaringly obvious in some of the clumsy and blindingly literal English translations produced by TASS and APN (Novosti Press Agency). Soviet translators and interpreters were well aware of these problems:

> К числу основных недостатков официальных переводов советской публицистики на английский язык, из года в год отмеченных зарубежными редакторами и рецензентами, относятся: многословие, описательность, цветистость, выспренность, претенциозность, структурная и синтаксическая рыхлость и беспомощность, искусственный, бесцветный, вымученный стиль.[25]

Here are a few examples:

Western media have been talking much of late about Western embassy personnel in Kabul hastily leaving.

Since Soviet journalists used to write according to scenarios they received from high on, so it would have been no sense in providing any additional information.

Reasonable, sober-minded people feel that the global problems have become common human problems. Therefore, solidarity with Armenia became the realization of this.[26]

And here are some examples from a textbook on translation:

I insist on a lawyer to be called in.

He is always making some or other plans.

Have you settled nicely in your hostel?
They are all impersonated by well-known Soviet actors.

The main part of the US presents four physical divisions.

In summer, did all their family travel without them?

But having visited the battle sites and learned about the appalling trials and sufferings, and the courage of the Soviet people, Burt Lancaster accepted the part in the film with joy.[27]

The point is not to make fun of these flawed linguistic products, but to demonstrate the very real problems which arise in translation and interpretation into a non-native language. These include poor knowledge of English grammar and of sequence of tenses, misuse of the definite and indefinite article, wrong prepositions and incorrect lexical and stylistic choices. The interpreter working into a non-native language may protect himself from errors by sticking to carefully prepared set phrases and a limited vocabulary; he may sacrifice stylistic accuracy and richness rather than venture into uncharted linguistic waters. At best, such an interpretation will be flat and uninspired, and at worst, wrong and incomplete. Such translators cling so closely to Russian constructions and syntax that the English-speaking reader is left to unravel the meaning of the sentence for himself. This is like presenting a dinner guest with a half-raw dish and inviting him to finish the cooking, adding and subtracting a few ingredients along the way. Many Soviet interpreters rendered literate, witty and sophisticated speakers of Russian into Dickensian or Orwellian English. (And Americans with a flawed knowledge of Russian do precisely the reverse when interpreting into Russian).

For most interpreters, therefore, working into a non-native language is fraught with risks. While there are several outstanding bilingual Russian and American interpreters with an in-depth knowledge of both languages and cultures, most professionals are acutely aware of the dangers of working into a non-native language: "Spontaneity of expression and ease of elocution are only really possible in the native language,"[28] commented one linguist. In Russia, however, interpretation is frequently done into a foreign language, a practice which runs counter to the "into native language" view favored at the United Nations and at most international conferences. "Teachers of interpreting in Moscow have maintained that it is better to interpret from the mother tongue... The United Nations case was based on the supposition that more stylish, fluent, and accurate interpretations will be made into a language spoken without accent, and of which one has the better grasp of vocabulary and grammar."[29]

The practical reason for this was the dearth of Soviet interpreters with a native knowledge of foreign languages. The theoretical argument for working into a foreign language holds that since the interpreter does not misunderstand anything he hears in his native language, he can devote relatively little attention to passive comprehension, and can therefore concentrate his full energies on active recoding into the foreign language. Theoretically, he will be able to retain material longer in his memory in his native language than in a foreign tongue. Some beginning interpreters have actually stated that they prefer working into a foreign language, and certain test situations claim to have produced "better" results with interpreters working into a foreign tongue rather than into the native language.[30]

These arguments seem extremely dubious. Sometimes an interpreter who is simply afraid he will not understand what is said in the foreign tongue prefers speaking it rather than listening to it. Some advocates of interpretation into a foreign language argue that interpretation in good listening conditions and on non-technical subjects should be done into the native language, but that the rendering of technical texts or interpretation in difficult listening conditions is best done into the foreign language.[31] The overwhelming majority of interpreters and listeners, however, agree that interpretation is easier to do—and to listen to—from a foreign language into the interpreter's native tongue. Serious grammatical errors, a limited vocabulary and halting delivery can make listening to interpretation into a foreign language an extremely tortuous process. Even the translator who argues that "when you translate from your own language you really understand the message: therefore, you cannot change the meaning" [! L.V.] admits that when she translates from her native Russian into English she needs an American native speaker to revise her work.[32] Despite the continuing stress in Russia on teaching interpretation into the foreign as well as into the native language, some Russian interpreters and researchers are now accepting the "foreign into native language" argument:

> при направлении "иностранный язык - основной язык" существует большая вероятность точного анализа и адекватного преодоления переводческих трудностей.[33]

There are distinct limitations on how well a non-bilingual interpreter can do working "the wrong way," as a Russian interpreter pointed out:

> Необходимо уяснить, что существует некий "потолок" возможностей научиться переводить на неродной язык. За редкими исключениями этот потолок – уровень газетно-информационного языка и язык газетно-журнальной публицистики.[34]

Though the interpreter can master set phrases and clichés in the foreign language, he will never achieve the lexical and stylistic levels, nuances and subtleties possible when working into his native language.

The interpreter who is constantly dealing with delegations obviously requires a minimum level of fluency in Russian even if he is only working into English in the booth. The better acquainted he is with the vocabulary, grammar, syntax and structure of Russian, the easier it will be for him to produce a smooth Russian-English translation. A more sophisticated knowledge of Russian will impact on his knowledge of his native English, for analyzing one's own language through comparison with a foreign tongue is a highly revealing and useful exercise. This is somewhat analogous to the American motorist who learns to drive on the left, and subsequently discovers that his grasp of traffic patterns in general—and of the behavior of people who drive on the right—has qualitatively improved. But since financial considerations often win out over linguistic criteria, more and more firms and delegations are economizing on interpreters and expect the interpreter to be able to work both ways—into Russian and into English.

The precision work and enormous pressure of simultaneous interpretation require absolute fluency in the target (active) language (the language(s) *into* which the interpreter is working), and excellent comprehension of the source (passive) language (the language(s) *from* which he works). Professional interpreters categorize their working languages as A, B, and C languages. A represents the principal active language(s) *into* which the interpreter works, and which he speaks as a native (e.g. for the Russian-English interpreter English is usually the A language), while B represents other active languages into which he interprets, e.g. an American of Russian background with near-native fluency in Russian might claim an A in English and a B in Russian. C languages are languages *from* which an interpreter works, e.g. an American Russian-English interpreter could claim Russian as his C language.[35]

Contrary to what most people think, many interpreters are not bilingual, and many bilinguals are incapable of simultaneous interpretation. Some bilinguals cannot interpret the simplest of conversations. "Most people believe that if you are bilingual, you can interpret," commented an official of the Administrative Office of the US. Courts, a frequent user of interpreters. "That's about as true as saying that if you have two hands, you can automatically be a concert pianist."[36] The chief of the interpreting division in the State Department Office of Language Services remarked to an interviewer, "Every day people walk in here who are totally bilingual—and are totally incapable of interpreting... They just can't do it."[37]

Bilinguals often suffer from interference of one language with another. "Too great a familiarity with a foreign idiom may render a man confused between that foreign idiom and his own," wrote the English writer Hilaire Belloc, explaining why he could not recall a single good bilingual translator. "It may make him at times run the two together within his mind, diluting and marring each with the properties of the other."[38] While many bilinguals cannot do instant linguistic or code switching, professional interpreters have learned to control their bilingual switch mechanism.[39]

Different language skills serve different purposes, and there is no automatic correlation between acquiring one skill and acquiring another. A person may speak Russian well and write it badly, or read with excellent comprehension but possess no oral fluency. These skills can be taught and developed separately. Some outstanding Russian-English interpreters would have a rough time in Moscow, for they cannot—or will not—speak the language from which they interpret. That simultaneous interpretation requires *oral comprehension* of the source language rather than the ability to *speak* it sometimes comes as a shock to would-be students of interpretation. As a Russian expert has pointed out,

> Каково же оказывалось недоумение студентов, когда выяснялось, что на практике хорошими переводчиками оказались лица, заурядно владеющие иностранным языком, и наоборот, люди, отлично знающие язык, зачастую оказывались неспособными к этому роду деятельности. Выходит, тут недостаточно умение более или менее полно и точно перелагать смысл с языка на язык, а нужно что-то еще.[40]

While the Russian-English interpreter must *understand* everything that is said in Russian, his command of spoken *English,* not of Russian, is of key importance. What the audience hears is an interpreter speaking in English, not Russian. For this reason he "needs to cultivate his native language with as much care as his foreign languages,"[41] and the interpreter "needs to be a person with fairly clear views on the use of English,"[42] as an English-language translator pointed out. The interpreter into English needs to think about expanding his *English* vocabulary and to work on his English style and syntax; he needs to read widely, and to listen to a variety of English oratorical and conversational styles. In fact, he needs to devote the same care to the study of English as to the study of the foreign language.

Lack of contact between professional interpreters and the academic world has contributed to this problem. From the first year through advanced-level courses many teachers of Russian are primarily concerned with cramming Russian vocabulary into their students rather than with teaching them how those words—and the sentences built on them—can properly be rendered into English. Slavists would do their students a great service if they stressed from Day One the importance of using good English when translating from Russian, even if the translation is only a drill on the use of participles or time expressions. The habit of literal—and bad—translation is not easily broken, and the language classroom is an ideal place to instill respect for English as well as for Russian. Students can practice translating the Russian press into stylistically as well as grammatically correct English, or try interpreting from Russian radio and television programs and films on videocassettes. There is also a broad range of Russian-language study materials available to the beginning interpreter, and over the last few years it has become quite simple to organize travel and language study tours to Russia.

This question of "knowing" Russian often causes confusion in hiring interpreters. All too often a conference organizer or television station jumps at Aunt Janet's recommendation of her bridge club friend who "knows" Russian, without checking whether the friend has ever interpreted in his life. Both the interpreter and the prospective employer should be perfectly clear as to the requirements: Russian-English, English-Russian, simultaneous or consecutive. Unfortunately, many organizations leap at the notion of "native Russian" for Russian-English interpretation. That can mean hiring a native speaker who, of course, "knows" Russian, but may have a very poor knowledge of English and/or be totally incapable of interpretation. Some large corporations have admitted to seeking interpreters through the Yellow Pages or hoping for "a good deal of luck."[43] There are two professional organizations, TAALS (The American Association of Language Specialists) and AIIC (Association internationale des interprètes de conférence), numerous professional freelancers who are not members of these organizations, State Department contract interpreters, and interpreters of many international organizations including the UN and its specialized agencies. Commercial so-called translation and interpretation "agencies" range from thoroughly professional organizations with a roster of highly competent people to a bumbling unemployed language student holed up in a cubicle with a fax and phone for company. In the US, unfortunately, anyone can still feel free to call himself an interpreter. *Caveat emptor.*

---

* All translations of quotations are mine unless otherwise noted.

** Though there are many women interpreters and translators, for simplicity's sake the male pronoun will be used to refer to all persons in these professions.

PART I
PRACTICAL PROBLEMS

CHAPTER I

THE SIMULTANEOUS INTERPRETER:
WHO HE IS AND WHAT HE DOES

Though modern simultaneous interpretation with its microphones, earphones, and sound equipment is a relatively new phenomenon, interpretation is as old as mankind.[1] In the first Letter to the Corinthians St. Paul orders, "If any man speak in an unknown tongue let it be by two, or at most by three...and let one interpret" (14:27). At various times interpreters have served as missionaries, liaison officers, military envoys, court interpreters, business couriers, and trade negotiators. Throughout history they have served as interpreters of culture and politics as well as language. During the Punic Wars negotiations were often carried on by interpreters, and the twelfth-century dragomans, the official interpreters appointed by local authorities, specialized in foreign affairs and were frequently entrusted with highly sensitive missions.

Interpreters have also been considered as resource persons by the side for which they work. The French drogmans (dragomans), who were trained in Oriental languages, were required not only to translate what was said but also to advise French officials as to the meaning of specific words or situations, to provide "cultural interpretation." Columbus sent young Indians from the New World to Spain to be trained as interpreters so that he could use them as go-betweens.

In medieval Europe Latin was the lingua franca, and until the appearance of the vernacular tongues there was less need for interpretation. Nor were interpreters always held in esteem. An *ukaz* of Peter the Great refers to *"переводчики и другая обозная сволочь."*[2] In nineteenth-century Europe there was little need for high-level interpretation, since French was the universal language of diplomacy and educated discourse. Consecutive interpretation was first used at the Paris peace conference of 1919, and simultaneous in 1928 at the sixth congress of the Comintern in Russia. The first patent for simultaneous interpretation equipment was given in 1926 to Gordon Finley at IBM for his device based on an idea of Edward Filene's (of Boston's Filene's department store fame), and in 1933 booths were used at the plenum of the executive committee of the Communist International.[3] In 1935 in Leningrad at the fifteenth international physiology congress Academician Pavlov's introductory speech was translated from Russian into French, English, and German. In the 1920s the use of simultaneous interpretation expanded rapidly. At the twentieth Party Congress interpretation was provided into six languages, and at the twenty-first Party Congress into eighteen.[4]

Simultaneous interpretation first emerged on the world scene in 1945 at the postwar Nuremberg trials. Many of the interpreters who worked there, emigres and refugees with a knowledge of Russian, French, German, and English, later went on to become staff members at the newly founded United Nations. A Russian scholar gave the following description of the Americans who interpreted at Nuremberg:

> Значительную часть их составляли эмигранты, прожившие много лет в Англии и США, люди, для которых два или три иностранных языка были в равной мере родными. В роли переводчиков подвизались и белые эмигранты. Некоторые из них долгое время жили во Франции, а затем эмигрировали в США и на процессе переводили с французского на английский и обратно. Эти люди, лишенные родины, разучились говорить по-русски. Их "русский язык" пестрит большим количеством иностранных слов и архаизмов, из-за сильного акцента иногда даже трудно понять, о чем они говорят.[5]

The need for interpreters became more urgent as international organizations and private conferences increasingly required their services. In 1948 the first school for interpreters was opened in Geneva, and Moscow's Thorez Institute began its interpreter training program in 1962. Today sophisticated and timesaving telecommunications networks, satellite technology, television spacebridges and videoconferencing have opened up new opportunities for simultaneous interpretation.

Most international conferences today would be unthinkable without interpreters. A conference using several languages works through a system of booths, each servicing a target language. Interpretation into English is carried out by the English booth, into Russian by the Russian booth, etc. The United Nations has six booths, one for each of the official languages: English, French, Spanish, Russian, Chinese and Arabic. The interpreters in the first four booths work solely into these languages, while the Chinese and Arabic booths interpret both into Chinese and Arabic and from them into English or French. There are therefore two people in the English, French, Spanish and Russian booths, and three in the Chinese and Arabic booths. In the English booth one person (known as a *russisant*) works into English from Russian and French, while his colleague (known as an *hispanisant*) works from Spanish and French. Similarly, in the French booth one interpreter works into French from English and Russian while the other works from English and Spanish. Work is generally divided into half hours. If a Russian-speaking delegate takes the floor while the *russisant* is out of the English booth, his colleague listens to the interpretation of Russian into French and translates that into English. Such an "interpretation from an interpretation" is known as relaying. Close coordination is required to ensure that both *russisants* or both *hispanisants* do not walk out at the same time. Elaborate versions of this game of "Telephone" can result at a meeting: e.g., Russian is interpreted into French, then into English, and then into Chinese—a triple interpretation within seconds. If a conference uses only Russian and English there will be a Russian and an English booth, or if both interpreters work both ways, they may share a single booth.

Relaying is occasionally inevitable, for no one is a camel and sitting in a booth for three hours at a stretch can be difficult. At a conference with many working languages it may be impossible to provide direct interpretation into all the conference languages. Since direct interpretation is considerably more accurate and reliable, however, most interpreters will avoid relay insofar as possible.[6]

In Russia a somewhat different system is generally used at conferences, with each booth working both into Russian and into a foreign language; the sound engineer must see to the switching of language channels. The interpreter works both from Russian into a foreign language and from that language into Russian. An extra booth is provided for speeches in foreign languages which are not covered by this system, with interpretation provided through relay from the other booths.[7]

Though interpreters hear the speaker through both earphones, many prefer to work with only one headphone so that they can also hear themselves. Learning to listen to oneself while concentrating on the speaker is crucial to successful interpretation. The interpreter's microphone is controlled by an on-off switch so that he can speak to his colleague when they are not working. The interpreter's voice should not bounce back at him, as this would drown out the speaker's voice and make it very difficult for the interpreter to follow what is being said. The temperature of the booths should be properly controlled, for boiling and freezing, as many an interpreter knows all too well, do not make for good communication and can lead to laryngitis. The booths are—or should be—provided with water, glasses, paper for note-taking, and pencils.

The simultaneous interpreter translates speeches, statements, documents, and informal conversations. At most meetings he finds documents awaiting him so that he can familiarize himself with specific vocabulary; these papers are usually available in all the meeting's working languages. Sometimes he may be sent documents or briefing papers in advance. The interpreter should also have the agenda, a list of speakers and relevant names and titles of individuals and organizations, as well as acronyms and abbreviations. Proper documentation is indispensable for drafting work, as it is impossible to follow a paragraph read off at top speed by a delegate burning with eagerness to make additions or deletions. A dictionary is always welcome, for even the most experienced interpreters can suddenly go blank on a specific term. It is a reference tool, a Peanuts blanket and also a kind of thesaurus which can prompt the interpreter in his choice of synonyms.

If delegates are discussing general ideas there may be no written texts. Texts of formal statements, however, are usually distributed in advance, allowing the interpreter to consult a dictionary—or colleagues—and to prepare the translation. Gorbachev's interpreter, Pavel Palazhchenko, called such texts a *"спасательный круг."*[8] If the interpreter has a great deal of time he may be tempted to write out entire sentences or difficult sections. If he is rushed, however, he will quickly read through the entire text, checking for names, numbers, acronyms and technical terms and syntactical difficulties. Special attention is paid to the very beginning and the very end of the speech, for here errors will be in the spotlight. An audience is generally eager to hear the beginning of a statement and may nod off during the middle, but interest is usually reawakened and snores broken off by the magic words "in conclusion." A flubbed ending instantly erases the good impression made by a half hour of brilliant interpretation.

Since there is no guarantee that a speaker will not make last-minute changes, additions, or omissions, many texts are marked "check against delivery." A delegate may also monitor the interpretation to see whether these changes have been included. While a text can be very useful in helping the interpreter catch up with a very rapid speaker, it is also a dangerous one. The text requires that the interpreter fracture his attention, that he listen and read at the same time.[9] If he has not been listening and the speaker departs from the text, in the words of one interpreter,

> the phrases of the prepared text are lost, the sense of the ad-libbed is not found, and the interpreter falls stumblingly between the two and hears himself mouthing contradictions, ill-mated phrases, and all their bastard offspring...Then the prepared text becomes a landscape with no landmarks into which intrudes surging at top speed complete confusion.[10]

Sometimes the interpreter is given both the original text and a translation into English, a "Van Doren." This appellation harks back to Charles Van Doren's apparently spontaneous performance on the "$64,000 Question" quiz show, for which the answers had in fact been rehearsed in advance. Even with a "Van Doren" the interpreter must remain alert, since there may be changes in the speech as actually delivered. The quality of the Van Doren may vary greatly. If there is time, the interpreter may edit out grammatical and stylistic infelicities, but there is always the risk of offending a delegation wishing to hear a speech exactly as it has translated the text. If he tries simultaneously to follow both the speech in the original language and the translation, the interpreter stands a good chance of becoming cross-eyed. Attempting to follow two texts while also listening to the speaker can try one's sanity.

In very formal meetings stenographers (verbatim reporters) may take down or record the interpretation for future publication or reference. The interpreter notes down the hour and minute at which he thinks he has made an error or omission, and then informs the stenographer of the necessary corrections.

Slides or short films are extremely difficult to interpret, and are becoming more and more common at conferences. If at all possible, the interpreter should ask to see the material before the meeting or request a transcript of the text. It is nearly impossible to interpret a film correctly at sight, since the speed of a soundtrack is generally far faster than that of a live orator. And the endless—and frequently inebriated—toasts which often follow a dinner can try the patience of both interpreter and audience.

Booth behavior has its own rules. Since it is difficult to hear external sound with earphones on, and conversation is impossible if one interpreter is working, interpreters often write notes rather that speak to their boothmates. Even while not working, the interpreter should stay alert, ready to fetch documents or water for his colleague, to write a note with a word or phrase to assist him, or to ask the engineer to adjust the sound. If eating and smoking in the booth annoy his colleagues, the interpreter will refrain from doing so. (An excellent list of suggestions for booth behavior for beginning interpreters, compiled by Professor Margaret Bowen and her colleagues at

Georgetown University, is included at the end of this book). But these are technicalities. In substance, asking interpreters what they do is like asking a centipede how it walks; the result is likely to be a breakdown of speech or locomotion. Within a few seconds the interpreter must listen, understand, react, analyze, memorize, rearrange syntax, select appropriate words, condense or expand a phrase, punctuate and articulate—without, of course, forgetting to breathe, and doing so as quietly as possible to prevent panicked gasps from shooting into the delegates' headphones.[11] The interpreter must keep up with an uninterrupted flow of material, rendering tone and nuance as well as meaning; he should speak smoothly, not in machine-gun bursts interrupted by seconds of silence. Nor has he any control over this material, for the vocabulary, syntax and speed are determined by the speaker. Generally speaking, anyone who proposed on a regular basis to carry out a dozen operations simultaneously—as does the interpreter—would be well advised to narrow his ambitions or, if he persists in his endeavors, to seek psychiatric help. Yet this juggling act is precisely what the interpreter must do. "There is no room for the slow thinker or the verbal plodder in the profession of interpreter."[12]

Since the delegate is speaking not to the interpreter, but past or through him to a listener, the interpreter must play the role of both receiver and dispatcher of the utterance, constantly switching roles to ensure communication.[13]

The advances of modern technology have isolated interpreters from conference proceedings. Instead of sitting with the participants, interpreter teams are often locked away in glass booths perched high above the meeting hall, which provide an excellent view of the backs of delegates' heads but little contact with the listeners. The interpreter is invisible and anonymous, exiled from the field of action. By flicking a dial a delegate can disconnect that human conduit for communication. Little wonder that the interpreter's disembodied voice is sometimes taken as part of the equipment. Delegates' remarks about the "conference facilities" often refer to interpreters and sound engineers as well as to the physical conference site. "Communications aids" and "electronic translation" are other euphemisms for interpreters which imply that the machinery itself is doing the interpretation, buttressing the notion that the interpreter is a mechanical robot, and that anyone who has memorized a good part of the dictionary could do as well. (Interpretation moreover, is often called a "service" profession). Satellite communications and teleconferencing can further depersonalize the interpreter by keeping him several thousand miles away from the actual conference.

Though exiled to his booth, the interpreter is generally part of a team. But once he has opened his mouth, even with his colleague sitting right next to him, he is totally alone. "He can only count on himself, on his intellectual resources, his cultural reserves and his own energy. He works alone, for himself. The greater the number of his listeners, the more likely it is that his feeling of isolation will grow."[14]

As opposed to children, interpreters should be heard and not seen. The less noticeable the interpreter's presence, the more natural the act of communication. *"Перевод считается...тем лучше, чем меньше ощущается присутствие посредника."*[15] It is when he fails rather than when he performs brilliantly that this professional is noticed. While no interpreter has yet found himself on page one of a major newspaper because he did an outstanding job, a *contresens* or slip in a sensitive situation may earn him plenty of unwanted publicity.

It has been said that to interpret is first and foremost to understand. The interpreter's finished product is an amalgam of ability, talent, training, intellectual understanding, careful preparation and study. His work requires excellent long and short term memory, concentration, iron nerves, endurance, curiosity, intuition, the ability to improvise and grasp tone and nuance, to adapt to the style of individual speakers without eclipsing them with prima donna antics. He must have a pleasant voice free from speech defects; he must be punctual and, since many meetings deal with confidential material, discreet. To keep the confidence of the delegates he must avoid the temptation to recount interesting anecdotes or tidbits which may include confidential material; at negotiations he must remain neutral and avoid showing his personal feelings regarding the delegates' positions.

The interpreter must try adapt to the speaker's accent and take into account his nationality and cultural background, whether he is being ironic, dispassionate, or deliberately vague. No matter what he may think of the speaker or his ideas, while he is working the interpreter *is* that speaker, and must convince the listener that he is that person. The interpreter should use the first person singular, i.e. "I think," "I wish to say," rather than the third person. "He thinks" sounds unprofessional and insulting. The third person would be used in interpreting a criminal investigation: "he says that he was not at the murder scene," and can be used when the speaker corrects himself, e.g. "The speaker apologizes," to make it clear that it is the speaker and not the interpreter who is doing the apologizing.

The interpreter's nerves may also be tested by Russian delegates who monitor the interpretation and correct the interpretation. Sometimes the speaker may want a specific term to be used; sometimes he may in fact have heard a mistake in the translation; but at other times, unfortunately, he may be showing off what he thinks is an excellent knowledge of English. It is particularly embarrassing for an Anglophone interpreter to be forced to say something in English which he knows is wrong; in that case he can say, "the speaker says" and repeat the word or phrase the speaker wants to hear. While after the meeting the interpreter may (calmly!) approach the delegate and discuss the term in question, he should never allow himself to show irritation or anger. Such corrections, however—particularly when they are unfounded or just plain wrong—can rattle even the most highly experienced interpreters.

Even more anxiety-provoking than erroneous "corrections" is the interpreter's realization that he has forgotten to turn off his microphone while making a negative (i.e. thoroughly nasty) comment about a delegate, or using various kinds of expletives. It cannot be sufficiently stressed how important it is for the interpreter to turn off the microphone *immediately* once he has finished speaking. A carelessly opened microphone has ruined more than one interpreter's career—or that of his colleague who was unaware that the microphone was still on. Above all, the interpreter must remember that his job is a life-long learning process—for languages never stop changing – and it is his duty to keep reading, listening, and learning, to try to keep pace with the linguistic developments of both Russian and English.

In his witty memoir *Faithful Echo,* Ekvall gives a brilliant description of the interpreter's psychology:

> To be really successful, the interpreter must paradoxically combine in his character and personality two contradictions: he may not be stolid and at the same time he must grimly and successfully refuse to panic. Interpretation at its best...is based on something very close to inspiration. And that flares its brightest when the nerves are taut and the sharp impact of the unexpected spurs mind and tongue to creative response...[16]

If and when he does panic, the interpreter must not allow his audience to sense his difficulty, and should maintain an even flow of words:

> ...точно так, как балерина, танцуя с видимой легкостью, вызывает
> доверие как балерина, и переводчик, делающий свое дело с легкостью, т.е.
> четко и уверенно, вызывает доверие как переводчика.[17]

Small wonder that many interpreters display strong personalities with sharply defined character traits and quirks:

> with some justification, exasperated bureaucrats and administrators call us prima donnas, too temperamental for any good use. We are nothing if not artists and we operate under terrific pressures. Those pressures, the sources from which they spring, and the interpreter's reaction to them have a very large place in the problem of interpretation.[18]

Another observer gave an even less flattering description of the interpreters at the Nuremberg trials: "Touchy, vain, unaccountable, puffed up with self-importance of the most explosive kind, inexpressibly egotistical, and as a rule violent opponents of soap and sunlight."[19]

Perhaps the interpreter is so touchy because he is often caught in the crossfire between warring or sparring delegates. On occasion he serves as a useful scapegoat, for a delegate may prefer to sarcastically remark "I can't believe what I just heard coming out of the English booth," "If I can believe the interpretation," or "There must be a problem with the translation" rather than to declare "Sir, I think you are an idiot and totally disagree with your proposal." Regardless of his personal convictions, in a discussion between two violently opposed parties the interpreter must not let his voice betray his own point of view. He must be a linguist, actor, verbal acrobat and diplomat, with a good knowledge of parliamentary procedure, the language of political negotiations, and a wide variety of fields. It is imperative that he keep up with current events and have a good background in history, geography, and world literature. Few interpreters have been spared quotes and misquotes from Shakespeare, Cervantes, Dante, Lenin, or the Bible, to name only a few sources. A good grounding in science is also useful. For technical conferences the interpreter must carefully study the documents in advance, as few people are born experts on the vocabulary of natural gas or blood cancers. "The life of a conference interpreter is a perpetual briefing," writes one professional.[20] And each group—be it makers of plastic boxes, rice growers, shoemakers or rocket scientists—is utterly convinced that its work is of the greatest and most universal importance.[21]

Naive laymen all too often expect that "since he knows the language," this genius can translate anything and everything. The interpreter must try to truly grasp the subject, for if he does not understand what he is saying he will quickly give himself away.[22] An interpreter who lacks any knowledge of the topic discussed has been aptly compared to a person who sees a photo taken by someone on a safari. While he may recognize the animals or objects in the picture, he has no clues regarding the associations or meaning the picture evokes for the photographer.[23]

Certain technical or even physical problems add to the interpreter's difficulties. The speaker's speed of delivery is beyond the interpreter's control. Many delegates are not used to working with simultaneous interpreters, and cannot—or will not—slow down. Excessive speed is one of the interpreter's major headaches. An extremely slow speaker presents another kind of danger, too, since the interpreter may have to wait for the subject or the object of a sentence before he can start to translate.

> При очень медленном темпе речи оратора некоторые переводчики заполняют длительные паузы в своей речи, используя "пустые" фразы и выражения, развивая и уточняя идеи оратора и дополнительно эксплуатируя логические связи между высказываниями и их частями.[24]

When a speaker is racing along, however, omission rather than addition becomes the major problem. The English-Russian interpreter may have a harder time with a galloping speaker than does his Russian-English counterpart, since the sheer length of Russian words and the structure of the language make English-Russian interpretation thirty-three per cent longer than Russian-English. Regardless of how fast the speaker is going, however, *it is of paramount importance that the interpreter finish or "wrap up" his sentences.* A dangling phrase, unfinished sentence or excessively lengthy silence will cause the listener to lose confidence. While some interpreters manage to maintain their own, moderate pace regardless of the speaker's delivery, most interpreters will rush to keep up for fear of being left behind.

Several studies have tried to determine the maximum speed at which interpretation is possible, and the optimal speed for adequate interpretation.[25] While such reearch is of little practical significance for the working interpreter, it is of considerable theoretical and scientific interest to neurologists and psycholinguists. For example, an extremely slow speaker of English would deliver at a rate of approximately 166-180 syllables per minute, with the interpreter into Russian following at about 206 syllables per minute.[26] In a faster speaker's range of 200-240 syllables per minute the interpreter would work at an approximate rate of 210-225 syllables. The speed of Russian speech covers a range of 120 to 405 syllables per minute, with the average discourse of radio announcers clocked at 250 syllables.[27] No wonder direct interpretation of radio programs is so hard, for above 250 syllables interpretation becomes hopelessly difficult and generally requires condensation or editing if the interpreter is to keep up.

Several researchers have focused on the speakers' pauses as the key to simultaneous interpretation, believing that it is here that the interpreter catches up and actually "does his job." A related question is the extent of the interpreter's lag, or how far he can allow himself to fall behind the speaker.[28] This lag between the interpreter and speaker ranges from 200 milliseconds to ten or even fifteen seconds, with an average of two to ten seconds. Ten seems to be the upper limit for effective interpretation, and two to three the most comfortable length.[29] Studies demonstrate that the interpreter is in fact talking in a continuum with the speaker, and does not make special use of pauses to catch up. One researcher shows that only 20-30% of the text is uttered by the interpreter during the speaker's pauses, and that 60-70% of the time they are in fact speaking simultaneously.[30]

An interpreter who does *not* lag slightly behind is not necessarily a good interpreter. "Jumping in" too soon may force the interpreter to commit himself to an awkward grammatical or syntactical structure which could have been avoided by waiting a few extra seconds. The more possibilities the interpreter leaves open, the greater his chances of landing on his feet, and the less the likelihood he will have to back up and correct himself. Jumping in too soon is often a mark of a nervous or new interpreter who is terrified of losing the speaker. The experienced interpreter makes use of the first few seconds to mentally encode the information he is receiving and to formulate his utterance before speaking.

A device used by interpreters both to catch up with and to anticipate the speaker is the "probability of prediction" or "probabilistic prognosis," *"вероятность прогнозирования."*[31] This means that "the interpreter as listener makes probabilistic inferences about the future development of a sentence on the basis of what he has just heard; his own utterances are then based on these predictions, becoming more determined as the source language proceeds."[32] This theory comes close to Chomskian notions of generative grammar, the generation of sentences through certain laws the speaker intuitively senses. *Вероятность прогнозирования* is defined as:

> Иерархическая система трех уровней – уровня лингвистической вероятности сочетания двух слов как наименьшей смысловой единицы..., уровня вероятности смысловых связей внутри предложения и уровня вероятности предикативных отношений во всем сообщении. Каждый верхний уровень прогнозирования увеличивает надежность вероятного прогнозирования на более низкий уровень.[33]

On this basis the interpreter can theoretically predict the semantic-structural development and conclusion of a speaker's utterance, and while listening can formulate his sentence in the target language. This predictive probability is particularly strong in highly inflected languages such as Russian or German which have strong verbal government, prepositions which dictate a limited choice of case endings, and a relatively predictable syntax. The importance of such probability prediction has been heavily stressed by Russian specialists such as Chernov, who believes that an unbroken "chunk" of interpretation depends primarily on this factor.[34] Excessive anticipation of verbal cues can, however, be very risky.[35] The notion of "probability prediction" comes close to the concept of an intuitive perception which replaces rational judgment.[36] Such "intuition," however, may be the result of extensive experience with verbal clichés, particularly if the interpreter is working in a familiar field or one with highly stylized vocabulary, or in ritual situations such as greetings, farewells, expressions of thanks, approval and disapproval. Here the interpreter's knowledge of accepted situational clichés makes for a significant degree of anticipation.[37] One Russian expert believes that such fixed expressions and idioms form the heart of the simultaneous interpreter's utterances:

> Гарантия успеха в синхронном переводе...заключается в самой широкой автоматизации языковых средств выражения...В несколько грубой форме, идеальный синхронный переводчик –это человек, в совершенстве владеющий

искусством штампа…Язык синхронного перевода изобилует штампами, да иначе и быть не может –поскольку невозможно переводить быстро и правильно, не прибегая к избитым выражениям.[38]

While clichés and fixed expressions are obviously a recurring phenomenon, particularly in technical prose and in certain types of political discourse, such as Soviet Marxist jargon, the assumption that they form the basis of the interpreter's work seems rather strange. A speaker may play with a cliché, distorting or even reversing its original meaning, and an interpreter who limits himself to a vocabulary of ready-made clichés is like an aspiring writer who limits himself to Basic English.

While all interpreters, good and bad, experienced and inexperienced, make mistakes, some errors are far more serious than others. Most common are errors of omission. Something may be left out because the interpreter has not heard it, has heard but not understood, or has made a conscious choice to eliminate certain words because he is compressing material when the speaker is talking very quickly. While decisions to edit and compress are an extremely important part of the professional's bag of tricks, omission of substantive material is quite a different matter.[39]

Another kind of error involves combining elements from two different parts of a sentence, e.g. *Выступая в городе, делегат говорил о том, что...*becomes "The city's delegate said that…" Or the interpreter may "substitute:" *французский делегат сказал* turns into "The British delegate stated." Another kind of error consists of the addition of material, when an interpreter uncertain of how to render a word provides two or three variants. *"Ужасная политика расизма"* becomes "the horrible, terrible—uh—atrocious policy of racism." Such self-correction by listing synonyms only serves to undermine the listener's confidence in the interpreter. While a serious error, omission, or *contresens* should—if possible—be corrected, the search for perfection often becomes the path to confusion. A frantic scramble for the perfect adjective may cause the interpreter to lose the building blocks of a sentence—the noun and the verb. Or the interpreter may feel that his addition provides badly needed semantic clarity:

> The temptation to add, if not a sentence, just a phrase or even a word, can be very strong. The interpreter often feels as though he were the only one with hearing ears, listening to a dialogue of the deaf where just one more word—the right one, of course—would clear up all misunderstanding; he may even deceive himself into believing that such addition is the best and highest form of interpretation.[40]

Such temptation, however, should be avoided. There may very well be diplomatic reasons why something is left unsaid or hinted at instead of explicitly stated.

Occasionally the interpreter comes out with something that is not in *any* way a part of the original text, an addition known as *"отсебятина."*[41] This may result from conscious or unconscious verbal associations with other parts of a statement or with something in the interpreter's mind that has nothing whatever to do with the speaker's text. An interpreter who has been trained to finish every sentence may do so even when the speaker does not, and thereby change the orator's intent. Sometimes an interpreter may reverse the order of items in a sequence or list simply because he remembers a later item better than an earlier one.[42]

Certain linguistic pitfalls invite errors from the interpreter. Non-native speakers of Russian such as Georgians, Mongolians, Armenians and Latvians may have difficult accents in Russian, and may make grammatical as well as phonetic errors. If mumbled or swallowed, the critical particle *не* can lead the interpreter into a *contresens*—the direct opposite of the speaker's meaning. Singular and plural case endings require very close attention, for sound similarity and vowel reduction can make the difference between *наше предложение* and *наши предложения* difficult to grasp at high speed. Verb singulars and plurals can also be tricky: *решает* vs. *решают*, or homonyms such as the ever-present *мир* can cause errors.

The keys to a sentence are the nouns and verbs, for these will unlock the doors to the speaker's thought. The interpreter must be alert to cues given by conjunctions or parenthetical expressions that a new idea is coming: *но, поэтому, однако, с другой стороны.*[43] Yet, in the verbal game of minimizing losses and maximizing gains which all interpreters must play, words are both best friends and worst enemies, aids and obstacles.[44] They are merely building blocks for the expression of thoughts and ideas, and disappear into the broader framework of context and meaning. Stripped of semantic and cultural context, words can have enormous destructive force. One need only recall Khrushchev's famous *"мы вас похороним"*—"We will be present at your funeral" (and therefore survive you) mistranslated as the threatening declaration "We will bury you."

Deprived of context, a word's meaning can become totally unclear. The word "shot," for example, can refer to a gun, a camera, some vodka, outer space or an injection. *Место* can be rendered as place, area, spot, locality, locale, role, post, turn, job, seat, birth, space, or room, depending on the meaning of a particular sentence. *Вид* can mean sight, air, appearance, look, prospects, view, mind (*иметь в виду* = to have in mind), aspect (of a Russian verb), type, species or form. In various word combinations (collocations) or *словосочетания,* the meaning can change completely: *быть на виду*—to be highly visible, in the public eye, or *делать вид*—to pretend.

Various word combinations with *взгляд* provide good examples of the variety of meanings—and different renderings—a single lexical item can engender when combined with other words:

беглый взгляд	a passing glance
бессмысленный взгляд	a vacant stare
неподвижный взгляд	a fixed gaze
смелый взгляд	bold view
торжествующий взгляд	triumphant air
укоризненный взгляд	reproachful look
взгляд на жизнь	outlook on life
обмениваться взглядами	to exchange glances
отречься от своих взглядов	to renounce one's opinions[45]

Since words do not appear in isolation, memorizing vocabulary lists is no panacea for the interpreter's ills:

> It is not enough for the interpreter to understand the semantics of individual words, phrases or sentences...it is necessary for him to get the ideas beyond the words and convey those ideas and not the word content of the original language.[46]

Interpretation should be a recoding and reexpression of a message rather than a mechanical translation of individual words. For example, in English *анкетные данные* is not "questionnaire data," a rather meaningless phrase, but biographical/personal data or information.

Interpretation involves the identification of relevant concepts and their rewording in another language in such a way that original and target language wordings may correspond only in their temporary meaning in a given speech performance without necessarily constituting equivalent language units capable of reuse in different circumstances.[47]

Literal, *mot-à-mot* translation requires considerably less mental effort but produces far worse results. Only in the case of fairly technical terms does literal interpretation come through with flying colors, when "the use of a term is restricted to a limited number of persons and represents a clearly defined notion which does not vary with context."[48] Such are the terms of technolects or sociolects, specific jargon used by groups of professionals. An interpreter reading off a list of various kinds of semiconductors is obviously expected to give the correct term and not to use his literary imagination. In delicate negotiations or in dealing with sensitive material the interpreter is well advised to stay close to the original text.

Not literal, but semantic or conceptual fidelity, known in Russian as *адекватность перевода,* is the interpreter's goal. His number one task is to make Russian prose sound like normal English and, given the enormous grammatical and syntactical differences between the two languages, this can be extremely difficult . He must see to it that frozen phrases which sound acceptable in Russian do not jar the anglophone's ear. It has been correctly noted that "the fact that a word or combination of words is commonly used in Russian…if it is reproduced mechanically as it usually is as a straightforward carbon copy, does not mean it will be understood in the same way as the Russian is, or even understood at all."[49] Such expressions as "our principled position" *наш принципиальный перевод* or "the goal-orientedness of this decision" *целеустремленность этого решения* require reworking. "Our basic or fundamental point," "the advisability/purpose of this decision" sound a good deal more idiomatic. "*Я хочу высказать несколько соображений*" is better rendered as "There are several points I would like to make" than by "I wish to express several considerations."

What may sound pompous or bombastic to a foreign listener may be perceived as a commonplace or as a cliché by a Russian audience. Many fixed expressions have lost their original force and elevated tone:

Мы хотим достойно встретить этот большой и радостный для нас праздник.
We want to celebrate this great day.

Статья посвящена проблемам рабочих.
This article deals with/relates/tells of/is about the workers' problems.

Он говорил о пафосе созидания новых заводов в нашей стране.
He spoke of the excitement/drama/thrill (the exciting/dramatic/thrilling work) of building new schools in our country.[50]

The interpreter must control the text, and not vice versa; his job is to knead raw linguistic material into a fully finished dough. A Russian translator's injunction, "Do not abandon your reader halfway"[51] can be reworded for the interpreter as "Do not abandon your listener halfway." Of course, the interpreter must proceed with reasonable prudence and caution. Recoding or restructuring does not mean disregarding meaning or letting the imagination run wild. But the interpreter who insists on literal interpretation will find himself producing Tassisms:

> Stalin came to power not only thanks to his intriguing and perfidy—but because of many objective circumstances.

> We deem it our duty to turn attention to the catastrophic state of the collections. This is a continuation of the provocative activities which happened last August.[52]

The use of short, Anglo-Saxon words: "make," "get," "do," "place," rather than "implement," "obtain," "receive," will help to avoid such awkward English. As the chief of the State Department interpretation section commented, "Why say 'is converted into becoming' or 'is in the process of becoming'…Why not say 'get'? 'It's getting cold!'"[53]

The ability to rethink, to use short words, and to transform a Russian text into good English is a function of the interpreter's skill, talent and experience as well as of his knowledge of English. He must be extremely careful in dividing his attention between listening, understanding, recoding and delivering. Careful attention to context and meaning are of enormous practical importance. If the prime minister of an African country refers to the *продолжение ____политики расизма,* an interpreter who has missed the adjective can with confidence insert any negative epithet such as "terrible," "horrible," or "odious." Even if the interpreter has missed or failed to understand *углубление,* when a speaker refers to the improvement in relations between our countries, *выступая за расширение и _____контактов,* he clearly has in mind some kind of increase, expansion or intensification,. And if the all-important verb is missed, context can come to the rescue: *Имея в виду возможные последствия, возможное уничтожение всей человеческой цивилизации, мы должны делать все возможно, чтобы _____ угрозу ядерной войны.* The speaker obviously wishes countries to do all they can to "prevent," "stop" or "avert" the outbreak of nuclear war.

To follow context and meaning the interpreter must recode syntactic chunks or segments rather than individual words. As scientists have shown, breaking up the material into logical segments also puts less strain on the memory:

> …the span of absolute memory imposes severe limitations on the amount of information that we are able to receive, process, and remember. By organizing the stimulus input simultaneously into several dimensions and successively into a sequence of chunks, we manage to break (or at least stretch) this informational bottleneck.[54]

The entire interpretation process of listening, understanding, remembering, recoding and uttering is a function of the nature of human language and speech. It has been theorized, along the lines proposed by Vygotsky, that in going between two lexical-semantic systems (e.g. Russian and English) words of the source language are decoded on an abstract or symbolic plane before being recoded in the target language.[55] Though the interpreter is thus going from surface structure to deep structure and back to surface structure, he may short-circuit the descent to the abstract plane by selecting frequently occurring surface structure correspondences. But the more familiar he is with the deeper levels at which languages correspond, and with the principles governing the generation of word combinations and sentences, the smoother and better his interpretation.

CHAPTER II

HOW HE WORKS:
THE TRICKS OF THE TRADE

Condensation, deliberate omission and addition, synecdoche and metonymy, antonymic constructions, grammatical inversion and the use of semantic equivalents are a few of the tools which help the interpreter do his job. As one professional noted, deliberate omission and condensation are quite different from omission errors resulting from non-comprehension:

> There are so many tiresome repetitions, such a great number of pyramided systems, that the interpreter feels it certainly will do no harm, maybe even help, if a few words are left out. How strong this temptation may be can well be appreciated by anyone who has sat through after-dinner speeches or other similar long-winded discourse and wished, in a rage that had to remain unspoken, that there were some way to amputate the wildly sprouting verbiage. The interpreter has that power.[1]

While purely subjective omissions and gratuitous editing obviously are to be avoided, the very nature of simultaneous interpretation is predicated on a certain amount of cutting and pruning. One study has shown that the average length of sentences in simultaneous interpretation is one to two words shorter than in written translation, and that syntax tends to be simpler.[2] If the Russian material is redundant, adds nothing to meaning, or if the speaker is racing along, the interpreter must resort to lexical or syntactical compression *(речевая компрессия)* to keep from falling too far behind or omitting important segments. He may drop one or more of a series of adjectives, or may engage in semantic condensation: *на международном, национальном и местном уровнях* may become "on all levels" or "on several levels." Abbreviations such as UN for the United Nations or CPRF for the Communist Party of the Russian Federation may be useful timesavers. Though he may try to find shorter words or drop superfluous words, the interpreter must use great care in deciding what precisely *is* superfluous and what can be omitted without doing violence to the text. The more experienced the interpreter, and the greater his familiarity with the material, the better his editing.

The ability to condense is crucial to successful interpretation. A specialist in interpreter training has written that "an interpreter who cannot abstract is very much like a soldier who, once out of ammunition, doesn't know any better than to surrender."[3] A flair for editing is particularly important for Russian-English interpreters because Russian tends to be more verbose and English more condensed: *"В целом в русском языке преобладают более развернутые, а в английском – более редуцированные или компрессованные способы."*[4] Both the length of the individual words and the grammatical constructions make for longer phrases in Russian.

For example, *решение начать забастовку* becomes "strike decision;" *программа космических исследований* can reduce to "space program."[5]

While key nouns and verbs must be translated, adjectival phrases and modifiers are prime candidates for condensation or omission. In simultaneous interpretation as opposed to written translation, *"чаще употребляют существительные, глаголы, прилагательные и наречия за счет уменьшения доли местоимений, числительных, предлогов, союзов и частиц."*[6] But here, too, context is the decisive factor: in some situations a noun or verb may have to go. *Госсекретарь предложил созвать конференцию* can become "The Secretary of State proposed a conference" (which is obviously going to convene and not to disband).[7] *Просмотр состоится 22-го сентября:* "The showing is on September 22" rather than "will take place on," an economy of several syllables. *Мы хотели бы съездить к вам в Канаду* can shorten to "We would like to visit you" (or "your country") rather than the clumsy "We would like to come to you to your country," as one interpreter announced. *Это было опубликовано в газете Нью-Йорк Таймс* sounds simply silly as "This was published in the newspaper the *New York Times.*" "This appeared in the *New York Times*" is more idiomatic and saves syllables. If the publication is not well-known, however, the word "newspaper" should be retained.

Expressions such as *в области* – e.g. *в области экономики, в связи с этим, в частности, как известно, при этом,* can also easily be dropped. *В области экономики* reduces to "in economics."[8] Connectives and superfluous interjections, along with such verbal *вода* as *ну, видите, и так* and other devices which allow the speaker to prepare his next utterance can safely be dropped. Adjectives such as *представленный, вышеупомянутый,* or *существующий* can often safely be dropped and replaced by the English definite article or by "this."

> Представленный доклад получил поддержку большинства делегатов
> The/this/draft was supported/backed/by the majority of the delegates.
>
> Рассматриваемый доклад содержит пять глав.
> This report contains/has/five chapters/sections.

With a very rapid speaker more drastic cuts may be needed:

> В своем послании всем делегатам нашей конференции президент
> Соединенных Штатов Америки Билл Клинтон сказал:
> In his message to us, President Clinton said:

or

> Перу, Аргентина, Уругвай, Боливия и многие другие страны
> латиноамериканского континента выступили за...
> Many countries of Latin America favored...

Natalya Strelkova used the following types of examples to teach her students at the former Maurice Thorez Institute how to turn literal translations into idiomatic English. Though these sentences are intended for translators, interpreters can "edit" orally, taking care not to drop important points:[9]

Russian text:

> Этот визит, подчеркивается в коммюнике, является важным вкладом в
> дело дальнейшего укрепления и развития дружественных отношений и
> братского сотрудничества.

16

Literal translation:

The visit, stresses the communique, is an important contribution to the cause of further strengthening and developing friendly relations and fraternal cooperation.

Edited version:

The visit is an important contribution to friendly relations and (fraternal) cooperation, says the communique.

In the last sentence "fraternal" can be omitted to save time. Or the interpreter could begin the sentence thus: "The visit, states the communique, is an important contribution," etc.

Russian text:

Эти соглашения предусматривают создание необходимых условий для дальнейшего развития экономического сотрудничества и использования преимуществ международного разделения труда.

Literal translation:

These agreements envisage the creation of the necessary conditions promoting the growth of economic cooperation and the utilization of the advantages offered by international division of labor.

Edited version:

These agreements will promote economic cooperation and make full use of the advantages offered by international division of labor.

Russian text:

Эти меры подчинили производство интересам удовлетворения потребностей народа.

Literal version:

These measures have subjected the interests of production to the interests of satisfaction of the needs of the people.

Edited version:

These measures have geared production to the needs of the people.

Though the interpreter does not have time for reflection and review and is less likely than the translator to risk major rearrangements of the components of a sentence, such oral editing is crucial for the generation of an idiomatic English sentence.

While Russian-English interpretation tends to condense rather than to expand, English grammar and structure may require the addition of articles, auxiliaries or modals in compound tenses (e.g. we shall have been doing this) or pronouns and possessives: *Подняла руку* – "She raised her hand." What the Russians term *реалии* – various phenomena of Russian or Soviet life – may need fleshing out for clarification:

Днем они пошли с друзьями в ЗАГС, а вечером свадьбу справили в ресторане "Арбат".
In the afternoon they went to sign the marriage registry, and in the evening they had a reception in the Arbat restaurant.

В понедельник пионеры уезжали в лагеря.
On Monday the Pioneers—members of the Soviet children's organization—were leaving for summer camp.

A literal translation, "the pioneers went off to camp," might convey some strange ideas of wild west explorers visiting concentration camps. Of course, the type of clarification required depends on the audience's familiarity with Russia and the former Soviet Union. A group of State Department analysts would not require the same explanations as a New Jersey housewives' gardening club.

Another technique involves metonymy and synecdoche, making the general specific and the specific general. When there is no equivalent in English for a general concept in Russian, or if the interpreter has missed a word, substitution of a more specific term is a good solution. *Нужно добавить зелень в суп* could be rendered as "parsley and other herbs."[10] And a specific term can often be successfully used to replace a general one. The interpreter who fails to understand *айва* in a list with *яблоки, груши и персики* would be quite safe in referring to "another fruit." "A bird" is better than saying nothing for *ласточка,* and translating *черемуха* as a "flowering tree" is better than embarrassed silence if "bird cherry" does not spring to mind. "We've eaten" will do nicely for *мы позавтракали,* particularly if the interpreter is not sure whether the speaker has in mind breakfast or lunch, and the English "student" can cover *студент, ученик* or *учащийся.*

An approximate synonym can also cover an interpreter's sudden memory blank. If the speaker is going on about the need for *разрядка напряженности в интересах мира* and the interpreter has forgotten "detente," he can talk about the need to improve relations. Or if "as wise as Solomon" does not come to mind for *семь пядей во лбу* the interpreter can say "he paid him a compliment." The ultimate degree of such descriptive avoidance of specific items occurs when the interpreter simply has no idea of what the speaker has said. Following a delegate's statement, "*А сейчас я хочу говорить о ————————*" if "————————" is incomprehensible, short of shutting off the microphone and bursting into tears, a solution is, "There is another point I would like to raise," or "There is something else I wish to say." More often than not in the next sentence the speaker will go into detail and clarify his thought.

Antonymic inversion, changing positives to negatives and vice versa, is a very useful device for avoiding literal translation. *Я все помню* can be rendered as "I haven't forgotten anything," or *Вы должны молчать* as "You mustn't say anything" rather than the more literal and awkward "You must be silent." *Там очень неплохо* can be "It was great there" or "things were fine."[11] Such flips, of course, depend on context, and there is often no reason to reverse a positive or negative statement. This is a matter of idiomatic usage. Take the Russian *Я их понимаю.* "I understand them" would be perfectly acceptable for explaining why people did something fairly neutral—decided to study English or moved to a bigger apartment. But if these people were being criticized for their apparently rational actions, then "I for one/myself/personally don't blame them" comes closer to the real meaning. Or *Это нередко бывает* implies "This happens often."[12] A few more examples:[13]

> Мы надеемся, что он от нас не убежит.
> We hope he'll stay.
>
> Не беспокойтесь.
> Take it easy/Relax.
>
> Им предложили не торопиться.
> They were told not to rush.

Этот диалект вышел из употребления в семнадцатом веке.
This dialect has not been spoken/used since the seventeenth century.

Без пиджака
In shirtsleeves

Не терять голову
To keep one's head

Ляжем поздно.
We'll stay up late.

Не унывай.
Keep at it/Stay with it.

Antonymic inversion can be particularly useful with certain *словосочетания* (word combinations) involving verbal negation:[14]

Не иметь себе равных	To be second to none
Не придавать значения	To overlook
Не принимать всерьез	To take lightly
Не соглашаться	To take issue with
Не содержать	To be free of
Не уступать	To be as good as
Не требовать пояснения	To be self-explanatory
Не отставать от	To keep up/pace with
Не поддаваться воздействию	To be immune to
Не принимать во внимание	To disregard/discount

Grammatical inversion and the switching of grammatical categories, translating a verb by a noun, a noun by a verb or an adjective by an adverb is another way of avoiding *mot-à-mot* interpretation. For example:[15]

Подняться оказалось легче, чем он ожидал.
The climb was easier than he had expected.

И в промышленном, и в военном отношении, эти планы нашей страны…
Militarily and industrially, our country's plans…

Их было больше.
They prevailed.

Он человек начисто лишенный моральных ценностей.
He has no moral values at all/whatsoever.

Этот форум мог бы квалифицированно и с необходимой глубиной рассмотреть всю совокупность вопросов разоружения.
This forum could engage in/provide competent and in-depth consideration/ analysis of the whole/entire/full range of disarmament questions.

Мы с пониманием относимся к их стремлениям.
We feel for/empathize with/side with/support their desires/wishes/aspirations.

Interpretation often requires syntactic inversion, which will be dealt with in the section on syntax. A few simple examples:[16]

В этой стране много проблем.
There are a lot of problems in this country/This country has a lot of problems.

Фильм шел с переводом?
Was there interpretation for the film? Was interpretation provided?

Because of the time required to successfully transpose all the elements of a long sentence, complex syntactic inversions are more often found in written translation than in simultaneous interpretation. Such a transformation may also result in a longer sentence, which is not in the interpreter's interest:

> Они завоевали эту территорию.
> The/This territory fell to them.

The use of semantic equivalents and the search for expressions which avoid *mot-à-mot* renderings are vitally important to sounding idiomatic. Russians are *глубоко убеждены,* but Americans are firmly—rather than deeply—convinced. A *содержательный* report is "informative" to an English speaker. *Идти кому-то навстречу* is to accommodate someone. *Не кажется ли* does not necessarily require the verb "seem." "Isn't it likely?" will get the point across. *Случайные люди в политике* are not random individuals but laymen or outsiders in politics; *белые пятна* in our knowledge are "gaps." *Политическое лицо мира* can be rendered as the political realities, situation, or configuration in today's world. A few more examples:[17]

> зловещие планы – sinister prospect(s)
> он снял трубку – he answered the phone

Syntactic and/or semantic equivalents can provide an idiomatic English rendering of the Russian:[18]

> Он сказал ей свое мнение о них.
> He told her what he thought of them.
>
> Послали за врачом.
> The doctor has been summoned/called/sent for.
>
> Ваша жена прекрасно готовит.
> Your wife is an excellent cook.

Here nouns replace verbs (*готовит*/cook), syntax and active and passive moods are reversed (*послали*/has been summoned), and a noun replaces a verb (*мнение –* thought). Fixed formulaic phrases can be rendered through carefully chosen equivalents:[19]

Объявляю заседание открытым.	I call the meeting to order.
Не вешайте трубку.	Hold on/Just a minute.
Я вас слушаю.	Hello (if on the phone)/What can I do for you?/I'll take your order (if in a restaurant).

These Russian and English idioms are so different that literal translation would sound comic. Hardest of all is the search for *cultural* rather than for purely linguistic or semantic equivalents, for though these are often vastly different in the two languages, the role of an interpreter of culture is the interpreter's most important and most difficult function.

CHAPTER III

INTERPRETING CULTURES

Звучат во всех краях планеты
Без перевода, как Москва,
Большевики, Октябрь, Советы,
Мир, Спутник – русские слова.

А. Твардовский[1]

The specific nature and structure of a language determine the way its speakers view the world, and serve as an organizing principle of culture. As Whorf has posited, "Facts are unlike to speakers whose language background provides for unlike formulation of them."[2] Of crucial importance to the interpreter is the fact that "the grammatical pattern of a language (as opposed to its lexical stock) determines those aspects of each experience that must be expressed in the given language."[3] For example, the Russian sentence *я нанял работницу* conveys immediate information concerning the sex of the employer, the sex of the employee, and the verb tense, which are lacking in the English statement "I hired a worker." (Masculine or feminine speaker? Male or female worker? Hired or has hired?) The effect of grammatical categories on the semantic impact of such a Russian sentence is enormous and, as Jakobson has pointed out, "naturally the attention of native speakers and listeners will be focused on such items as are compulsory in their verbal code."[4] An excellent example of the problems grammar imposes on semantics—and on the interpreter—is the sentence, *"Ты откуда пришла, с верху, из Нижнего, да не пришла, по воде-то не ходят "* from Gorky's *Детство*. Gender, aspect, motion verbs and the play on upper-lower *верх-Нижний* create a chain of translation problems.[5] The absence—or existence—of entire categories of words in one or another language creates a major problem for the interpreter. Russian lacks articles and a complex tense system. English does not have aspect, case endings, or the Russian system of prefixation. *Я искал жену* through the accusative ending indicates that the speaker is searching for his wife, while *я искал жены* can imply that he would have liked to get married. The article may be indicated by words such as *один* or *тот*:

Тот мужчина, который только что вошел – ее брат.
The man who just came in is her brother.

Один его друг сказал мне это.
A friend of his told me that.

A series of words which are specific in English are non-specific in Russian: *рука* hand/arm), *нога* (leg/foot), *палец* (finger/toe), while there are no words in English replicating the Russian distinction between *свекровь* and *тёща*, both of which are rendered as "mother-in-law," or between *жениться* and *выйти замуж*.[6]

Literal interpretation which ignores such aspects of the language can produce grammatically wrong or confusing statements. "The struggle for detente and friendship among nations got *a* considerable support," writes *Moscow News* (2/5/89). Or take the sentence, *"По праздникам и воскресеньям муж работает в гараже."*[7] The translation "in *a* garage" would give the impression that the speaker's husband has a second job on weekends and holidays, when she in fact means that he tinkers with the car in *the* (their) garage in his spare time.

Words which characterize the life, culture and historical development of any given country often have no precise equivalents in other languages. It has even been argued that only proper names, geographic, scientific and technical terms, days of the week, months and numerals have full lexical correspondence in several languages.[8] If a term does not convey the flavor of the original language and is entirely anglicized all cultural connotations are lost. The interpreter's or translator's greatest difficulty lies in idiomatically transposing a text into the culture of the receiver while somehow maintaining the color of the original.[9] *Обед* translated as "lunch" may suggest a sandwich and a cup of coffee to an American but oily chunks of beet and carrot, a watery soup, a slab of meat and fried potatoes to a Russian. The taste and texture of *котлеты* are closer to American meat loaf than to "cutlets" or even to hamburgers. This difficulty of cross-cultural equivalents has been beautifully illustrated by the translator Richard Lourie:

> The translator's heart sinks at the sight of words like *коммуналка* which he knows he must render as "communal apartment." He is willing to lose all the coloration of the original—the slightly foreign *коммун,* as in *коммунист,* made Russian by the kiss of the diminutive suffix *ка,* here expressing a sort of rueful affection. The English term conjures up an image of a Berkeley, Calif., kitchen, where hippies with headbands are cooking brown rice, whereas the Russian term evokes a series of vast brown rooms with a family living in each, sharing a small kitchen where the atmosphere is dense with everything that cannot be said and the memory of everything that shouldn't have been said, but was.[10]

The interpreter's role as a mediator between cultures as well as languages is of critical importance, and here his work is hardest and most rewarding. As one corporation executive noted, "You can manage foreign languages. It's the culture that trips you up."[11] Or as a Russian writer commented, *ведь перевод – это не только взаимодействие языков, но и взаимодействие культур… Процесс перевода 'пересекает' не только границы языков, но и границы культур."*[12]

Hence the need in the interpreting field for "mediating men" or "persons with inter-cultural experiences."[13] The fact that cultural differences act as a block to understanding, however, is often blithely ignored by both conference participants and interpreters. If the interpreter "knows" the "language," then everything should be just fine. This problem of cross-cultural communication was nicely demonstrated by a Japanese-speaking American professor who assumed at the end of a faculty meeting he had chaired on a strike-torn Japanese campus that the group had finally reached agreement, since all the professors had spoken in favor of the item under discussion. "All this may be true," his Japanese colleague remarked at the end of the meeting, "but you are still mistaken. The meeting arrived at the opposite conclusion. You understood all the words correctly, but you did not understand the silences between them."[14]

This problem of cultural communication was particularly complex in Soviet-American contacts, and is still an issue in Russian-American relations today. Edmund Glenn gives an excellent example in his brilliant essay, "Semantic Difficulties in International Communication."

> It is too often assumed that the problem of submitting the ideas of one nation or cultural group to members of another national or cultural group is principally a problem of language...Soviet diplomats often qualify the position taken by their Western counterparts as "incorrect" *неправильное*. In doing so, they do not accuse their opponents of falsifying facts, but merely of not interpreting them "correctly." This attitude is explicable only if viewed in the context of the Marxist-Hegelian pattern of thought, according to which historical situations evolve in a unique and predetermined manner. Thus an attitude not in accordance with theory is not in accordance with truth either; it is as incorrect as the false solution to a mathematical problem. Conversely, representatives of our side tend to promote compromise or transactional solutions. Margaret Mead writes that this attitude merely bewilders many representatives of the other side, and leads them to accuse us of hypocrisy, because it does not embody any ideological position recognizable to them. The idea that 'there are two sides to every question' is an embodiment of nominalistic philosophy, and it is hard to understand for those unfamiliar with this philosophy or its influence.[15]

This heavy use of *неправильное* led many Western diplomats to see the Soviet side as stubborn and dogmatic, while Soviets perceived the American insistence on looking at both sides of the question either as deliberate attempts to avoid taking a position or as a way of covering up a stand. Unless the interpreter had time to explain Hegelian theory to Western listeners, he could say "we disagree" or simply "no," instead of "that's wrong" or "that's incorrect," thus rephrasing the Soviet position in Western linguistic-cultural terms. Soviet references to *определенная стадия* of a historical process or a meeting could mean "this particular stage," "another stage" or nothing more than "some stage." The words "definite" or "determined"—all too frequent translations of *определенный*—sound odd and dogmatic to a Western listener. "It fits in with the Marxist interpretation of history according to which evolution proceeds necessarily from one 'well-determined phase' to another," writes Glenn.[16] In Marxist political writing *определенный* does and can convey a notion of determinism, but in ordinary speech the word is semantically quite neutral and should be translated as such: *определенные идеи*"—certain ideas," *определенные люди*—"some people." Here a problem arises when a text (or term) oriented towards the bearer of one culture is aimed at a foreign receiver. A Soviet listener would have had no problem with *неправильно* or *определенная стадия*.[17] It is ironic that so many texts aimed at foreign audiences—e.g. *Moscow News, Soviet Life,* speeches delivered abroad—were written using a terminology intended for Soviet readers and listeners.

The cultural knowledge and attitude of the interpreter can play an extremely important role in communication situations, particularly in those involving small groups, and may impact on the outcome of the conversation. Though today the majority of Russian texts are free from Marxist clichés, the language still bears the stamp of the Soviet past, and words such as *правильно* and *неправильно* still pop up, a linguistic legacy which can easily be rephrased for modern Western listeners.

The question of linguistic and cultural identification is particularly relevant for compound and coordinate bilinguals.[18] While compound bilinguals have acquired their two languages from childhood, they are not generally familiar with the culture of one of the languages—e.g. an American who learned Russian entirely in the US in a Russian-speaking home but had little or no contact with Russian life. Coordinate bilinguals acquire the second language somewhat later than the first, associate words with empirical referents and maintain two distinct linguistic systems—e.g. an American of Russian background from a family with a strong interest in Russian culture, who, even if Russian was not spoken a great deal at home, has spent much time in Russia. Theoretically, the coordinate bilinguals will produce interpretation with greater equivalency than the compound group because of their separate referent systems for the two cultures.[19] To a compound Russian-English bilingual the word *ресторан* as used for an eatery in Soviet Russia may conjure up the image of a place where people gather to eat and drink, while a coordinate will see the huge smoke-filled room, dance floor, orchestra, din and lengthy meals which were part of Soviet dining out. Both groups may be subject to role strain if for intellectual, emotional or psychological reasons they identify more strongly with one of the cultures and try—consciously or unconsciously—to tilt the outcome of negotiations in that side's favor. The interpreter who substitutes his own thinking for that of the parties to negotiations, imparts privileged knowledge to either side, or takes advantage of his knowledge of the language and culture to influence communication, is the opposite extreme of the automaton locked up in the glass booth. He must use his grasp of the two languages and cultures to impartially and objectively explain each side to the other. Such objectivity is particularly important in Russian-American relations, for even in the post-cold war era the two side still view each other through the prism of deep-rooted prejudices and stereotypes.

A Russian-English interpreter must have an excellent knowledge of *реалии,* the phenomena of daily life, politics and culture in Russia and the US. Such Russian *реалии* have been defined as "words that stand for realities that do not exist in the West and have no ready verbal equivalent in English (e.g. *председатель колхоза, субботник,* " or "those words that, though they do exist in English, mean something else, and… are used in a different context *(пафос созидания)*."[20] *Идеализм* used by a Soviet speaker referred to a philosophical trend of thought opposed to materialism, while for an American the word means the advocacy of lofty ideals over practical considerations.

The cultural context of *реалии* must be maintained in the English translation. Just as a Chinese-English interpreter would not turn rice into bread, the Russian-English interpreter should not turn Russian *лимонад* (fruit-flavored soda) into American lemonade, or the Komsomol into the Boy Scouts. For a Russian, *общественная жизнь* means various kinds of civic and public activities, including volunteer or community work, while, as a Russian commentator noted, in the US, "'social life' *означает всякое отношение с людьми, включая посещение платных курсов, театров и ресторанов."* Nor does Russian *общественная работа* with its political and educational connotations have much in common with English "social work," which *"означает, в основном, помощь беднякам, обычно оплачиваемую местными властями."*[21] Today, however, as Western concepts and words intrude into Russian life and language, an enormous number of English-language *реалии*

24

require translation into Russian, but aside from recognizing them in order to translate them from Russian back into English this is not our subject here. Many of these English words have already taken firm root in Russian, e.g. *брифинг, имидж, холдинговая компания, дисплей, плейер.*

The interpreter's job is to make these *реалии* understandable to his listener. In the sentence *Они решили пожениться и пошли в ЗАГС,* rather than struggling with "Registration Bureau" or "Palace of Weddings," the interpreter can say "they took out a marriage license," "they signed the register," or simply, "they got married." *Реалии* highly specific to a culture may require description. *Он получил путевку в дом отдыха*—"He got a voucher for his vacation trip/center." "Rest home," as Strelkova has pointed out, "sounds like something for the old or the ill, an expensive establishment to stay at while recovering from a long illness."[22] If pressed for time— and on the assumption that saying less is always safer than saying too much—the interpreter may simply say "He went off on vacation." The sentence *мы долго стояли в очереди на квартиру* was once translated by an interpreter as "We stood on line for a long time for an apartment," creating the impression that one could obtain housing by patiently standing in the street. What is meant is "For a long time we were on a waiting list." The interpreter must both know his *реалии* and be able to recode quickly. A woman saying, "*У нас две комнаты и общая кухня с соседями*" is not referring to a "common kitchen,"—a phrase with a possible double meaning. She means "We share the kitchen with the other people in our communal apartment." *Соседи* is a *ложный друг переводчика,* for to the American ear "neighbors" imply only the people in the next apartment, not in one's own. Or take a complaint about the *низкая культура противозачаточных средств у нас.* The "culture of contraceptives" sounds bizarre indeed. The speaker is referring to poor quality and lack of knowledge concerning birth control devices. "Our problems with birth control devices" would cover both categories.

A word such as *коллектив* needs explanation. *Наш школьный коллектив* might refer to a class or a sports team, depending on context, while *коллектив нашего института* is the staff and *коллектив нашего завода* the employees. The word could mean group, personnel, staff, colleagues, co-workers, associates, or all those who work at X.[23] The eminent Russian interpreter G.V. Chernov has suggested descriptive translations for a series of such *реалии:*[24]

рабочий поселок	industrial settlement, workers' community
стаж	seniority, period of service
детская консультация	child welfare center
медалист	honor student
вредная профессия	hazardous occupation
поликлиника	health center, outpatient clinic
ЗАГС	civil registry office
курсы повышения квалификации	refresher courses, advanced training courses
субботник	an unpaid weekend stint/volunteer effort/ community effort/donation of a day's work.[25]

This list could be continued indefinitely. The interpreter must be familiar with the specific phenomenon and recode it into English rather than translating literally. Description may replace translation:

> Они пили чай из пиалок.
> They drank tea from small china cups with no handles/small Central Asian china teacups.

In those rare cases when the interpreter is not pressed for time he can give both the Russian word and the English definition: "They drank tea from *pialki,* Central Asian china teacups with no handles." In *Он объяснял эти идеи в своем автореферате* the word *автореферат* means nothing to the average American listener: "He explained these ideas in his *автореферат,* the published summary of his thesis/dissertation."

L.A. Cherniakhovskaia, a Russian specialist on Russian and English syntax, gives several good examples of translation-explanations of *реалии:*[26]

> Они надеются, что недалек тот день, когда в стране будут открыты
> крупные залежи.
> They hope that large deposits will soon be discovered in Kazakhstan.

We know from context that Kazakhstan is the particular republic referred to, and the name is much less confusing than "the country." *Недалек тот день* could, of course, be rendered literally—"the day is not far off when"—but English usage tends to bring this kind of lofty Russian prose down to earth. Cherniakhovskaia suggests "they hope eventually to discover," but "soon" is shorter and closer to the original *недалек.* Or:

> 22 июня он ушел добровольцем на фронт.
> On June 22, the day Nazi Germany attacked, he went to/volunteered for the front.

The interpreter's decision here must be based on his audience. For an audience of historians adding "On the day Nazi Germany attacked" would be insulting, but to say only "On June 22" to a group of American farmers might be confusing.

The interpreter may also change Soviet historical terms to those used in the West, e.g. rendering *Великая Отечественная Война* as "World War II."

Contemporary *реалии* as well as historical references may require such cultural conversion of terms. For example,[27]

> Наши курорты функционируют круглый год.
> Our health resorts are/stay open all year round/year round.

The literal rendering, "Our resorts function the whole year," does not work. Or:

> Эти три года дали нам главное, что необходимое для молодых людей –
> поле для активной деятельности.
> These three years gave us what (the) young people needed most/what was most important for young people, a chance to do big/important/great things/to build the country/to make full use of their abilities/gave young people a chance to work and grow.

The literal rendering, "a field for active activity" is comically repetitive. While to a native speaker a Russian fixed expression may sound quite normal, to the English listener it may seem pompous or odd. Recoding can even out such stylistic differences.

The dangers of cross-cultural *mot-à-mot* rendition is particularly clear for those cognates which are *ложные друзья переводчика*. Here are a few examples of such words which can—and do—regularly entrap interpreters:[28]

адресный	targeted, specific (адресные рекомендации, санкции)
актуальный	topical, pressing, relevant, immediate, important
аргумент	reasons, convictions (not disagreement)
артист	any performing artist
авантюра	a shady or risky undertaking
декада	ten *days,* not ten years
декорации	stage sets
диверсия	military diversionary tactic, subversion, sabotage
экономный	thrifty, frugal, practical
фальшивый	artificial, forged, imitation, counterfeit
характер	nature, disposition (a character in a work of literature is a *персонаж*)
характеристика	description, a letter of recommendation
конкретный	actual, specific, positive, definite
курьезный	amusing, odd, intriguing, funny
манифестация	public mass demonstration
митинг	mass public demonstration, rally (never a get-together of a few people)
момент	period of time, element, point, aspect (*один из моментов его выступления*)
нормально	well, properly (*он вел себя нормально*)
оперативный	effective, quick, practical, current, timely
пафос	excitement, inspiration, enthusiasm, emotion, thrill
персонаж	character in a literary work
перспективный	promising, future, long-range
поэма	a long epic poem, not short verses
претендовать	lay claim to, have pretensions to: *Он претендовал на имущество своего соседа*
симпатичный	nice, pleasant, sweet
титул	title for the nobility (e.g. duke, count)
циничный	crude, shameless, ruthless, amoral

Many of these cognates are clearly very far apart in meaning. Correct translation of these words and translation-explanations of *реалии* will go a long way in successfully conveying to the listener what the speaker is trying to say.

CHAPTER IV

POLITICAL TERMINOLOGY

The language of Soviet political discourse posed a special set of problems for interpreters. Tass and Novosti had listeners used to such oddities as "It is not in vain that," or "Western countries' solidarity, forgetting all ideological boundaries, was all the more effective, since the Soviet authorities agreed to accept the aid and removed bureaucratic obstacles."[1] The Russian-English interpreter had to be particularly sensitive to literal renderings and do his best to recode Soviet political clichés in idiomatic English. Here the danger of hanging on to individual words became glaringly apparent. Russian political texts in international organizations such as the United Nations (occasionally written in what is known as UNese) also often suffer from the influence of English, resulting in highly un-Russian constructions. Despite a tendency in post-perestroika Russian towards greater use of colloquialisms and more informal speech, these texts may still be weighed down by clumsy phrasing, turgid syntax, and lengthy, lumbering clauses.

There are plenty of Russian-English cognates—and *ложные друзья*—in political terminology, e.g. *революция* and revolution. In Russian the word still implies a radical and progressive—i.e. positive—change, while in English it may refer to a progressive or a reactionary event. A sentence such as "Revolutions are a common occurrence in Latin America" would be rendered in Russian as *Государственные перевороты – обычное явление в Латинской Америке*. Speaking of a palace revolution, English might prefer "coup d'état."

Эксплуатация and exploitation can also have different meanings. Exploitation of an oppressed people is quite different from *эксплуатация минеральных ресурсов*. Other political terms may be emotionally charged. In Russian *круги* meaning "circles" very often has a pejorative tinge, *империалистические* or *капиталистические,* or, more neutrally, *официальные* or *деловые*. But *круги* are clearly negative in a sentence such as *Эти круги делают ставку на безудержную гонку вооружений*. In English "circles" is not always the most idiomatic translation; "quarters," "sections," "community," "forces," "elites" or another synonym may be more appropriate.

Это предложение не встретило сочувственного отклика в официальных кругах.
This proposal did not find favor in official quarters.

Деловые круги
business circles (neutral)

международные научные круги
the international scientific community

правящие круги
the ruling elite, officialdom, power circles, policy makers[2]

Общественный, государственный and *публичный* do not directly correspond to English "social," "state," and "public." *Государственная библиотека* is a state library if we are talking about the Moscow State Library (formerly the Lenin Library) but a public library if the reference is to a local institution. *Общественное мнение* is public opinion, and in the U.S. the *государственный сектор* is the public or government sector vs. the private *(частный)* sector. An *общественный деятель* is not a social or "public" worker but someone active in local or community affairs or a public figure; in America such a person might even be a philanthropist.[3]

Russian social and political terms which have no direct equivalents in English can be invented, described, or left in transliteration. The choice of word depends on context. *Служащие* can be employees or white-collar workers. *Отсутствие безработицы* can be lack of unemployment or, more commonly, its antonym in English—full employment. If a word is well known to English speakers the interpreter may choose to leave it in Russian, e.g. *kolkhoz* rather than collective farm. In the case of a less familiar word such as *область* he may say "oblast'" or "region."

The interpreter must use care in putting Russian translations of American terms back into English. The US *министр обороны* referred to by a Russian delegate is the Secretary of Defense, while the *министр юстиции* is the Attorney General. *Политика поощрения/продвижения национальных меньшинств* may be Affirmative Action. Russian political terms which do not exist in the American system require descriptive explanation: *наказ* means instructions or requests from voters to an elected official, and *секвестр* refers to budget cuts. [4]

The political terminology introduced by the Gorbachev era provides excellent examples of the need for such description and transliteration. For several months until *гласность* and *перестройка* were absorbed into English the newspapers wrote of "openness" and "restructuring." Such terms as *выводиловка* (juggling or padding figures and statistics) or *администрирование* (the abuse of administrative power or authoritarianism), however, require recoding.

The following example of recoding Soviet political prose to avoid literalisms lists various kinds of people involved in political activities. While the Soviet Peace Committee has been relegated to the past, the linguistic problems posed by this sentence are still relevant.

> Советский комитет защиты мира, являясь самой массивной неправительственной организацией, объединяет в своих рядах десятки миллионов людей – рабочих, крестьян, представителей интеллигенции, ученых, художников, артистов, религиозных деятелей, ветеранов войны, молодежь.[5]

Literal translation:

> The Soviet Committee for the Protection of Peace, being the most mass Soviet nongovernmental organization, united in its ranks tens of millions of people.

Now for some reworking. The first four words can be reduced to "The Soviet Peace Committee." *Являясь* here means "as," not "being," and can safely be omitted. *Самая массовая* is a fancy way of saying "biggest" or "largest." *Объединяет в*

своих рядах boils down to "brings together" or "unites." "Tens of millions" would be more idiomatic in English as "dozens," but neither "tens" nor "dozens" is really necessary. The point is that a great many people are involved.
Recoded version:

> The Soviet Peace Committee, the largest Soviet nongovernmental organization,
> brings together millions of people.

The original Russian test had 34 syllables, the literal rendering 44, and the reworked text 33. The recoded text is both more idiomatic and saves eleven syllables, a considerable economy when a speaker is talking quickly.

Continuing with the text: the eleven-syllable *представителей интеллигенции* becomes a five-syllable "intellectuals." *Ученые* is broader than "scientists;" "scholars" is a possibility, but "academics" would better cover all those involved in teaching and research. *Художники* are painters, but if the interpreter has said "artists" and is then confronted by *артисты,* the *артисты* can become "performing artists." *Религиозные деятели* (nine syllables) reduce to "the clergy" (three syllables).

A difficult person to deal with in Russian texts is the ever present *собеседник.* "Interlocutor" is an awkward solution. The interpreter may refer to "the other party," "the other side," or insert the person's name or title:

> Как я сказал моему собеседнику…
> As I said to Mr. Ivanov/the Director…

Or a pronoun can be used:

> As I said to him/her/them

In some cases the word can be omitted:

> Я несколько раз подчеркивал моему *собеседнику,* что…
> I repeatedly made the point that…
> I emphasized several times that…[6]

English-speaking listeners were often struck by the plethora of words suggesting military action which dominated Soviet political and economic terminology: *арсеналы средств, вахта мира, борьба за производительность труда, новый фронт в промышленности, ударный труд.* Though this martial tone has become considerably less strident following the collapse of the USSR, decades of this aggressive political language have left an imprint on Russian political prose. Even Soviet commentators voiced concern that such "aggressive" terminology might give foreigners the wrong impression that their society was engaged in continuous preparation for war, and suggested more neutral English renderings:

борьба за производительность труда	labor efficiency campaign
боеспособность	efficiency, readiness
борьба за первое место	competition for first place

Though English does make use of certain military metaphors, these are not as widespread and are less jarring to the English native speaker's ear than the Russian "vocabulary of war." In a brilliant essay Susan Sontag has pointed out the heavy use of military metaphors in describing illness, especially cancer: tumors "invade," cells are "bombarded with rays."[7] "Disease is seen as an invasion of alien organisms, to which the body responds by its own military operations, such as the mobilizing of immunological 'defenses,' and medicine is 'aggressive,' as in the language of most chemotherapies."[8] In other contexts English speaks of the "battle for survival," "conquest of space," "going great guns," "war of nerves," "bite the bullet." Yet such expressions do not sound as stylistically high-flown as do many Russian military metaphors.[9] These "battle flags" require idiomatic equivalents:

> Вы приехали сюда после жарких дебатов, вооруженные наказами своих избирателей.

> You've come here bearing/bringing/with/encouraged by/backed by instructions/ requests of your voters/constituents.

Even texts which actually deal with military events may require some recoding. For example:

> Великая победа над гитлеровским фашизмом, имеющая всемирно-историческое значение, – наше общее достояние и она была одержана общими усилиями народов и армий стран анти-гитлеровской коалиции, партизанов, бойцов движения сопротивления, антифашистов, демократов и патриотов, миллионов борцов за свободу.

"Hitlerite" (but not "Hitler's") is often used for *гитлеровский,* though in Western parlance "Nazi" is more common.[10] The entire phrase can be translated simply as "the historic victory over Fascism," omitting "Hitlerite" as tautological with "Fascism." *Имеющая* does not require translation and the phrase can be simply rendered as "of historic (not historical) significance." The real verb lies in the dash between *значение* and *наше:* the great victory... *is* our common/shared legacy/heritage and was won/gained by the joint efforts of the peoples and the armies of (the countries of) the antihitlerite coalition." An even shorter version would suffice: "The war was won by..." *Бойцов движения сопротивления* can reduce to "the Resistance" or "the resistance movement," and "millions of freedom fighters" is shorter than "millions of fighters for freedom." Under severe time pressure, the interpreter could reduce the entire list to "antifascists and freedom fighters," categories which basically cover all the other groups:

> The historic victory over the Nazis is our common/shared legacy/heritage and was won by the peoples and armies of the anti-fascist coalition, partisans, the Resistance movement, antifascists, (democrats and patriots) and millions of freedom fighters.

"Military" or "aggressive" terminology, however, should be toned down or neutralized only when it is inappropriate to the context of the English text.[11] Otherwise, strong words demand equally strong terms:

> Ничего они не жалеют, чтобы поддержать режим своих ставленников...совершающих кровавые преступления против этого маленького народа..

"Stooges" or "henchmen" are *ставленники,* and the crimes they are committing "bloody," or "horrendous." To save time *кровавые преступления* can be reduced to "atrocities" (nine syllables to four). As an exercise in interpretation technique, let us assume that the interpreter has forgotten or does not understand *ставленники,* and needs a word neutral enough to cover any context. "Their men" or "their supporters" would work as a filler.

Unfortunately, "military" terms used in a "civilian" context appeared with indefatigable regularity in Soviet political prose. Strelkova has rightly commented that *борьба* and *бороться* were so frequently used "that they have lost their power of denotation and have become purely functional… Unless the context includes some reference to a genuine struggle in the literal sense (such as the struggle for freedom, national liberation, or power) these words are really symbols."[12] To the English speaker, however, *борьба* sounds aggressive, a particularly odd oxymoron when they are "fighting" for peace:

> Для жителей нашей страны *борьба за мир* остается одним из наиболее важных дел.

Since presumably no one is actually out shooting for peace, the "campaign for peace," "the peace movement," "work for peace," or the "drive for peace" would be more appropriate. A *борец за мир* is a campaigner or a peace activist rather than a "fighter." The *борьба с наркотиками* is the "war on drugs" (now the accepted military metaphor in English) or a "campaign to combat drugs," and a *борьба мнений* may be a clash of opinions, while a *борьба противоположностей* is a clash of opposing views.[13] *Мы боремся за это* can be rendered as "we want this/we are striving for this" rather than "fighting" or "struggling."[14] Or *бороться против* can be "to contend with."

In some contexts, however, an actual struggle or fight is precisely what is meant:

> Поддержка справедливой борьбы этого народа против иностранных наемников.
> Support for the just struggle of this people against foreign mercenaries.
> Борьба за свободу – the fight for freedom

Context may take the interpreter even farther afield:

> Становится все яснее, где главное очаги противодействия и кто хотел бы создать фронт *борьбы* против новых подходов во внешней политике.

Очаги—"hotbeds" (as in hotbeds of tension)—can be neutralized to "focal points/ centers of resistance," and *фронт борьбы* to "those who wish to oppose/resist/create an opposition/resistance movement to new foreign policy approaches/tactics."

Another commonly used and heavily charged word is *острый*. Newspaper accounts often refer to the "sharp problems" we are facing. A textbook on Russian-English translation informs us that "they all felt acute joy,"[15] and change in Poland is described as "sharp, deepgoing, highly promising…and discussed all over the world."[16] A speaker referring to the need to *высвободить средства для решения острых экономических и социальных проблем* is speaking of "urgent" or "pressing" rather than "sharp" or "acute" problems. Acute is better used for geometric angles, awareness, or attacks of appendicitis. Or:

> Эти проблемы сегодня самые *острые* для всех нас.

While "urgent," "pressing" or "drastic" would work, "these problems are the worst," "the most important," "the gravest" or "most serious" would also be appropriate.

> Положение там не улучшается, а становится еще более острым.
> The situation there is deteriorating/exacerbated/becoming more serious/grave/drastic.

The verb *заострить* stresses intensification of action:

Позвольте *заострить* внимание членов комитета на некоторых аспектах
нашего предложения.
Allow me to call/draw/focus the attention of members of the committee to/on certain aspects
of our proposal.

Like the adjective *острый,* the noun *острота* also conveys a notion of urgency:

Особую *остроту* вопрос о запрещении испытаний ядерного оружия
приобрел в условиях нарастающей военной опасности.
The question/issue of a nuclear test ban has become particularly urgent/pressing/serious/
crucial/critical because of/given the growing danger of war (not "military danger").

В условиях is better rendered as "because of/given the" rather than the awkwardly
literal "in conditions of." Political events frequently occur in *условиях* of various
sorts:

в условиях разрядки напряженности	given/during/at this time of detente
в условиях капитализма	under capitalism
в условиях современности	now/here and now/at this time/stage/today
в условиях буржуазного общества	in the context of bourgeois society (or
	simply: in bourgeois society)[17]

The huge globe of political terminology is often divided into two hemispheres:
Good Things and Bad Things. People are either doing things to help, assist, benefit
and promote welfare, security, safety, well-being, peace and detente, or they are out
to aggravate, complicate, damage, harm, injure, destroy, devastate and annihilate all
of the above, in the name of evil, dictatorship, hegemony, horrendous, obnoxious and
inhumane policies of repression, oppression, torture, genocide, mass murder and
other very unpleasant things.

Good things are done for someone or something. Here the word *польза* makes
regular appearances:

Антивоенное движение стало сейчас важным фактором *в пользу* мира.

"The antiwar movement has now become an important factor for peace" or
"working for peace" is more idiomatic than "for the benefit of peace." Sometimes *в
пользу* is best translated by a preposition:

Создание такого механизма позволило бы объединить усилия всех
государств *в пользу* безотлагательного политического урегулирования.
The establishment of such machinery would allow all states to unite their efforts
for an immediate just settlement. (*Урегулирование* is "settlement," not "regula-
tion").

There are, however, contexts when "benefit" is appropriate. In this example the
noun becomes a verb:

Открытие прививки против этой опасной болезни будет в пользу всего
человечества.
The discovery of a vaccine against this dangerous disease will benefit all mankind.

Several positive words describing Good Things became standard clichés of Soviet political language:

Информация будет служить духовному обогащению народов, углублению
и расширению сотрудничества между ними, созданию климата доверия и
добрососедства.

"Spiritual enrichment" is an awkward literalism, and "Information will serve/help to raise the moral level of/uplift/enlighten peoples" would work better. "Intensification" is better than "deepening" for *углубление*. "A climate of trust and goodneighborliness" is fine for *доверие и добрососедство*. *Меры доверия* are confidence-building measures, not trust, and the way to trust lies through *разрядка напряженности* (relaxation of tensions). *Разрядка* is a synonym for detente.

Another very important issue is the question of security, in particular *всеобъемлющая безопасность* – comprehensive security, and *принцип ненанесения ущерба безопасности сторон* – undiminished security of both sides/without detriment to the security of the sides. To provide such security countries must act with *сдержанность*, restraint, not to be confused with the policy of *устрашения*, deterrence.

Negotiations are part of a positive process which helps provide security and other Good Things:

> Начаты и ведутся переговоры. Руководство нашей страны положительно
> оценивает этот процесс.

The interpreter should exert care regarding several adjectives commonly used to describe negotiations. *Односторонний* can mean unilateral, but in certain contexts is "lopsided" or "slanted": *Односторонний и узкий подход к этой проблеме*. *Двусторонний* is bilateral, and *многосторонний* is multilateral when referring to negotiations, but "multifaceted" or "varied" in other contexts: *многосторонний анализ этой проблемы*. *Оценивать* is all too often translated as "assess," e.g.:

> We were one in assessments of art and literature and of everything we were told
> to assess.[18]

Rather than "Our leaders positively assess" this problem, they might approve of, like, appreciate, or take a favorable view of it. A *целенаправленная политика* is a deliberate, planned, focused or purposeful policy rather than a "goal-directed" one. Or take *целесообразность*:

> Мы поддерживаем предложение о *целесообразности* подготовки
> содержательного исследования о пагубных последствиях милитаризации
> космического пространства.
> We support the proposal for a study/we support the proposal concerning the
> usefulness/point/purpose/advisability of an informative/thorough study on the
> negative/pernicious consequences of the militarization of outer space.

In this sentence the word "content" does not work for *содержательный*. If the study contains *обновленные данные* these are best rendered as "updated" rather than by variants of "renewed" or "new," since the implication is that it contains both older data and new additions. *Убедительные причины* for us to do something may be cogent, persuasive, telling or simply good reasons as well as the overused "convincing" ones. If we approve of something and wish to help, *мы солидарны с*, e.g.:

> *Мы солидарны* со справедливой борьбой этого маленького народа.

Rather than being "in solidarity with," we can associate ourselves with or back a just struggle or cause, which in Russian is often *дело*. This noun can be omitted if it adds nothing to the sentence:

Это вносит клад в *дело* упрочения международной безопасности.
This is making a significant/considerable contribution to ("the cause of" can be omitted) consolidating international security.

Законный is another good thing, but also a troublemaker, since depending on context it can mean legal, legitimate, or lawful: *законные действия,* lawful acts; *законные интересы этого народа,* the legitimate rights of this people; *его законное право подать в суд,* his legal right to sue.

What do good things do? They promote or encourage *(поощрять, содействовать)* positive measures, and they *содействуют* or *отвечают интересам народа:*

Политика нашего правительства полностью соответствует интересам и устремлениям широких масс нашего народа
The policy of our government is fully in keeping with the interests and wishes of our people/all of our people.

"All of our people" is more idiomatic than "masses." "In keeping" works in most cases for *соответствует,* while "corresponds" can sound awkward. "Is consonant with their interests" is a possibility, but, as shown by this Moscow Newsism, the construction does not always fit: "The December 29 resolution is not consonant with this ideology."[19]

Here is another kind of *соответствует:*

Этой цели *соответствовало бы* создание международной рабочей группы.
This goal would be advanced/helped/promoted by the establishment/creation of an international working group.

Or *отвечает интересам* can mean "serves the cause/interests of/works for/ promotes" or simply, "is in the interests of:"

Эти предложения *отвечают интересам* всех стран Африки, стремящихся жить в мире.
These proposals are in the interests of all African countries which want to live in peace.[20]

Ответственный is another common word that can cause trouble. Rather than "responsible," an *ответственный пост* or *решение* can be key, pivotal, or, simply, important. And *участие* is not necessarily participation; *наше участие в этом движении* can be rendered as "our involvement in this movement." Unfortunately, in the world of politics Bad Things happen a great deal more than Good Things. When everyone agrees, there is not much to debate. Big bad words can cause big bad problems for the interpreter:

Столь же очевидна несостоятельность и противоправность попыток этого правительства обосновать совершенный акт агрессии какими то ни было предлогами.

Несостоятельность can be rendered as "inconsistency" or "groundlessness," and the adjective *несостоятельный* – as in *несостоятельные принципы* or *аргументы* – as unfounded, untenable, wrong, unworkable. *Противоправность* refers to the legal system, so "illegality" would do. Or a country may perpetrate a *грубейшее надругательство,* a flagrant outrage or brazen act, or a *грубое нарушение,* a flagrant, crude, gross *вопиющее* (glaring) violation of someone's rights. "Outrageous" is a possibility here and as a translation of *политика разбоя* (outrageous policy), rather than a policy of "piratry" or "banditry."

Bad Things, like good things, often come in series:

> Психологическая война с полным набором присущих ей средств – провокаций, подлогов, клеветы и замалчивания реальных фактов – подталкивает мир к опасной грани...
>
> Psychological warfare with its full set/array/panoply of devices/tools/means, provocations, distortions, forgeries/deceptions, slander and deliberate silencing/ignoring/omission of the facts—is dragging the world to a dangerous brink/abyss.

Those who engage in these *неблаговидные* (reprehensible, deplorable, improper, shady, unsavory) activities try to avoid taking on/shouldering responsibility, but

> Им не уйти от осуждения их авантюристических действий всеми миролюбивыми государствами.
>
> They will not be able to/cannot (much shorter!) avoid/evade condemnation of their risky/shady/reckless ventures by all peace-loving states.

Fabrications *(измышления)* are often *клеветнические* (slanderous) or *надуманные* (trumped-up, invented, false). Things get particularly bad when countries begin to act with *безнаказанность* (impunity). Or they may wish to *разжигать очаги напряженности* or play with *горячие точки* (inflame/kindle/whip up/fan the flames of hotbeds of tension all over the globe.

A common Bad Thing among nations is *вмешательство во внутренние дела суверенных государств* (interference in the internal affairs of sovereign states) which is *недопустимо* (inadmissible) and *бесцеремонно* (high-handed). Or they may engage in *сделки* (deals).

People who are oppressed (*угнетенные*) try to throw off the yoke (*ярмо*) and fetters (*кандалы*) imposed on them. Their oppressors then resort to *жестокие репрессии*—brutal reprisals, *запугивание* (intimidation), *давление* (pressure), *принуждение* (coercion), *нажим* (pressure), and *домогательство* (power bids, extortion). Here are various combinations of such terms:

> Культ превосходства, грубой силы, разжигание вражды и ненависти к другим народам, организованная преступность неизбежно трансформируются в попрание социальных и экономических прав человека, его личной безопасности и свободы.
>
> The cult of superiority, crude/brute force, fanning the flames of hostility and hatred/encouraging/promoting/advocating hostility/hatred/enmity of other peoples, and organized crime inevitably lead to trampling underfoot man's human rights, his personal security/safety and freedom.

Several other "bad" adjectives appear regularly in Russian political prose. The interpreter who is equipped with an *арсенал* of synonyms will have no trouble pulling one of them out of his quiver at the appropriate moment:

вызывающий (наиболее вызывающая форма расизма)	inflammatory, glaring, brazen
зловещий (зловещие намерения, зловещий альянс)	evil, ominous, sinister, brazen
произвольный (произвольные действия этих стран)	arbitrary, capricious, illogical, tyrannical
разрушительный (разрушительная война)	devastating, ruinous, calamitous
нечистоплотный (нечистоплотная игра, оправдывающая военное вмешательство)	unsavory, dishonest, dirty
неуступчивый (неуступчивая позиция)	stubborn, unyielding, intransigent

непомерный (непомерные амбиции)	wild, insane, unbounded
подрывной (подрывная деятельность против демократических сил)	subversive
отживший (отжившие стереотипы)	obsolete, outdated, archaic, ancient
воинствующий (воинствующая пропаганда)	glaringly violent, arrant, militant

Bad Things are dangerous and threatening because they can lead to conflict or war. A Bad Thing *таит в себе опасность/чревата опасностью*, is fraught with the danger of something. A dangerous tactic is *балансирование на грани войны* (brinkmanship) or making a country a *плацдарм для агрессии* (beachhead for aggression). Attempts are made to *вводить народы в заблуждение*, to mislead people. War is equally evil be it *быстротечная* (blitzkrieg) or *затяжная* (protracted). The most dangerous threat is to *развязать ядерную войну*, to unleash/start a nuclear war. A Bad Thing relies on/counts on/force *делает ставку на силу)* and tries to turn back the course of history *повернуть историю вспять)*. A *нападение* (attack), *вторжение* (invasion), *захват* (capture, seizure, occupation) are all equally deplorable. Those who do Bad Things *чинят помехи* (create obstacles) to Good Things. Or they can *поднять шумиху* (raise a fuss/hullabaloo/start a campaign/make noise over something). In the worst of cases:

> Измышления, небылицы, злорадство, идущие вразрез с элементарными нравственными нормами, приобретают масштабы непристойной пропагандистской кампании.
>
> Fabrications, fantasies, and malicious glee/gloating which run counter to/contravene moral norms/the norms of society become/turn into an undignified/despicable/contemptible propaganda campaign.

All of this is done *в обход* (circumventing, evading, sidestepping) the Good Guys, e.g. *Все это делается в обход Совета Безопасности* (All this is done behind the back of/sidestepping the Security Council).

A number of verbs describe how situations become bad: *ухудшаться, обостряться, осложнять, усугублять*.

Положение внутри Руанды резко *ухудшилось*.	The situation in Ruanda has deteriorated badly/gotten much worse.
Ситуация в этом районе еще больше *обострилась*.	The situation has been further aggravated/exacerbated/has deteriorated further.
Они это делают с целью *осложнить* ситуацию в Африке.	They are doing this to aggravate the situation in Africa.
Международная ситуация за последнее время *осложнилась*.	Recently the international situation has deteriorated.
Переговоры не приблизили урегулирование конфликта, а лишь еще более усугубили его.	The negotiations did not help in bringing about a settlement; rather, they aggravated the conflict.

Other nominal and verbal forms such as *ухудшение, обострение, обостренный* operate along similar lines:

заметное ухудшение экономического положения	a noticeable/clear deterioration/worsening/aggravation of the economic situation

продолжая линию на *обострение*   continuing the policy of exacerbating/
международной обстановки   aggravating the international situation

but:

обостренная обеспокоенность политических деятелей экономическим состоянием развивающихся стран
heightened/increased/enhanced/greater/more intense concern of politicians/statesmen/ officials over/about/regarding the economic state of the developing countries

Avoiding Good Things is also a Bad Thing: *Они уклоняются от переговоров с этой страной* (They are avoiding negotiations/refusing to negotiate). *Увести* in such contexts means to divert or distract: *Эти предложения – попытка увести в сторону от практического решения насущных проблем разоружения* (These proposals are attempts to divert/distract attention from the search for real/realistic solutions to disarmament issues/problems/questions).

Bad Things are done openly or secretly, overtly or covertly: *Те, кто прямо или косвенно* (overtly or covertly) *способствует продолжению этой кампании...* "Direct" does not always work as a translation of *прямой*:

Прямой неприкрытый шантаж в отношении этой организации продиктован политическими мотивами.

Blatant and open/overt/shameless blackmail of this organization comes from/results from/is caused by/is dictated by political reasons/motives.

Bad Things cause suffering and claim victims:

Эта агрессия несет нашему народу неисчислимые страдания.
This act of aggression has caused our people unspeakable/untold/infinite suffering.

В результате землетрясения имелись значительные человеческие жертвы.
The earthquake caused significant loss of life/many deaths/claimed many victims.

The word "casualties" covers wounded, dead and missing and can be used for both military conflicts and natural disasters.

Bad Things are usually someone's fault, and the word *вина* often causes problems. In sentences such as *И это ухудшение международных отношений произошло не по вине нашей страны,* the interpreter tends to reach for the words "fault" or "guilt." The "it's not my fault" mentality sounds a bit childish here. "For this deterioration of international relations our country is not to blame" would be better. Or:

Безусловно, большую часть *вины* за положение на Ближнем Востоке несет одна страна.
Clearly, most of the blame for the situation in the Middle East must be born/lies with one/a certain country.

To cope with the Bad Things we must deal with the situation *перед лицом:*

Стремление ослабить Анголу *перед лицом* военной угрозы со стороны агрессоров
The desire to weaken Angola given the military threat/danger of war from the aggressors

A related but different word is *налицо:*

Налицо зависимость развития этих территорий от финансовой помощи обеих держав.
The dependence of these territories on financial assistance from both these powers is obvious/clear.

39

In Russian Good and Bad Things often "convincingly attest" or "testify" (*свидетельствуют*) to something: "This initiative, the same as many others, testified to the feelings of solidarity which the whole world expressed in connection with the tragedy in Armenia."[21]

> События последних лет убедительно свидетельствуют о том, что администрация США избрала эту страну в качестве одного из объектов своей агрессивной политики.
> Events of recent years clearly show/prove/demonstrate/point to the fact that/ are convincing proof that…

Яркое свидетельство can be convincing, compelling or dramatic proof, a good/ clear example/indication, a case in point.[22]

Countries are constantly "turning to" or "addressing" each other: *Десятки стран Азии и Африки обратились к нам за помощью.* What they were in fact doing was asking for or requesting help. An *обращение* of a head of state to a meeting or conference is a "message" or sometimes an appeal.

Positions of states, if the speaker considers them correct, in Tassese are "well-founded" (*обоснованную*), although there are a number of other possible translations of this word:

> Поддерживая обоснованную позицию Афганистана, наша делегация выступила…
> In support of the just/correct/legitimate position/stand of Afghanistan, our delegation took the floor/stated/said…

Or:

> Рекомендации 13-15 вполне обоснованно конкретизируют функции важного элемента…
> Recommendations 13-15 spell out in detail the functions/give the reasons for/give the arguments for/explain in detail…

Positions also often explain *специфика*

> С учетом специфики нынешней обстановки на мировой арене необходимо, чтобы работа сессии велась в конструктивной атмосфере.
> In the light of/Given the special nature/specific/unique/distinguishing features/particular characteristics of the international situation…

A *сдвиг* or *поворот* in position or policy is not necessarily a "shift" or "turn:"

> Это обусловлено резким *поворотом* в политике США..
> This results from/is determined by/depends on a major/sudden/radical/fundamental change/about-face/shift/step/swing in US policy.

Facing Bad Things is not enough, and something must be done about them:

> Мы должны оказаться на уровне ответственности…
> We must meet/ take on//discharge/shoulder/carry out/act in a manner commensurate with our/ responsibilities/the responsibilities given us…

A favorite word when one is taking action is *активизироваться:*

> Очень важно *активизировать* нашу роль в этой организации.
> It is very important that we intensify/step up/enhance/expand our role in this organization.

In some contexts the colloquial "speed up" is also possible:

> Следует *активизировать* деятельность по распространению информации на эту тему.

We should step up/speed up dissemination of information on this subject/the program should be accelerated/intensified/speeded up.

To get things done individuals and organizations often try to say a *веское слово*:

Наша организация призвана сказать свое *веское слово* в этом вопросе.

Rendering *веское* as "weighty" or even "important" does not work:

Our organization must/should/has a duty to make its voice heard/make its contribution to/speak out on/take a firm stand on/make its opinion known on/bring its weight to bear on this matter.

Веский also causes trouble in the phrase *веские основания*:

Для этого шага есть *веские основания*.

Again, "weighty" does not work.

There are good reasons/good grounds for this step.

Весомый also needs reworking:

Государства осознают ту *весомую* роль, которую призвана играть наша организация.
States recognize/acknowledge/are aware of the important/significant/authoritative role our organization must play.

To make our point we must sometimes

открыто и во весь (в полный) голос сказать: эта проблема еще не решена.

Anything "loud" here would suggest a shouting match.

We must clearly/forcefully/emphatically/publicly state that this problem has not yet been resolved.

A key word for getting anything done is *осуществление*—to implement/carry out/ conduct/put into effect/take measures/accomplish:

Впереди самое трудное: *осуществление* нашей программы.
The most difficult work/hardest part lies ahead: the implementation of our program/ to carry out our program.

Positive goals must be pursued in all possible ways,—*всячески*:

Данные державы *всячески* тормозят процесс освобождения этих территорий.
These powers are doing their best/all they can/all in their power/in every possible way/everything possible to slow down/are slowing down/curbing/impeding the process of liberation of these territories.

We need to take measures, *принимать меры* and *ответные меры* (countermeasures) to get things done. Sometimes action must be taken *немедленно и безоговорочно,* immediately and unconditionally. A synonym for *немедленно* is *безотлагательно*:

Безотлагательный, безусловный и полный вывод всех войск из Анголы.
The immediate, unconditional and total withdrawal of all troops from Angola.

In political language the Russian superlative *скорейший* is usually not rendered as "speediest" or "the most speedy":

скорейшее и полное осуществление Декларации о деколонизации
the speedy and full implementation of the Declaration on Decolonization

For things to get done we need to express ourselves vigorously or forcefully:

Мы решительно осуждаем эту агрессивную политику.
We firmly/vigorously/forcefully (but not decisively) condemn this aggressive policy.

To express our positions on Good and Bad things we need to *выступать за,* or *против. Выступать за* has several possible meanings: favor, wish to see, back, to be for, stand for, speak out in favor of, take a stand in favor of, or would like to see. For example:

Страны-члены ОАЕ твердо *выступают* на стороне молодых независимых государств.
The member countries of the OAU (Organization of African Unity) firmly back/are for/are on the side of the young independent states…

Or:

Мы *выступаем* за добрые отношения со своими соседями.
We favor/we back/we wish to see/we are for good relations among neighbors.

Renderings of *выступать против* include to oppose, be against, do not favor, do not wish to see, speak out against:

Вот почему наша делегация *выступает против* включения этого вопроса в повестку дня.
This is why our delegation opposed/was against the inclusion of this matter/item/issue/question on the agenda.

Also very common in political terminology are *исходить* and *исходя.* Rather than "basing ourselves on the fact that," *исходить* can simply mean that the speaker believes, assumes, or thinks something:

Наша страна *исходит* из того, что для ограждения собственной безопасности…
Our country believes/thinks/is convinced/assumes that to protect its own security…

Исходя can also be rendered without "basing ourselves on:"

Уже сейчас надо подумать о том, как обеспечить безопасность в процессе разоружения. *Исходя* из этого, наша страна выдвинула предложение о создании всеобъемлющей системы международного мира и безопасности…
Therefore/for this reason/on this basis/guided by this/bearing this in mind our country has made a proposal…

While "vystupating," a delegate may *выражать надежду:*

Мы *выражаем надежду* на то, что вслед за заключением указанного договора, Советский Союз и Соединенные Штаты придут к соглашению о 50-процентном сокращении стратегических выступательных вооружений.

Rather than literally "expressing hope" the interpreter can say "we would hope that" or simply, "we hope that." "We hope that" represents a saving of four syllables over *выражаем надежду* (three vs. seven).

We hope that following the conclusion of this treaty, the Soviet Union and the United States will reach agreement on a 50 per cent reduction in strategic offensive weapons.

Or a delegate may *позволить себе сказать,* which is often closer to "I venture to say" than to any implication of "allowing" or "permitting."

One of the most important and commonly encountered words in Soviet political language in describing what must be done is *задача*. For the most part, the interpreter should steer clear of the literal "task."

> Наши народы готовы вместе решать непростые *задачи* перехода к
> рыночной экономике.
> Our peoples are ready together to resolve the difficult questions/problems/issues
> of the transition to a market economy.

"Task" is too limited a term, suggesting washing the dishes rather than restructuring a country. Or:

> Самая важная *задача* сейчас – это прекратить гонку вооружений.
> Our most important goal/objective/aim/target now is to stop/halt the arms race.

Or, colloquially:

> Our biggest job now is to curb the arms race.

While *вещь* in Russian has a very limited range of meaning—a concrete item or thing or a piece of clothing, "thing" in English can refer to abstract as well as concrete nouns. It is therefore an extremely useful word, particularly for the interpreter who under pressure has forgotten a specific term.

Задача appears in other contexts, too:

> Главную *задачу* такой организации мы видим в координации деятельности
> комитетов.
> We see the major purpose/function of such an organization as the coordination of
> the activity of the committees.

Задачи (problems) are solved by taking advantage of possibilities *(возможности)* for solution. The word *возможность* appears in social science prose almost as frequently as *задача*.

> *Возможности* для устранения напряженности имеются.
> There are possibilities for eliminating tensions.

Often, however, it is "opportunities" or "potential" which are meant rather than "possibilities," e.g. opportunities for eliminating tensions."

> Народы не оставляют забота о том, как *обеспечить* возможности для развития
> и прогресса.
> Peoples are constantly/continually concerned as to how to/with ways to ensure op-
> portunities/the potential/ for development and progress.

In a sentence such as *Мы должны полностью реализовать все эти возможности*, resources, potential or abilities may be meant as well as opportunities. Or in a context such as *Это откроет возможности для переговоров*, the interpreter might say "This will open the door to/pave the way for negotiations."

In any discussion of Good or Bad Things we will hear that *речь идет о…*Here a number of English expressions do good service:

> Думаю, в этом зале согласятся с тем, что *речь идет* не только об опасном
> симптоме, но и о целенаправленной государственной политике.
> I think many of those present here will agree that we are speaking of/I am referring
> to/ this is not only a dangerous symptom, but also a deliberate state policy.

Or:

> *Речь идет* о том, чтобы энергия атома использовалась в мирных целях.
> The point is/The/My idea is/I mean that nuclear energy should be used for peaceful purposes.

*   *   *

Russian political prose features a series of very common and very tricky words. The interpreter who has several solutions in hand can devote more attention to difficulties of tense, grammar, and syntax. Here are a few examples:

Направление

It is extremely difficult to find a Russian speech without *направление,* usually automatically translated as "direction," e.g. *В каком направлении вы идете?* "Where/ what direction." In the language of social science, however, "direction" is very rarely meant:

> Предстоит совместно определить основные *направления,* где должны быть сосредоточены усилия стран в области экономики.
> We need jointly to determine the major/basic areas in which countries should concentrate their ecological efforts.

> Это *направление* в их политике – опасное.
> This trend/mentality/way of thinking/outlook of theirs is dangerous.

> Мы говорим здесь не о временном явлении, а об основных *направлениях* нашей экономической политики.
> We are talking not of passing issues/temporary questions but of the basic/fundamental objectives/aims of our economic policy.

Or:

> Мы хотим, чтобы решения сессии ориентировали государства в *направлении* коренного решения этих проблем. Мы рассмотрим любые предложения, идущие в этом *направлении,* которые будут здесь рассмотрены.
> We would like the decisions of the session to serve as guidelines/to guide states towards a radical/fundamental solution to these problems. We shall consider any proposals to that end/along these lines/any such proposals which may be submitted.

Closely related to *направление* is *направленный*

> Нужны четкие временные рамки проведения дальнейших мер, *направленных* на обеспечение независимости этого народа.
> A clear schedule should be drawn up for further measures aimed at/designed to grant/ensure/give independence to this people.

While Russian requires *направленный* or a similar qualifier after words such as *действия* or *меры (направленные на то, чтобы…)* English can get away with simply "measures/steps/actions/to do/ensure/bring about/. When used in the sense of "designed to" or "aimed at," *направленный* often does not need to be translated:

> Некоторые государства предпринимают действия, *направленные* на подрыв общественно-политического строя других стран.
> Certain states are doing things/taking action/measures to undermine the socio-political systems of other countries.

Or:

> Меры, *направленные* на дальнейшее совершенствование учебного процесса.
> Measures/ways to improve teaching methods.[23]

Quite a saving in syllables!

Путь

Путь is another Russian favorite, and it has far more meanings than "path:"

Тяжел был *путь* к победе.
The road to victory was arduous.

Реакционеры пытались силой оружия заставить их свернуть с избранного *пути*.
Reactionary forces tried by force of arms to sway/divert them from their chosen course.

Дискуссия продемонстрировала широкое понимание того, что *путь* военной конфронтации не может привести к миру.
The discussion showed general understanding of the fact that a policy of military confrontation cannot bring about/lead to peace.

Путь can cover broad territory, as in these congratulations on an official's election to high office:

Наша страна желает Вам успехов на этом *пути*.
Our country wishes you success in this work/task/endeavor/field/in this.

Путь can also mean ways in the sense of ways and means, and *путь к решению вопроса* can be an approach to a solution or even the process for resolving an issue:

Мы выступаем за то, чтобы активизировать коллективные поиски *путей* разблокирования конфликтной ситуации, за конструктивный поиск *путей* и средств скорейшего выполнения решений нашей организации.
We would like to see intensification of the/a joint search for ways/joint approach to defusing/a process for resolving/ to defuse this conflict situation, and a search for ways and means to implement the decisions of our organization as soon as possible/ in a speedy manner/to bring about speedy implementation of the decisions of our organization.

Путь can sometimes mean "direction," the word all too often used in rendering *направление:*

Важным шагом на этом *пути* была бы подготовка плана.
An important step in that direction/in making progress would be the preparation/ drawing up/drafting of a plan.

In the instrumental *путь* can simply mean "through:"

Путем грубого экономического давления эта страна навязала соглашение.
Through crude economic pressure this country imposed an agreement.

The plural instrumental of *путь* can be rendered as "how:"

Давно не скрывается и то, какими *путями* закупленное оружие попадает в руки террористов.
It has long been obvious (antonymic translation) how the weapons which were purchased ended up in the hands of the terrorists (time-saver: got to the terrorists).

Путь can be swallowed up by a neighboring word, making translation unnecessary:

В продвижении на *пути* к реальному разоружению
In making progress towards real disarmament

Все препятствия, которые стоят на *пути* к разоружению
All the obstacles to disarmament

These omissions make the English both more idiomatic and shorter, saving syllables for the interpreter.

Ряд

The English speaker tends to reach automatically for a literal rendering, "series." Yet there are a number of more idiomatic choices:

> Они совершили террористические нападения на ряд государств.
> They carried out/conducted terrorist attacks on several/certain/a number of states.

Целый ряд is not necessarily "a whole series:"

> Социализм распространился на целый ряд стран.
> Socialism has spread to quite a few/very many countries.

> Имеется целый ряд свидетельств, что эта организация пытается инициировать новые изменения.
> There is a great deal of/a lot of/plenty of evidence that...

Очередной

While *очередное заседание комитета* is a regular or scheduled meeting of a committee, in other contexts *очередной* is not always easy to render:

> В очередной раз, вопреки справедливым протестам, эта тема обсуждается нашим комитетом.
> Once again/yet again despite just protests...

Or:

> Готовность сделать очередной шаг навстречу партнерам
> Readiness to take yet another/still another/one more step to accommodate our partners

> Не помогает и очередное голосование
> Nor does the regular/routine/annual/monthly/weekly (as the case may be) vote on the draft resolution help.

Очередной can also mean "usual round of," as in *очередное нападение на эти предложения*—the routine, customary, usual round of attacks.

The word *очередь*, in the expression *в первую очередь,* can also cause trouble if it is automatically rendered as "in first place" or "first and foremost." More idiomatic choices include mainly, chiefly, primarily, most importantly, above all, or in particular.[24]

Сама жизнь

This expression sounds particularly awkward in English, as in the Moscow Newsism, "Life might again force us to take emergency measures."[25]

> *Сама жизнь* диктует необходимость срочно добиться устранения напряженности в Центральной Америке.
> Life itself is dictating the need urgently to eliminate tension in Central America

sounds rather odd. What is meant is that the course of events/recent events/this situation shows the need to achieve an immediate reduction/lessening of tensions in Central America. Or the expression can be rendered as "Time has shown this to be so/to be true/the course of events/the past has shown this/what we have seen/experience has shown this."

*   *   *

The following group of common trouble-causing items is particularly dangerous because these words are English cognates.

Актив

This word has nothing to do with "active:"

> В *актив* работы сессии следует отнести существенный прогресс…
> On the credit side of the session's work we see substantive progress/to the credit of the session is/Among the credits/achievements of the session are…

Активы in economic terms means "assets," and this carries over into metaphorical use:

> В *активе* нашей организации накопилось немало всесторонних исследований.
> Our organization has to its credit/chalked up/on its balance sheet/among its assets many/a considerable number of/quite a few comprehensive studies.

Заинтересованность

This does not necessarily mean "interest," although sometimes the meaning comes close, as in *Комитет не очень заинтересован в анализе итогов дискуссии*—the committee is not very concerned about/does not display much interest in. *Заинтересованные стороны*, however, are nearly always the parties concerned or involved.

> Включение этих положений в резолюцию позволило бы всем *заинтересованным* сторонам выступить в её поддержку.
> The inclusion of these provisions in the resolution would allow all parties involved/concerned to support it/take a stand in favor of it.

The noun *заинтересованность* expresses a concept halfway between interest and concern, or the idea that the party involved has a stake in the outcome and stands to benefit from this situation:

> Наша *заинтересованность* в этой проблеме известна всем.
> Our interest in /concern for/ this problem is well known.

Принципиальность

Perhaps no word is more hated by Russian-English interpreters. In most cases the English word "principled" does not work.

> Этот *принципиальный* и последовательный курс встречает поддержку народов мира.

This principled policy? No. This fundamental and consistent policy. Or:

> *Принципиально* важно сравнить два направления в подходе к проблеме ядерного оружия.
> It is of great/fundamental/crucial importance to consider two views of/approaches to the problem of nuclear weapons.

A *принципиальный человек* can be a person of integrity or moral fiber. (A "man of principle" is possible but a bit high-flown.)

Результативный

The notion here is that something constructive or positive has yielded results:

Это стало возможно благодаря *результативному* развитию русско-американских отношений.
This was possible/came about because of the/thanks to the positive/constructive development of Russian-American relations.

Солидный

To use an oxymoron, this is a true false friend. A *солидный человек* is a reliable, experienced and trustworthy person. Or:

Солидным шагом стало заключение в 1972 между СССР и США временного соглашения об ограничении стратегических наступательных вооружений (ОСВ-1)
A serious/significant/important step was the conclusion in 1972 between the USSR and the US of the SALT-I Agreement.

Серьезный

Here is a partially false friend. *Это серьезный человек* doesn't mean that he is totally lacking in humor. Rather, he means business, knows what he is talking about, is an experienced professional. *Это серьезная ученый*—he is a reputable and eminent/knowledgeable and professional scientist. *Эта организация нуждается в серьезной реформе*—this organization needs a thorough reform. *Это серьезная работа*—this is a solid piece of work. Should we take a decision after such brief consideration of the matter? *Нет, это несерьезно*. No, that would be irresponsible/nonprofessional/wrong. *Это несерьезно!* You don't/can't mean that/You must be kidding!

Мы ожидаем, что американская сторона со всей *серьезностью* отнесется к изложенным соображениям.
We expect that the American side will give serious/careful consideration to the views expressed here.

Such a mistranslation of *серьезный* occured when former Soviet Foreign Minister Shevardnadze was asked for his response to US Defense Secretary Cheney's expression of his doubts concerning perestroika and Gorbachev's political fate:

Shevardnadze: That particular statement is incompetent and not serious. I think President Bush understands the situation quite well when he says perestroika is an irreversible process.[26]

As a translator subsequently pointed out,

Whoever translated Shevardnadze's words in the above passage was tripped up by two "false friends…" In Russian *некомпетентный* does not mean "incompetent" but "out of one's area of experience or jurisdiction." And *несерьезный* does not mean "not serious"; rather, it means "thoughtless" or "flippant."[27]

Such misrenderings can cause "serious" communications problem.

Актуальный

This animal is not the equivalent of English "actual." If anything, it is closer to the French "*actuel*," meaning present-day or current. Both the noun *актуальность* and the adjective *актуальный* recur frequently in political texts:

Проблема предотвращения гонки вооружений в космосе ныне приобретает все большую *актуальность*.

> The problem of preventing an arms race in outer space is now becoming ever more urgent/pressing/important/relevant.

The word conveys the meaning of something which is taking place here and now and which demands our attention because of its intrinsic importance.

> А разве сегодня работа по укреплению мира не менее *актуальна,* чем вчера?
> Is work today to strengthen peace any less urgent/important/needed/pressing/relevant than yesterday?

Практически/й

"Practical" can sound extremely awkward as a translation of *практически/й:*

> При обсуждении здесь *практически* все выступавшие подчеркивали необходимость приступить к *практическим* мерам по осуществлению решений комитета по всему комплексу проблем.
> Nearly/virtually all the speakers emphasized the need for realistic/genuine measures to implement the committee's decisions on the whole range/set (not complex) of problems.

Or:

> Главное – положить начало *практическому* движению в направлении всеобщего урегулирования.
> The most important thing is to begin making real progress/to take real action/start in fact taking steps towards (omit *направление*) a comprehensive settlement.

Практика does not always mean practice:

> Мы уже демонстрировали на *практике,* что мы за интенсификацию работы международных форумов.
> We have already in fact/through our actions shown…/We have demonstrated that…

Практический often comes along with *конкретный,* meaning individual or specific rather than "concrete:"

> В *практическом* плане это означает, что комитету необходимо рассмотреть *конкретные* вопросы.
> In actual fact this means/this really means that the committee must consider specific items/issues/questions/matters.

Вопросы are issues, matters and problems as often as they are questions. The journals *Вопросы языкознания* or *Вопросы философии* would be better translated as "Problems of Linguistics" or "Problems of Philosophy" than as "Questions."

Комплексный

While *комплекс вопросов, предложений,* etc., means a range or a set of whatever, *комплексный* implies comprehensive or far-ranging, not complex in the sense of difficult or problematical:

> Этот документ содержит *комплексную* программу строгих мер.
> That document contains/spells out a comprehensive/wide-ranging/full program of urgent measures.

*   *   *

A few words should be said concerning the language of *perestroika.* The last few years have seen the introduction of scores of new words into the Russian political vocabulary, headed by *гласность* and *перестройка.* The speeches of Gorbachev and his colleagues resurrected words which had lain unused for years and created neologisms to express the concepts of *новое мышление* (new thinking). Some of these words left the stage along with Gorbachev and have already been relegated to the archives of linguistic history, but others are still appearing in the press today. Here is a very brief overview of some such terms:

What went before *perestroika* were *годы застоя,* years of stagnation. Russia had to *выстрадать* (a favorite verb of Gorbachev's) *свою историю* (her history was born of travail/born in suffering/she endured an ordeal), and reached an *исторический перелом* (historic turning point, crucial point). The process of *перестройка* was to be made *необратимый* (irreversible), and had its *закономерности* (logic, pattern, norms which regulate it). People were confronted by a host of evils: *вседозволенность* (all-permissiveness), *всепрощенчество* (all-forgiving attitude), *бездельники* (idlers), *тунеядцы* (parasites), *прогульщики* (idlers), *лодыри* (loafers), *бракоделы* (hacks) all acting with *безнаказанность* (impunity), *местничество* (parochialism, regionalism) and *ведомственность* (overdepartmentalization, narrow institutional interests). The *командно-административная* (command-administrative/administration by fiat) system and *администрирование* (abuse of administrative authority, authoritarianism) had to be done away with, as well as total *уравниловка* (lack of differentiation/leveling/ equalization of all).

In economics *хозрасчет* (cost accounting) became the principle for most enterprises, and there were *бригадные* and *арендные подряды* (team and leasing contracts). Concepts of *самофинансирование* (self-financing), *самоокупаемость* (cost recovery), and *себестоимость* (production cost/price cost) became increasingly important. And *кооператоры* (people in the cooperative movement) had to fight against *рэкетиры* (racketeers, mafia) who were (and many still are) engaged in their own *разборки* (internal quarrels, shoot-outs).

CHAPTER V

VERBS AND THEIR PROBLEMS

Russian verbs, with their limited tense system, aspects, prefixation, impersonal, participial and gerundive constructions, pose a large potential stumbling block for the interpreter. Since the highly reduced Russian tense system of present, simple past and future does not provide the variety of forms which are possible in English, and since there is no formal grammatical equivalent in Russian for many English tenses, the Russian-English interpreter must weigh carefully his choice of a simple or compound tense. Though the Russian perfective or imperfective aspect occasionally gives the interpreter a nudge in the right direction, at the moment he launches into an English sentence the best rendering is not always obvious, and a later clause may make him wish he had set off in a different direction.

The English of TASS was filled with incorrect use of tenses and verbal forms:

> For many centuries now, Spaniards are living without paying attention to what is happening beyond their country.

> This is a successor to the association which was active for nearly a decade recently.

> The play was banned from being performed at the Taganka.

> We were recommended to spend our holidays in the mountains.[1]

The Russian-English interpreter must fight the tendency to reach automatically for a simple instead of a compound tense:

> Социалистическая Республика Вьетнам, героически перенесшая все тяготы многолетней и суровой войны, теперь мужественно отстаивает свой суверенитет.
> The Socialist Republic of Vietnam, which heroically bore the burdens of a terrible war which raged for years, *is* now courageously *defending* its sovereignty.

The translation of a sentence such as *Вы меня раздражаете* depends on context. If the person in question is an annoyance seven days a week, "You annoy/irritate me" is fine. But if at the moment he is being a pest though generally he is well behaved, "You are irritating/ annoying me" is preferable.

When Russian repeats a verb in two tenses to emphasize continued action a literal interpretation sounds clumsy. Here is such a present/imperfective-future combination:

> Мы поддерживаем и будем поддерживать прифронтовые государства Африки
> в их усилиях по достижению урегулирования этого вопроса.

"We support and will support the front-line African states" is very awkward. More idiomatic would be:

We have always supported the front-line states.
We are continuing to support the front-line states.
We shall continue to support the front-line states.

Or the verb can be changed to a noun:

We shall continue our support for the front-line states.

In these examples the verb "continue" or the compound tense "have supported" cover the notion of past action continued into the present and future. This device also works for a present-perfective future combination:

Россия не ослабляет и не ослабит усилий, направленных на то, чтобы отвести от человечества военную угрозу.
Russia will not slacken its efforts/will persist in its efforts/will continue its efforts to protect mankind from the threat of war.

Военная угроза is better rendered as "threat of war" than as "military threat." *Направление* does not require translation; "aimed at" or "designed to" adds nothing.

The Russian repetitive verbal construction with an imperfective past and present can also be rendered by a single English compound tense:

Мы никогда не искали и не ищем себе выгод – будь то экономических, политических или иных.
We have never sought profits/advantages for ourselves—be they economic, political, or any other kind.

"Have never" covers both the past and present of *не искали и не ищем*.

The imperfective past-present construction can also be rendered by the verb "to continue:"

Мы предлагали и предлагаем договориться о полном запрещении ядерного оружия.
We are continuing to propose/continue to propose/continue to favor/we have always favored/always proposed agreement on a total nuclear weapons test ban.

A perfective past-future construction can be rendered as a past or future:

Наша страна не допустила и не допустит вмешательства в свои внутренне дела.
Our country has never allowed/will never allow/will continue to prevent/oppose interference in its internal affairs.

Because of the imperfective aspect's stress on process over completed action, imperfective past-future constructions tend to be future-oriented, and should be translated as such:

Мы выступали и будем выступать в их поддержку.
We shall continue to support them.

is more appropriate than "We have always supported them."

A doubled present or past tense Russian verb form can be rendered by "keep + verb" or can be rephrased:

Я иду-иду, уже сил нет, а все еще далеко до перевала...
I keep/kept on going, but it is/was still a long distance to/far to go to the crossing/pass.
On I went/I walked and walked, but...

Or:

> Он смотрел-смотрел, не мог разглядеть никак.
> He kept on looking but/No matter how he looked he could not make it out.[2]

Another kind of "false future" and "false past" are conveyed through *впредь,* *прежде,* and *по-прежнему,* which make the interpreter look for an English past or future tense to express the notion of "in the future," "earlier," or "formerly." Since the Russian verbs are imperfective, however, these constructions stress process and continuity rather than completion of action.

> Мы будем и *впредь* с другими странами действовать в интересах оздоровления международных отношений.
> We shall continue to act/work with the other countries to improve international relations.

В интересах adds nothing. By dropping it the interpreter gains several syllables and produces a more idiomatic sentence. Or:

> Мы будем, как и *прежде,* содействовать выполнению этой организацией ее миссии.
> We will continue to encourage this organization to carry out its mission/in carrying out its mission.

Or:

> Расисты *по-прежнему* продолжают незаконную оккупацию этой территории.
> The racists are continuing/have not ceased/are going on with/are carrying on with the illegal occupation of this territory.

In some constructions the Russian infinitive can be rendered in English by a future tense:

> Дети есть дети.
> Children will be children.[3]

A future tense or imperative used in a Russian conditional clause may require a present tense in English:

> Если завтра будет хорошая погода, мы пойдем гулять.
> If the weather *is* good tomorrow, we'll go for a walk.

> Случись так, что расходы превысят доходы…
> If expenditures exceed revenue/income/if expenditures should exceed revenue/income…[4]

The English sequence of tenses can vary when the singular imperative is used as a conditional:

> Приди я вовремя, ничего бы не случилось.
> If I had come in time nothing would have happened.

This form of the imperative may also imply obligatory action or protest on the speaker's part:

> Тебе хорошо с гостями чай распивать, а я дома сиди.
> You're having fun drinking tea with the guests while/but I've got to stay home.

> Сами гулять пойдете, а я пиши.
> Go off on your own, I've got to write/I'm stuck with the writing.

A third meaning of this form is sudden or unintended action:

> Он меня позвал – я споткнись, чашку разбил.
> He called to me and I stumbled and broke a cup.

> Дорога ровная – а он возьми и упади.
> The road was flat/even when all of a sudden he fell.[5]

The Russian historical present can be translated by an English past:[6]

> Возвращаюсь я вчера вечером домой, иду по нашей улице, вдруг слышу знакомый голос
> Last night as I was going home, walking down our street, I suddenly heard a familiar voice.

And a Russian present tense can take an English present or future tense:

> Я уезжаю через неделю, завтра я весь день работаю, а вечером сижу дома.
> I'm leaving in a week—tomorrow I'll work/I'm working all day and in the evening I'll be home.

Russian perfective verbs used to express repeated action can be translated by an English continuous present tense:

> Сегодня мне весь день мешают – то кто-нибудь придет, то зазвонит телефон.
> I'm being bothered all day—people keep coming in and the phone keeps ringing.

A series of habitual actions which are expressed in Russian by a future tense requires a present tense in English:

> Вечер я обычно провожу так: приду поздно, сразу поужинаю, помою посуду, посмотрю телевизор и ложусь спать.
> Here's what I usually do in the evening: I come home late, eat supper right away, do the dishes, watch TV and go to bed.

Repeated past actions can also be expressed by a future tense in Russian and by a present tense in English:

> Он человек со странностями: зайдет к нам, сядет и молчит. Посидит так – и уйдет.
> He's a bit odd—he comes to see us and just sits there and says nothing. Just sits there and then leaves.

Such lists of verbs are often used to describe a person's characteristic or habitual mode of behavior:

> Он всегда прибежит, накричит, наскандалит, а потом удивляется: Почему меня не любят?
> He's always barging in/rushing in screaming/yelling at someone/causing trouble/insulting people/offending people/raising a row and then he wonders why/is surprised that/and then he asks why people don't like him.

> Маша всегда что-нибудь некстати скажет.
> Masha always says/has a knack for saying the wrong thing/something inappropriate.[7]

Past tense forms of *пойти* and *поехать* are used in colloquial speech to convey a future meaning:

> Я пошел.   I'm about to leave.
> Я поехал, буду через два часа.   I'm off/I'll be going/I'll be back in two hours.

Interpretation into English often requires the interpreter to provide modals which do not exist Russian, or to "soften" the force of a verb. Depending on context, *Мы хотим* may be better rendered as "We would like" than as "We want;" or *Я думаю* can be translated as "It seems to me." This will avoid making the speaker sound too dogmatic. "Might," "may," "could," and "should" often make for a smoother and more polite English sentence, and the use of these words is not prompted by Russian verbal-grammatical constructions.

Russian grammatical structure often produces much longer sentences than English. *Дело в том, что* and *чтобы* clauses frequently need condensation and transformation if the interpreter is to utter grammatical English sentences and keep up with the speaker. Careful attention must also be paid to tense:[8]

> Сложность этого эксперимента заключается в том, что он требует длительного времени.
> The problem with this experiment is that it requires a lot of time.

> Утешение было только в том, что он уезжал всего на несколько дней.
> The only consolation was that he would not be away for long/was leaving for only a few days.

The English gerundive construction is idiomatic and saves syllables:

> Мы начали вечер с того, что предложили всем потанцевать.
> We started the party/evening by suggesting/with the suggestion that everyone dance.

> Он начал с того, что лично познакомился со всеми.
> He began by introducing himself to everyone/by getting personally acquainted with everyone.

In many *чтобы* clauses the word *чтобы* is not translated and tense is determined by context:

> Я не видел, *чтобы* он чистил зубы..
> I didn't see him brush his teeth/I never saw him brush his teeth.

> Я хочу, *чтобы* вы меня правильно поняли.
> I want you to understand me correctly/to get what I mean.

Чтобы may be rendered as a simple "to + infinitive," rather than by the clumsier construction "in order to" or "so as to:"

> Я вернулся с тем, *чтобы* предупредить вас.
> I came back to warn you.

> Я не пришел с тем, *чтобы* спорить с вами.
> I didn't come to argue with you.

Sometimes "so that" can replace *чтобы*:

> Говори, *чтобы* все поняли.
> Speak so that everyone understands/gets the point.

Как and *как бы* clauses can be rendered by an English conditional or a gerund:

> Я люблю смотреть, *как* он выступает.
> I like watching him perform/I like to watch him perform/I like watching him performing.

> Он боялся, *как бы* не простудиться.
> He was afraid of catching cold/He was afraid he might/could catch cold.

Не + infinitive *бы* requires an English "don't" or "see that X doesn't do Y:"

> *Не* простудиться *бы!*
> Take care/I'll take care not to/See that you don't catch cold.
>
> *Не* забыть *бы* его адрес!
> See you don't/take care not to/be sure you don't/I mustn't/I must take care not to forget his address.

While in some cases aspect may not play a critical role for the interpreter, e.g. *они это говорили* and *они это сказали* may be rendered identically in English, in others it is crucial. The difference between *мы две недели решали эту задачу* and *мы вчера решили эту задачу* is vitally important to the negotiators of the solution to that *задача,* since in the first case the problem may or may not have been resolved while in the second a solution has definitely been found. The classic examples *Колумб был счастлив, не когда он открыл Америку, а когда он её открывал,* or *Он умирал две недели, очень мучился, а умер вчера вечером* illustrate the distinction between imperfective-perfective/process-completed action, a difference which must be rendered by the use of compound and continuous tenses in English: "while Columbus was discovering America," "he was dying for two weeks." Or there is the example cited by Catford:

> Что же *делал* Бельтов в продолжение этих десяти лет? Все или почти все.
> Что он сделал? Ничего или почти ничего.
> What did Beltov do during these ten years? Everything, or almost everything.
> What did he achieve? Nothing, or almost nothing.[9]

The interpreter should continually bear in mind that English may require completely different verbs for the two members of a Russian aspect pair. "What did he succeed in doing?" is awkward and much longer than "What did he achieve?" The importance of conation for certain Russian imperfective verbs has been stressed by Townsend:

> A Russian conative verb is an imperfective verb which, in addition to other aspectual meanings (e.g. it may admit durative or iterative meaning, or both), signals an attempt to carry out an action whose successful conclusion is expressed by a formal perfective partner, e.g. *уверять* "try to convince" vs. *уверить* "convince;" *решать* "try to solve" vs. *решить* "solve." English may have altogether different verbs as its most common translations of these Russian aspectual partners; e.g. *учиться* "study" vs. *научиться* "learn," *отыскивать* "look for" vs. *отыскать* "find."[10]

Common examples of such pairs include *сдавать/сдать экзамен* (to take/pass an exam) or *поступать/поступить в университет* (to apply to/be admitted or get into a university). Certain imperfectives with conative meaning require translation which emphasizes the notion of trying to do something:

> Войска *брали* крепость целый месяц.
> The troops tried for a whole month to take the fortress.
>
> Я к нему долго *привыкал,* но наконец *привык.*
> For a long time I tried to get used to him, and finally did.
>
> Не *оправдывайся!*
> Don't try to justify yourself!/Don't try to make excuses![11]

Townsend also points to a related category of verbs for which the imperfective aspect indicates a state resulting from a perfective achievement:

Я понимаю is the result of *я понял,* and note that English "I understand" translates them both. The formal pair *разобраться/разбираться* are exactly the same; the verb in *я разобрался в этом* is an achievement with the change-of-state meaning characteristic of perfectives, while the verb in *я разбираюсь в этом* signals the state resulting from the achievement. They may both be translated as "I understand," but the former means "I have figured out (come to understand)," while the latter means "I understand (as a result of having figured out.)" These verbs belong to a very large group of perfectives whose change of state is inceptive, whose imperfectives denote the new, resulting state: *понял, понимаю, поверил, верю, понравиться, нравиться.*[12]

The interpreter should be alert to such distinctions and should not hesitate to use quite different words—and tenses—to translate the members of an aspect pair. On the whole, however, the highly reduced Russian tense system causes Russian-English interpreters more problems than does aspect.

Impersonal constructions which often require reworking can be difficult to interpret. *Здесь не курят* clearly cannot be rendered literally. "Smoking is/ not allowed/ forbidden here" or "No smoking" would make the point. Or a third person plural impersonal construction can be transformed into a passive construction:

Посетителей просят оставить верхнюю одежду в гардеробе.
Visitors are requested/asked to leave/Visitors must leave/check their coats in the coatroom.[13]

A personal subject may be used to render an impersonal construction:

Об этом часто приходится слышать.
I/he/we/they often hear about this.

Чувствовалось, что он доволен.
I/we/they felt/could feel that he was pleased.

Depending on context, reflexive verbs may acquire a subject when translated:

Под вакуумом понимается пространство, не содержащее вещества.
A vacuum is defined as space/By a vacuum we mean space/The definition of a vacuum is space/A vacuum is understood to be space free from/not containing/ devoid of matter.

В данном случае сложное движение рассматривается как результат двух движений.
In this case complex movement is considered as/considered to be/we see complex movement as/we define complex movement as the result of two movements.[14]

When a Russian pronoun is the complement of an impersonal verb construction, the interpreter can make it into a subject in English. Some expressions of this type (*меня знобит*—I am feverish) are so common that the interpreter may barely be aware of the transformation, while others require a conscious reworking:

В ушах звенело, во рту пересохло.
His/my ears were ringing, his/my throat was dry.

Меня неудержимо клонило в сон.
I felt an irresistible urge to sleep/I just couldn't stay awake/I felt horribly/terribly/ awfully sleepy.

Ей потянуло в Париж.
She felt an urge to go to Paris/Paris was calling to her/She felt like going to Paris.

Мне жаль мою подругу.
I'm sorry for my girlfriend.

57

But:

> Мне жаль потерянного времени.
> I regret/begrudge the time lost/wasted.

Though students are traditionally taught that present active participles are translated by an -ing form (*Девушка, читающая книгу, очень красивая*—The girl who is reading the book is very pretty), the interpreter can save time and words by using a prepositional phrase or short subordinate clause, or by dropping the participle:

> Группа, *имеющая* такие блестящие результаты, является гордостью нашего института.[15]
> The group with such outstanding results is the pride of our institute.

> Вопрос, *входящий* за рамки данной статьи.
> A matter/issue/question beyond the scope of this article.

A reflexive participle can be rendered by a prepositional phrase:

> *Строящийся* завод является одним из новейших в стране.
> The factory under construction is one of the newest in the country.

Принадлежащий can be rendered by a simple possessive:

> Книга, принадлежащая ей
> Her book

Russian present passive participial constructions can be translated as adjectives rather than participial clauses:

> *Проводимая* страной политика одобряется всем народом.
> The policy pursued (not "which is being pursued") by our country has the backing/approval of the entire people.

In some cases such a participle can simply be left out:

> Ясно определились позиции, *занимаемые* обеими сторонами по таким жизненно важным вопросам.
> The positions of both sides on such vitally important questions are now clear.

The participles *имеющийся, сложившийся,* and *создавшийся* require reworking and can often be rephrased or omitted:

> Нам нужно вскрывать *имеющиеся* резервы.
> We need to exploit the available reserves/the reserves at our disposal/the existing reserves.[16]

Though to the English ear *сложившийся* suggests something that has been formed or put together, this does not work in translation:

> *Сложившаяся* ситуация требует укрепления существующей правовой основы.
> The present/today's/this situation requires a strengthening of the existing legal basis.

> Необходимо на все 100% использовать *сложившиеся* благоприятные условия.
> 100% use must be made of today's/present/existing conditions.

Sometimes *сложившийся* or *создавшийся* are little more than synonyms for "this:"

> В создавшейся обстановке наш комитет должен выполнить свой долг.
> In this situation our committee must do its duty.

Назревший, often used in the phrase *назревшие проблемы,* can be rendered as longstanding/pressing problems/issues.

Gerunds also cause translation problems. Two Moscow Newsisms show the misuse of a gerund and the failure to use a gerund when necessary in English:

> Every country must build its own economy based on its own ideas rather than copying foreign technological developments.
>
> Many of us have hundreds of times experienced the need for a reference book and the utter impossibility to find one.[17]

A Russian past tense may become an English gerund:

> Мы видели, как дети купались в реке.
> We saw the children swimming in the river.

Or a Russian present tense gerund may become a past construction in English:

> Раза два в год бывал в Москве, и *возвращаясь* оттуда, рассказывал об этом.
> He would visit/used to visit Moscow a couple of times a year, and after returning home/on his return home tell/would tell about it.[18]

A Russian past gerund may be rendered in English as a present:

> *Сев* за рояль, она заиграла вальс.
> Sitting at the piano, she played a waltz.

Translation of a Russian gerund may require explanation of cause, reason, or time:

> *Выслушав* меня внимательно, вы быстро меня поймете.
> If you listen to me carefully, you'll understand quickly.
>
> *Почувствовав* голод, они решили обедать без гостей.
> Because/since they were hungry, they decided to eat without/without waiting for the guests.
>
> *Переехав* в собственную квартиру, он стал гораздо более самостоятельным человеком.
> When/after he moved to his own apartment he became a lot more independent.

In descriptive gerundive constructions "with + noun" can often replace the gerund:

> Он сидел, *закрыв* глаза..
> He sat/was sitting with his eyes closed.
>
> "Это очень смешно!" –сказал он, *засмеяв*.
> "That's very funny," he said with a laugh.[19]

So-called "subjectless" gerunds, which are quite common in Russian technical language, may be changed to nouns or require a preposition in English:

> *Используя* эти данные, можно приближенно предсказать процесс.
> Use of this data allows us to make an approximate prediction of the process/By using this data, we can make…
>
> *Изучая* эту таблицу, легко видеть,что…
> Study of this table makes it clear that…
> In studying this table we clearly see that…[20]

The interpreter should be particularly sensitive to lengthy Russian verbal constructions which can be reduced to a word or two in English: *утверждать то, что оказалось чистейшей чепухой* (to talk utter nonsense), *располагать что–то в алфавитном порядке* (to alphabetize).[21] A Russian verb and adverb or descriptive phrase may be condensed into a single verb: *злобно смотреть*—"glare," *заставить грубой силой*—"bludgeon." A verb with a complement can lose the complement in

English: *приводить в систему, распределять по категориям*/list, categorize; *лишать законной силы, делать недействительным*/invalidate; *выводить из строя, делать непригодным*/incapacitate; *поймать в ловушку*/entrap; *расстегивать пуговицу* unbutton; *превосходить количеством*/outnumber; *ударять молотком*/to hammer; *резать ломтями* to slice; *сделать вывод*/to conclude; *неправильно использовать*/to misuse; *двигаться с грохотом*/to rumble. In many cases prefixation or suffixation (en-, un-, -ize, -ate) allow the English verb to capture the meaning of the Russian phrase.

The following common expressions can be interpreted in ways that save interpreters time and syllables:

быстро/стремительно расти	to mushroom, jump, soar, spiral
резко падать/сокращаться	to dwindle, slump, slash[22]

The extra syllables in English compound tenses can be offset by careful condensation of Russian verbal constructions. Some of the most useful verbs in English are one-syllable words: do, make, get, work, write, come, go. There is no need to "attempt to obtain" when one can simply "get," or to "implement" what one can "do." The use of these short but clear words helps produce a cogent and understandable interpretation—and a grateful listener.

CHAPTER VI

YESTERDAY, TODAY, AND TOMORROW:
TIME EXPRESSIONS

Time expressions often require a good deal of rethinking on the interpreter's part. Everyone knows that *вчера вечером* is not "yesterday in the evening" but last night. But take the innocent-looking

> Центральная Америка *как никогда* нуждается в мирных условиях.

"Central America needs peace (better than peaceful conditions) as never before" does not work. "More than ever," or "now, more than ever" or simply "desperately needs peace" would be preferred.

Or take the following reference to the immediate future:

> Прямой долг организации – принять все необходимые меры для того, чтобы *в самое ближайшее время* добиться осуществления своих резолюций по этому вопросу.

"In the near future" sounds too vague for what the speaker perceives as an urgent situation. Possibilities include:

> It is the clear/bounden/unquestionable/obvious duty of our organization to take all measures necessary for speedy implementation/the implementation as soon as possible/implementation of its resolutions as rapidly/quickly as possible/the speediest possible implementation of its resolutions.

The frequently occurring phrase *в эти дни* is better rendered as "now, today, at present, at this time" than as "these days" or "during these days."[1] A very common expression referring to the immediate past, *в последнее время,* which would seem to translate naturally as "in recent times," usually sounds more idiomatic as "recently:"[2]

> *В последнее время,* благодаря распространению спутниковой связи, большую популярность получили разного рода теле - и радиомосты.
> Recently, thanks to increased/expanded satellite communications, various types of TV and radio spacebridges have become very popular.

"Recently" is also a possible translation of *на днях*. A sentence such as *Я видел его на днях,* however, does not provide much information as to precisely when the action took place. Qualifiers and context may be needed to make that clear.

> Буквально *на днях* был сделан очередной, крайне опасный шаг по обострению ситуации в Центральной Америке.
> Just a few days ago yet one more/yet another very/extremely dangerous step was taken/move was made/which aggravated/to aggravate the situation in Central America.

A time expression may require antonymic translation:

> Выдвинут, и *не сейчас*, вопрос о сокращении военных бюджетов.
> The question of reducing military budgets was put forward quite some time ago/a long time ago.

A compound verb tense can express the concept of time passing which is implied in *в свое время:*

> Это идет в разрез с интересами длительного значения, которые *в свое время* были положены в основу данного соглашения.
> This runs counter to/contravenes those long-range interests, which have been the basis for this agreement/had been the cornerstone of this agreement.

Careful choice of English verb tense to indicate a Russian action in the past is particularly important when a Russian time expression indicates past tense even though the verb is in the present:

> *Из года в год* растет и ширится международная поддержка справедливой борьбы этого народа.
> Year by year/The years have seen/Over the years/Every year there has been/we have seen the growth and expansion of international support for the just struggle/campaign of this people.

Such continued action in the past is particularly tricky in sentences involving negative time constructions:

> *Не один год* сохраняется напряженность на Кипре.
> For many/several years there has been continuing tension on Cyprus.

> *Не один месяц* мы обсуждаем этот вопрос.
> We have been discussing this question for months now.

Который + time period implies repetition in the past:

> Однако противники ядерного разоружения уже *который* год твердят, что якобы не существует приемлемых условий для проведения переговоров.
> How often/for how many years now have the opponents of nuclear disarmament asserted/claimed/propounded that the conditions for negotiations are unacceptable.

The construction *уже не* + time period when applied to days, weeks, months, years and decades can be rendered as "for many/several Xs now:"

> *Уже не одно десятилетие* эта страна продолжает игнорировать решения нашей организации.
> For decades/for several decades now this country has been ignoring/has continued to ignore the decisions of our organization.

> *Уже много лет* не сходит с повестки дня вопрос о выводе иностранных войск из этого района.
> For years/many years now the issue/question/item of the withdrawal of foreign troops from this region has been/remained/stayed on our agenda.

Translation of *уже* as "already" in time expressions should be avoided:

> Вот *уже сорок лет* мы занимаемся обсуждением этого вопроса.
> For almost/nearly/for some forty years (now) we have been discussing/have been engaged in discussion of this question.

The compound past tense covers *уже,* since here a Russian present tense cannot be translated by an English present.

Уже and *еще* followed by a specific date have the meaning of "as long ago as," "as far back as:"

> *Уже* в январе 1985 года обе стороны договорились о том, что целью их переговоров по ядерным и космическим вооружениям будет выработка эффективных договоренностей...
>
> As long ago as/as far back as/back in January 1985 both sides agreed that the objective of their negotiations on nuclear and space weapons was to draw up/conclude effective agreements...

A verb such as "draw up" or "conclude" works better than a noun in rendering *выработка.*

In this context *еще* works the same way as *уже.* Here is an example in an English-Russian translation:

> As long ago as 1841 a Royal Commission directed the attention of the British government to the advantage of establishing a decimal system of coinage.
>
> *Еще в* 1841 королевская комиссия указывала английскому правительству на преимущества введения десятичной системы денежного обращения.[3]

Another possibility for *еще* or *уже* + date is "as early as:"

> Это было известно *еще/уже* в 1910 году.
> This was known as early as/back in 1910.[4]

Еще/уже in certain contexts can mean "even:"

> *Еще/уже* ребенком он был выдающимся скрипачом.[5]
> Even as a child he was a superb violinist.

Problems which have been around for a long time and still require solutions in Russian are described as *давно наступила пора:*

> *Давно наступила пора* смыть позорное пятно, лежащее на совести человечества.

"It is high time" is shorter and simpler than "the time has long been ripe:"

> It is high time to erase/remove/dissolve that shameful stain/blot (the participle can and should be omitted, as in English stains and blots do not "lie") on the conscience of humanity/mankind.

The same construction works with *назрела пора:*

> *Давно назрела пора* для четких рекомендаций по вопросу о сокращении военных бюджетов.
> It is time for clear recommendations on the issue/question of reductions of/reducing military budgets.

Or the sentence can be rephrased:

> The question of reducing military budgets is a longstanding one/long overdue/has been with us for a long time.

Antonymic translation is also possible: "This question is hardly a new one/hardly new/hardly new to us." For this particular sentence that solution would be more useful to the translator than to the interpreter, who will probably not have time for such a lengthy inversion.

CHAPTER VII

SAYING "HET": NEGATIVE CONSTRUCTIONS

In English translation, many constructions which are negative in Russian sound far more idiomatic when they are rendered as positive constructions. A series of questions asked daily by millions of Russian speakers, such as

> Вы не скажете, сколько времени?
> Не подскажете, как проехать к (Большому театру, etc.)?
> Не хочешь вечером в кино?
> Вы на следующей остановке не выходите?

would sound most bizarre if translated as negatives. "Will you not tell me what time it is" is certainly not what the speaker has in mind, but "Do you have the time?" Can you (not can you not) tell me how to get to the Bolshoi, do you (rather than don't you) want to go to the movies, and, obviously, are you (not are you not) getting off at the next stop? Or *больше не болейте* can be rendered as "stay well" rather than "don't get sick again."

The same principle of antonymic rendering holds for more formal sentences, such as:

> Нелишне напомнить, что дискуссии подобного рода создают опасный прецедент.
> It should be recalled that such discussions create a dangerous precedent.

> Не менее важно соблюдать уже подписанные договоры.
> It is just as/equally important to comply with treaties already signed.

> Прошедшее обсуждение не было бесполезным.
> The discussion was useful.

> Не прекращаются провокации против Вьетнама.
> The provocations against Viet Nam are continuing.

Particularly tricky are *не раз* constructions, which must be carefully distinguished from *ни разу* (not a single time). Failure to do so can lead to a serious *contresens:*

> Наша страна *не раз* заявляла о том, что готова принять участие в обеспечение мира на Ближнем Востоке.
> Our country has repeatedly/frequently/on several occasions declared its readiness/ that it is ready to help bring peace to the Middle East.

> Делегаты знают, что мы *не раз* приходили этим странам на помощь, оказывая политическую, экономическую и военную поддержку.
> The delegates know/are aware that we have often rendered assistance to these countries, providing political, economic and military support.

The extra seconds the interpreter spends waiting to ensure that what the speaker has said is *не раз*—and not *ни разу*—are well worth it.

Similar in meaning to *не раз* is *неоднократно:*

> Наше руководство неоднократно излагало свои позиции по вопросам отношений с НАТО.
> Our leadership has repeatedly stated its position/made known its views on relations with NATO.

Не один, as in *не один год, не один месяц* can also easily lead to a *contresens:*

> Не одному поколению дипломатов пришлось заниматься этим исключительно сложным вопросам.
> More than one/Many/Several generations of diplomats have had to tackle/deal with/take up/been faced with/confronted by this extremely/extraordinarily/most/ very difficult/complicated/intricate/complex/involved problem/issue/question.

As anyone who has ever dealt with Russian statements and speeches knows (*как всем известно*)—as everyone is well aware), the phrase *не случайно* is a perennial favorite. Depending on context, this warhorse can be rendered positively or negatively:

> Не случайно, молодежь составляет значительную часть международного движения.
> It stands to reason that/It is not fortuitous that/No wonder that/It is no surprise that…

> Не случайно, что при обсуждении этого вопроса все выступающие подчеркивали необходимость перейти к практическим мерам.
> There are good reasons why/It is understandable why/It stands to reason that/It is not fortuitous that/Understandably…

> Все эти факты носят *не случайный* характер.
> This is not a random collection of facts/These facts are not unconnected/These things did not just happen/There is a reason for these events/developments/things/ These things are linked/connected.[1]

Equally common expressions are *нет тайны* or *ни для кого не секрет:*

> Нет тайны в том, кто насадил и вскормил кровавый режим Пол Пота.
> Everyone is well aware/Everyone knows/It is perfectly clear/It is no secret who imposed and fostered the bloody Pol Pot regime.

The negative words *напротив* and *наоборот* do not necessarily have to be rendered literally as "on the contrary" or "the opposite is true:"

> Однако этот факт не означает, что рассмотрение данного вопроса не дает результатов.
> *Напротив,* это лишь подчеркивает, что эта страна оказалась в изоляции.

"In fact" would work for *напротив,* and saves time as compared to "the opposite is true." Or a simple "No" would do it. The same is true for the following:

> Это не приближает урегулирование конфликта. *Наоборот,* речь идет о новом шаге, затрудняющем справедливое решение этой неотложной проблемы.
> This is not helping to resolve the conflict. No/In fact/Frankly speaking/Indeed this is a new step which is hampering/impeding/holding up/delaying a just solution to this urgent problem.

The verb "fail to" is extremely useful in rendering both single and double negative constructions:

> Расовые отношения в Южно-Африканской Республике неизбежно будут ухудшаться.

This could be translated as "Racial relations in South Africa will inevitably worsen/ deteriorate," or "Racial relations cannot fail to worsen."[2]

"Must" or "cannot fail to" can help resolve the problem of double negatives, and "must" saves syllables:

> *Нельзя не* видеть, что данная акция является произволом.
> We cannot fail to see/We must see/It is clear that this action is arbitrary.
>
> *Нельзя не* согласиться с замечанием в докладе о том, что...
> We cannot fail to agree/cannot but agree/We must agree/It is clear we agree with the comment in the report...
>
> Существование арабского народа – объективная реальность, и не считаться с этим *не имеет* право *никто*.
> The existence of the Arab people is an objective reality which no one can fail to take into account/everyone must accept/which no one can ignore.

This notion of "ignoring" something works well with things which are being done— or should *not* be done *в отрыве* or *в стороне* from something:

> Наша организация не может стоять *в стороне* от активного обсуждения затронутых вопросов.
> Our organization cannot ignore/fail to engage in active discussion of these questions.
>
> Комитет пытается инициировать новые изменения в структуре этих органов *в отрыве* от утвержденных комиссией общих задач реорганизации.
> The committee is attempting to initiate new changes in the structure of these bodies, ignoring the/divorced from/in isolation from the/ general objectives of reorganization adopted by the commission.

Constructions with *как бы ни* can be translated as "regardless of" or "despite" rather than as "no matter how:"

> *Как бы ни* пытались доказать обратное...
> Despite/regardless of efforts to prove the contrary...

The verb "made" as in "efforts made" can be omitted.

Negative participial phrases may require reworking:

> Работа нынешней сессии комитета проходит в условиях напряженной международной обстановки, когда проблема безусловного и не терпящего отлагательства предотвращения нового опасного витка гонки вооружений...стала наиболее актуальной.
> The (work of the) present session/the present session ("work" can be omitted as redundant) is taking place in a tense international climate, when the problem of the unconditional and immediate (participial phrase reduced to one adjective) prevention of a new and dangerous spiral/advance of the arms race has become (the) most urgent/crucial/critical/pressing (problem).

The negative particle in the Russian subordinate clause may be shifted to the main clause in English:

> Боюсь, я не совсем ясно изъяснился.
> I don't think I've made myself quite clear.

"I'm afraid I haven't been quite clear" is of course also a possible translation. Or the sentence can be turned around:

Признаться, я не ожидал от него ультиматума.
I don't think I expected an ultimatum from him/Frankly, I wasn't expecting an ultimatum.[3]

Не исключено, что:
It may be that…/It may happen that

While each linguistic situation requires its own solution, that old American favorite, "the power of positive thinking" often works wonders in dealing with negative constructions.

CHAPTER VIII

SMALL AND SLIPPERY WORDS:
CONJUNCTIONS, PREPOSITIONS AND PARTICLES

Three categories of little words—conjunctions, prepositions and particles—can cause interpreters big problems. The tendency to translate prepositions literally—although the target language requires a different word—must constantly be fought. One study showed that errors in the use of prepositions accounted for 28% of all serious grammatical errors made by interpreters.[1]

The deceptively simple-looking conjunctions *и* and *а* are cases in point. *А* can mean "while" as well as "but" or "and":

> Где вы оба были? – Он ходил в кино, *а* я – в театр.
>
> He was at the movies *while* I went to the theater.
> He went to the movies *but* I decided to go to the theater.
>
> Летом я играю в теннис, *а* зимой хожу на лыжах.
>
> In summer I play tennis *but/and* in winter I ski.
> In summer I like tennis *while* in winter I like to ski.
>
> *А* охотой не увлекаешься?
> Не очень, *а* вот мой брат – охотник.
>
> What about hunting?
> Not really,—it's my brother who's a great hunter/my brother really likes that.[2]

A shift of intonation can change the meaning of an all-too-easy-to-forget conjunction:[3]

>   1
> И она ушла.
>
>   1
> И она ушла.

With the intonational center (IK-1) on the pronoun, the sentence means "She also left," i.e. "Some people left, and so did she." When the center shifts to *ушла*, the meaning changes to "And after that (whatever action is referred to) she left."

И functioning as an intensifier requires description-explanation in English:

> *И* куда мы только не обращались!
> We must have tried everyone/everything/left no stone unturned!
>
> Не знаю, что *и* думать!
> What am I supposed to think of this!/I'm at a total loss!/What is this supposed to mean?
>
> *И* хорош он! Весь белый, шерсть блестит (about a cat).
> He's absolutely gorgeous!/What a gorgeous cat!

In some contexts *и* in conjunction with *не* can mean "even":

> *Не* прошло *и* года со дня нашей последней встречи.
> Less than a year/not *even* a year has passed since our last meeting.

> Он *и не* улыбнулся.
> He didn't even smile.

И can mean "also," "too," or "as well:"

> Мы предложили *и* другой вариант.
> We also made another proposal/We proposed another version as well.

If the interpreter has failed to translate this *и* following a verb and needs to insert a word later in the sentence to compensate for that, "too" or "as well" work better than "also:"

> Такой мир может быть создан *и* на Ближнем Востоке.
> Such (a) peace can be established in the Middle East, too/as well.

Or:

> Хотелось бы надеяться, что *и* другая сторона садится за стол переговоров
> со столь же искренними намерениями.
> We hope that the other side *as well/too* is coming to the negotiation table with
> equally sincere intentions.

Sometimes it can be nearly impossible for the interpreter to know whether a first *и* will be followed by a second one, forming an *и – и* (both...and) construction. In that case he is better off omitting the first one and inserting "as well" or "also" after the second "and:"

> Наша страна добивалась запрещения ядерного оружия *и* тогда, когда не
> располагала им, *и* после того, как создала это оружие. Мы *и* теперь выступаем
> за незамедлительное принятие мер по сокращению, а в конечном счете –
> полной ликвидации ядерного оружия.
> Our country was working for/favored/was trying to achieve a ban on nuclear weap-
> ons *(both)* when we did not possess them *and* also/later/as well when we had manu-
> factured/produced/when we did have these weapons.

The second sentence contains an *и* stressing continuity of action:

> We (now) are continuing/continue to back/favor/press for the immediate adoption
> of measures to reduce and ultimately fully eliminate nuclear weapons.

Changing *сокращение* from a noun to a verb makes for a smoother sentence. Another possibility is to replace *и* and *теперь* by "still":

> Our country still favors the immediate adoption.../We are still backing the
> immediate adoption...

И in the sense of continued action is common in formal statements:

> Очевидно, что наша организация должна *и* дальше заниматься этим
> вопросом.
> It is clear that our organization must continue to deal with this question.

Не....и constructions can have the force of "nor":

> Администрация США *не* откликнулась *и* на предложение о моратории на
> любые ядерные взрывы.
> Nor did the US Administration respond/react to the proposal for a moratorium on all
> nuclear explosions.

If the interpreter has already said "The US Administration has not responded," once he hears the *u* he can insert "moreover," or "in addition," and then continue the sentence:

> The US Administration did not respond/has not responded/moreover/in addition/ to the proposal...

Or:

> *Нельзя не* остановиться *и* на той негативной роли, которую военно-морской флот играет во внешней политике определенных государств.
> Nor can we fail to dwell on/ignore the negative role played by naval forces in the foreign policies of some states.
> We cannot fail to dwell as well/in addition/moreover on the negative role...

Yet another type of *u,* in the opinion of the Russian linguist Cherniakhovskaia, serves to weaken the force of the verb in a sentence by separating the subject and predicate, for here the omission of *u* would put greater emphasis on the verb:

> Изумляла *и* удивительная выносливость Льва Николаевича.
> Lev Nikolaevich had extraordinary stamina.[4]

Failure to insert "and" between the last two items of a list in English results in a sentence which sounds unfinished to the English listener; Russian often uses a comma instead of the conjunction *u,* particularly in a sentence describing two or more closely connected actions:

> Все устали, обозлились.   Everyone was tired *and* cross/angry.
> Он орал, кричал.   He was screaming *and* shouting.[5]
>
> Сушеная вишня была мягкая, сочная, сладкая, душистая.
> The dried cherries were soft, juicy, sweet *and* fragrant.[6]

Such listing is also very common in formal speeches:

> Мы считаем, что осуществление мер доверия применительно к этому региону имело бы большое политическое значение, содействовало бы предотвращению конфликтных ситуаций, укреплению безопасности морских коммуникаций в этом районе.
> We believe that the implementation of confidence-building measures concerning this region would be of great political significance, promote the prevention of conflict situations, *and* strengthen the security of naval communications in the region.

Sometimes the interpreter may not realize that a list has come to a sudden end:

> Такому урегулированию помогла бы глубокая перестройка международных экономических отношений, прекращение гонки вооружений.
> Such a settlement would be advanced/promoted/assisted by an intensive/in-depth/ fundamental (not deep!) restructuring of international economic relations *and* by the cessation/halting of the arms race.

If the interpreter has not inserted "and" and finds himself hanging on to an unfinished sentence, he can add on "and other things," "and other items," "and other goals" or even "et cetera."

In an English sentence, a preposition may replace the comma in a Russian sentence which precedes a participle:

Раздел, посвященный процедуре планирования бюджета, по своему значению заслуживает особого внимания.
The section *on* budget planning procedure deserves special consideration/is so important it deserves special consideration.

Prepositions are particularly tricky because of the tendency of interpreters to translate them automatically and literally rather than by selecting the correct word needed in English. This choice is made more difficult by a certain arbitrariness in the way languages describe the semantic features and functional relationships between two objects. In the use of prepositions we accept certain variations of generally accepted geometric and spatial conventions. "The pear is in the bowl" does not mean that the fruit is in fact located inside layers of glass.[7] In Russian one says *Я поехал в Бостон на машине.* While in English theoretically we can say "I went to Boston in the car" or "I went to Boston by car," more idiomatic solutions would be "I drove to Boston," "I took the car to Boston" or "I got a ride to Boston" depending on what the speaker wishes to emphasize.[8]

Prepositions which take the genitive in Russian do not necessarily require "of" in English. The interpreter's instinct is to automatically translate *для* as "for," whereas English may require the preposition "to:"

Было бы желательно создать международный фонд, открытый *для* всех государств.
It would be a good idea/desirable to establish an international fund open *to* all states.

The ubiquitous Russian *у* as in *у нас,* can refer to a part of the world, country, city, house or cultural group. In Russian *он живет у своих родителей,* while in English he lives *with* his parents. In Russian he is *у Петра* while in English he is "*at* Peter's/ place."[9]

Here are a few examples of Russian constructions with *от* and the genitive case which are translated by a whole range of different prepositions in English.[10]

Улицы были мокрые *от* дождя.	The streets were wet *with* rain.
зевать *от* скуки	to yawn *from, out of* boredom
прыгать *от* радости	to jump *with, from* joy
Мост разрушился *от* взрыва бомбы.	The bridge was destroyed *by* the bomb.
погибнуть *от* пожара	to die *in* a fire
тяжелые *от* плодов яблони	trees heavy *with* fruit
страдать *от* слабости	to suffer *from* weakness
страдать *от* бессонницы	*to have* (verb instead of preposition) insomnia

The preposition *от* is omitted if the word it governs becomes a nominative subject in English:

| *От* шума у нее заболела голова. | The noise gave her a headache. |
| *От* боли она вскрикнула. | The pain made her scream. |

The expression dative + *не до* needs reworking in English:

| *Мне* было *не до* них. | I couldn't deal with them/I didn't have time for them. |
| Завтра *мне* будет *не до* разговоров. | Tomorrow I won't have time to talk/ I'll be in no mood for talk. |

Мне сейчас *не до* этого.	I'm not up to that now/I can't do that now/I don't have time for that now/I'm in no mood for that now/ I don't feel like that now/I can't cope with that now.

The preposition *c* + genitive has numerous translations in addition to the literal "from:"

Он устал *с* дороги.	He is tired *after* his trip.
умереть *с* голоду	to die *of* hunger
выпить *с* горя	to drink *out of* grief, to drown one's sorrows *in* drink
со зла	*out of* malice

Translation of Russian prepositions governing the dative may also require a variety of English prepositions:

> *К* числу важнейших решений, принятых в Хельсинки, относится договоренность о развитии сотрудничества в области информации.
> *Among* the very important decisions adopted in Helsinki is the agreement on…

Here too, if the Russian noun governed by the preposition becomes the English subject, the original preposition is dropped:

> The important decisions adopted in Helsinki include an agreement on the development of cooperation…

Or:

> В Кабуле, например, *по* сообщениям печати, стало известно, что священнослужители готовятся основать исламскую партию Афганистана.
> In Kabul, for example, *according to* press reports, the clergy are preparing/ planning the establishment of an Islamic party of Afghanistan.
> In Kabul, for example, press reports stated that…

По requires a host of different prepositions in English:

по этому закону	*under* this law
по двору	*about* the yard
по шоссе	*along* the highway
по Волге	*down/up* the Volga
по равнине	*across* the plain
по крыше	*on* the roof
по всему миру	*throughout/all over* the world
ходить *по* магазинам	*from* store to store
отсутствовать *по* болезни	*because of/on account of* illness
по уважительной причине	*for* valid reasons
работа *по* метереологии	*on, about* meteorology
экзамен *по* химии	exam *in* chemistry, chemistry exam
работать *по* плану	*according to* plan
узнал *по* голосу	*by* his voice
по четвергам	*on* Thursdays
румянец разлился *по* лицу	a blush spread *over* his face
по совету врача	*on* the doctor's advice
по рассеянности	*out of* absentmindedness
по чьему приглашению	*on/at* whose invitation
по глупости	*out of* stupidity

Or the Russian preposition may be omitted in English:

Они разошлись по домам.	They went home
По чьей вине это случилось?	Whose fault is this/Who is to blame for this?

Prepositions with the accusative may also need reworking in translation. *За* + a noun can sometimes be rendered as an infinitive:

> Хотя особая ответственность *за* устранение ядерной угрозы ложится *на* ядерные государства, борьба *за* предотвращение ядерной войны – дело всех и каждого.
>
> Although particular/special responsibility *for* the elimination of the threat of nuclear war lies *with* the nuclear states/nuclear-weapon states/powers, the campaign *to* prevent nuclear war is the cause of each and every one of us.

Of course, the interpreter can also say "the campaign for the prevention of," but this is clumsier and takes six syllables instead of three ("to prevent").

O + accusative also has several translations:

птица бьется *о* стекло	*against* the pane
погасил сигарету *о* подошву	put out the cigarette *on* the sole of the shoe
спотыкался *о* камни	tripped *on/over* the stones

По and *перед* + instrumental can be particularly dangerous *ложные друзья* for the interpreter:

> Именно *под* этим углом зрения мы рассматриваем противоправное требование правительства США о сокращении персонала миссий ряда государств-членов ООН.
>
> It is precisely *from* this point of view that we are considering/this is the way we see the illegal demand of the US government for a reduction of staff...

Or:

> Такая точка зрения ставит *под* вопрос дальнейшие шаги...
>
> Such a point of view jeopardizes/challenges/threatens/calls into question...

In English *под*, like *по*, requires a variety of prepositions. In certain contexts it indicates proximity rather than "under:"[11]

жить *под* Москвой	to live in the outskirts of Moscow, near Moscow, in the suburbs of Moscow
дети *под* ногами	The children are getting in the way/are all over the place.

Под+ instrumental and accusative also takes a range of prepositions in English translation:

залы, отведенные *под* музей	rooms allocated *for*/earmarked *as* a museum
вернуться *под* вечер	to return *towards* evening
принять деньги *под* квитанцию	*against* a receipt
заснуть *под* музыку	to fall asleep *to* music
писать *под* диктовку	to write *from* dictation
быть загримированным *под* старика	to be made up *as* an old man
под свою ответственность	*on* his own responsibility
помещение *под* школой	premises used *as/for* a school
под предлогом усталости	*on* the pretext of fatigue

This last phrase, *под предлогом*, frequently trips up interpreters:

> Важно не допустить, чтобы *под предлогом* реорганизации были ущемлены права какого бы то ни было члена этой организации.
> It is important to prevent violations of rights of any member of this organization *on* the pretext of reorganization.

Or omission of the preposition and nominalization of the object of the preposition can restructure the sentence:

> It is important that the pretext of reorganization not be used to violate the rights of any member of the organization.

Перед + instrumental sometimes should be rendered as "to," or "in," rather than being automatically translated as "before" or "in front of," as in *перед обедом* "before dinner," or in *перед дверью*, "in front of the door:"

исполнить долг *перед* другими	to carry out obligations *to* others
Вы отвечаете *перед* заводом	You are responsible *to* the plant
Перед отцом он ничего	He is nothing compared *to* his father
(Variant: *Перед* Пушкиным все поэты ничтожны - *beside* Pushkin, compared *to* Pushkin)	
извинился *перед* ним	apologized *to* him

Preposition omitted:

виноват *перед* ним	owe him an apology
перед вами большая задача	a major problem is facing/ confronting you

It is very easy to give in to the temptation to say "before" rather than "to" in a sentence such as the following:

> Огромна ответственность средств массовой информации *перед* народами своих стран за правдивое информирование общественности о событиях международной жизни.
> The mass media have an enormous responsibility *to* the peoples of their countries – to give fair information to people/society/public opinion on/about world events.

Над used figuratively should not necessarily be translated as "on" or "over:"

насмехаться *над*	to jeer at
издеваться *над*	to make fun of, to mock, to abuse

And the garden variety *с* + instrumental frequently does not translate as "with:"

с пониманием, что	on the understanding that
бутылка *с* водой	a bottle of water
обращаться *с* просьбой	to make a request, to request
поздравить с днем рождения	congratulate someone on a birthday
У него *с* деньгами трудно	He has money problems
Делегация приехала *с* дружеским визитом	The delegation arrived on a friendly visit

The preposition *в* in *в*+ prepositional phrases can sometimes be omitted in expressions such as *в области, в деле*, or *в целях*, e.g. *в области сельского хозяйства* – "in agriculture," *в деле разоружения* "in disarmament," *в целях продвижения дела мира* "to advance the cause of peace." *В* can also be rendered as "about:"

Нет сомнения *в* его честности.	There is/can be no doubt about/ concerning/regarding his honesty.

На and *в* + prepositional are often best rendered as nominatives when they stand at the head of a sentence or clause:

На страницах газет и журналов в подробностях описываются многочисленные партии.
The pages of newspapers and magazines.../Even shorter: Newspapers and magazines give detailed descriptions of numerous parties.

There are a variety of translations for *o* + prepositional:

вспоминать *о* долге	to remember his duty
напоминать *о* долге	remind someone *of* his duty
упоминать *о* долге	to mention/refer *to*
призыв *о* помощи	appeal *for* help
заботиться *о* билетах	see *about* the tickets

При + prepositional is not always "in the presence of" or "under:"

при этих условиях	*under/given* these conditions
спросить *при* встрече	to ask *on* meeting someone
при всех его особенностях	*with/despite* all his abilities
при институте есть столовая	the institute has a cafeteria
ждать *при* выходе из метро	to wait *at* the subway exit
при участии всех	if everyone joins in
при всех его талантах – он дурак	*despite* all his talents...
при нашем университете	*at* our university
жить *при* дворе	to live *near/on* the grounds of the palace

Though *благодаря* + dative and *из-за* + genitive can both be translated as "because of," the former is positive and the latter negative in meaning. This distinction can be conveyed:

Благодаря твоей помощи, мы все успеем.	*Thanks to* your help we got everything done. *With* your help we got everything done.
Мы опоздали *из – за* тебя.	We are late *on account of* you.
Они поссорились *из-за* пустяков.	They quarrelled *over* trifles.

Since not all speakers make the correct distinction between these two prepositions, the interpreter should listen carefully before jumping in to translate *благодаря* as "thanks to."

Several compound prepositions can be rendered simply as "because:"

В силу того, что
В результате того, что не было кворума, заседание было отменено.
В связи с тем, что
Ввиду того, что

Because there was no quorum, the meeting was canceled.

* * *

Emphasis can be indicated in Russian both through intonation and through a series of conjunctions, adverbs and particles placed directly before or after the word stressed. In many cases the interpreter can use his voice to indicate stress—"It is *he* who did it." "*This* is what we want." Words such as *именно* and *ведь* signal that a particular item is being stressed:

Так *именно* поступает Россия.
And *this* is what Russia is doing.

Or "precisely," "exactly," "that," "that very" convey emphasis along with intonational stress:

And *this* is *precisely/exactly* what Russia is doing.

Or:

Именно данное направление в мировой политике нас интересует.
It is precisely *that* area/it is *that very* area of world politics (or global policy, depending on context) which is of interest to us.

Or:

Именно они прибегали к откровенному нажиму на коренное население.
It is *they* who resorted/They were the ones who resorted to outright/direct pressure on the indigenous population.

Как раз serves the same function as *ведь*:

Наша организация *как раз* и призвана явиться механизмом для решения всех этих проблем.
It is precisely/in fact/indeed/ through our organization/It is *our* organization...

Or:

Это *как раз* и демонстрирует истинное отношение правительства к вопросам прав человека.
This/in fact/specifically/just/precisely/reveals/It is *this* which reveals the real attitude of governments to human rights issues/questions.

Ведь can sometimes be a synonym for *именно*. Its meaning can also be conveyed through intonation or through "that" or "but:"

Ведь это отвечало бы собственным национальным интересам.
That, in fact/That, indeed/That, to be sure/That, after all/*That* would be in keeping with their own national interests.

Or:

Космос должен быть чистым, на него не должна распространяться гонка вооружений. Но *ведь* положение иное.

Here *ведь* has the notion of protesting or contradicting a previous idea:

Outer space should be kept clear, free from an extended/expanded arms race.
      But that is not the case.
      But the situation is different.
      The situation, however, is different/is in fact, different.

Ведь with an IK-2 intonation can emphasize a fact obvious to the speaker and to the person he is addressing. With IK-3 *ведь* sometimes serves as an explanation:

$$2$$
Я уеду рано, *ведь* я очень далеко живу.
I'll leave early because I live so far away.

$$2$$
Почему ты не позвонил? Ты *ведь* обещал.
Why didn't you call? You promised you would/after all/didn't you.

$$2$$
Надо к нему сходить. Он *ведь* болеет.
We should go see him—he's sick, after all/he's really sick/because he's sick.

77

2

Конечно у меня странный голос – я *ведь* болею.
Of course my voice sounds odd/funny—I'm sick, after all/it's because I'm sick/
you know I'm sick.

3

Зачем мне идти к врачу? У меня *ведь* только насморк и болит горло.
Why should I go see the doctor? I only/just have a cold and a sore throat (expla-nation).[12]

Ведь with *a* or *но* implies that the speaker is protesting or contradicting some-thing said earlier:

Ведь ты мог бы мне написать два слова.
You really could have dropped me a line.

Ты занят? А *ведь* мы собирались в музей.
You're busy? But we had been planning to go to the museum/but what about the museum?

Sometimes *ведь* combines explanation and protest:

Зачем тебе читать эту книгу? Ты ведь ее уже читал.
Why do you want to/why should you read that book? After all/when you've already read it.

The explanatory *ведь* occurs frequently in statements when the speaker wishes to emphasize a point:

Ведь эта угроза вынуждает рабочих мириться с произволом предпринимателей.
That in fact is the threat which is making/forcing the workers to accept/put up with the arbitrary actions of the employers.
It is that very threat/*That* is the threat which/But that is the threat which…
But *that* threat forces workers…

The particles *-то* and *же* are enclitic and emphatic. *-To* puts emphasis on the word which precedes it, a stress which in English can be conveyed through intonation:[13]

Он-*то* это сказал.   *He* said it.

Or an added word of intensification gets the point across: "*He's* the one who said it." For the interpreter, however, using intonation rather than extra words saves time and avoids an awkward sentence:

Наконец-*то* мы договорились   *Finally,* we agreed.

While close to *-то* in meaning, *же* usually implies some form of contrast or apposi-tion approximating English "but," "however," "otherwise" or "also." Or it may be rendered by intonational stress:[14]

Зимой они жили в Москве. Летом *же,* они жили за границей.
In winter they lived in Moscow. In summer, however, they lived abroad.

Почему ты ей не доверяешь? Она *же* твоя сестра.
Why don't you trust her? She's your sister, after all.

Я *же* не буду участвовать.
I want no part of it./For *my* part, I won't participate.

Он любит сына, и сын *же* опора ему в старости.
He loves his son and the son is also/it is the son who is his support in his old age.

In the sense of explanation or protest, *же* can be a synonym for *ведь:*

Я *же* тебе говорил.	I told you so, didn't I/after all.
Тебя *же* просили, не меня.	They asked *you,* after all/not me.
	It was *you* they asked.
Как, он не знает? Я *же* ему говорил..	He doesn't know? But I told him/I told him that.
Как, где она? Она *же* уехала.	What do you mean, where is she? She's left, of course/You know she left.
Ты *же* читал эту книгу.	You've read that book, after all.

Же can be purely emphatic:

Она *же* некрасивая, эта девушка.	*That* girl isn't pretty.
Воскресенье *же* он дома сидеть не будет.	On *Sunday* he certainly won't stay at home.

Как же can imply a contradiction of another speaker's assertion:

Вы не ездили в Москву? – А как *же!* Были два раза.
You've never been to Moscow? Of course we have! Twice!

Кто же, когда же imply a request for more information:

Если не он, тогда *кто же* это сделал?
If he didn't do it, then who was the person who did it/who on earth did it?

Когда же он это поймет, в конце концов?
When is he ever going to understand that?

Же can serve to indicate disagreement with the expected or implied answer to a negative question:

Ты не сможешь сегодня пойти с нами в кино?
Почему *же* не смогу? Обязательно пойду.

Can you come with us to the movies today?
Of course! Absolutely!

Following a sentence such as *Это не Анна пришла* the phrases *А кто же (а как же, а что же)* indicate a desire for more information—"Then *who* came? Well, *who* was it, then? How come? Why?"

The exclamation *Ну что* + pronoun also implies contradiction, surprise or indignation:

Это, наверно, стоило тебе очень много денег. – *Ну что* ты!
That must have cost you a fortune. Not in the least!

> No way!
> Come on!
> Not at all!
> What are you talking about!

Я надеюсь, что я вас не обидел. – *Ну что* вы!
I hope I haven't offended you. Not at all!

> Certainly not!
> Absolutely not!
> Not in the least!
> No way!

Russian questions are indicated by an interrogative word such as *что, кто, когда, как, где,* etc., or by intonation: *Это ваша* (IK-3) *книга?* Syntax and tense may need to be reworked in English translation of such sentences. In rhetorical questions the word *разве* introduces constructions which can be tricky for the interpreter, since they may require him to wait before beginning the sentence. For example:

> *Разве* кто-нибудь хочет ядерной войны?

A *разве* sentence can usually be resolved through "does" or "is:"

> Does anyone really want nuclear war?
> Is there anyone who really wants/wants nuclear war?

Разве can express surprise, distrust, suspicion, or indignation:[15]

> *Разве* вы не знали?   Did you *really* not know?

The interpreter can express this sense of surprise through intonational stress as well as through "really:"

> *Разве* у вас нет моего телефона?   You *really don't* have my number?

While *неужели* is close in meaning to *разве,* it expresses a slightly stronger shade of surprise: *Неужели у вас нет моего телефона?* (You *really don't* have my number—how odd!) In some contexts *разве* can imply distrust or inability on the speaker's part:

> *Разве* мне переплыть?   Do I really have to swim across?
>   (because I probably can't)
>
> *Разве* мне выступать?   Do I really have to speak? I don't h
>   have to speak, do I?

In both these cases the speaker does not want to or doubts he can perform the action. A shorter interpretation would be: "Do I *have* to do that?"

Intonational stress can emphasize the speaker's surprise:

> *Разве* это случилось в прошлом году?
> Did that really happen *last year*?
>
> *Разве* вас это обидело?
> *That* offended you?

Or, if there is time: "Were you really offended by that?" "Could that possibly have offended you?"

> *Разве* ты не пойдешь со мной? – Конечно!
> Aren't you coming with me? Of course I am!
>
> *Разве* он это сказал?
> *Did* he say that?

If the interpreter has rendered the first question in the negative the answer must be adjusted accordingly:

> You aren't coming with me? Why not? Of course I am!

This example shows how much simpler—and shorter—it is for the interpreter to rephrase a negative question as a positive one in English.

Как...разве expresses a strong degree of surprise:

> Я жду его завтра. *Как, разве* ты не знаешь? Он уже приехал..
> I'm expecting him tomorrow. What??/Really?/Don't you *know*? He's here/He's
> already arrived.
>
> Я не знаю, как проехать в этот театр. – *Как, разве* вы еще там не были?
> I don't know how to get to that theater. What/You mean/You really haven't gone/
> been there/yet?

In colloquial interrogative sentences surprise or misgiving can be expressed by *a вдруг:*

> *А вдруг* он не приедет?   What if he doesn't come?
> *А вдруг* это не то, что я хотел?   What if it isn't what I wanted?

Разве can also indicate direct contradiction:

> Вы мне очень много кладете. – Да *разве* это много? Это ничего.
> You're giving me a lot. Nothing of the sort/not at all. That's nothing/a tiny portion.

In a very long sentence the interpreter can risk beginning a *разве* sentence with "that" and add the interrogative at the end:

> *Разве* кто-нибудь хочет ядерной войны?
> That anyone would want nuclear war—is that possible?

Or take a longer sentence:

> *Разве* сегодня дело мира менее актуально, чем вчера?
> Is work for peace/the cause of peace/to strengthen peace any less urgent/pressing/relevant today? ("than yesterday" can be omitted)
> Does work for peace today seem less relevant…
> That work for peace is less relevant today than yesterday – could that be so?

The construction with "that" is awkward, but provides a means for launching into a sentence right away if the interpreter cannot—or is afraid—to wait. "Can" is also a possible solution:

> Can work for peace be less relevant today…

"Can" also works in the following:

> *Разве* это справедливость?
> Can this be /called/ justice?/Is this really justice?

Another rhetorical qualifier is *вряд ли.* The speaker is usually asserting something he feels *вряд ли* will be contradicted:

> *Вряд ли* кто возьмет на себя смелость сказать, что эта ситуация не чревата опасностью нового взрыва.

The literal translation, "Hardly anyone would dare to say," is quite awkward. An impersonal construction is frequently the easiest solution, with the sentence turned into an interrogative: "Would anyone dare to say…" This is a bit different from the speaker's intention, however, and if the sentence is long can lead to awkward phrasing. Easier solutions are:

> Probably no one would venture/dare/want to say…
> It is unlikely anyone would/There is probably no one who would…

Or:

> *Вряд ли* кто-либо станет отрицать, что завоевание этой страной независимости является в наши дни одной из более актуальных международных задач.
> Probably no one/It is unlikely that anyone would deny that the achievement of independence by this country is one of the most pressing/urgent/critical problems of our time.

The adverbs/particles *разве что, иначе, лишь* and *только* in certain situations act as synonyms. *Разве что* can convey the sense of "solely," "only," "perhaps," "except perhaps," and sometimes "but only:"

> Это серьезный вызов, сопоставимый по своему масштабу *разве что* с теми возможностями, которые открываются перед человечеством.
> This is a serious challenge, comparable only/perhaps/solely in size/magnitude/scope/ scale to the opportunities opening up to mankind.

In colloquial Russian *лишь* and *только* can be synonymous:

> *Лишь бы* успеть! *Только* бы с ним ничего не случилось!
> If only we make it/get there in time! If only he's OK!

Иначе used with *не* in a negative clause has the meaning of "only:"

> Объявленная этой стороной акция не может квалифицироваться *иначе* как несовестимая с нормами международного права.
> The action announced by this party can only be described as incompatible with the norms of international law.

> Близорукой – *иначе* не назовешь – является политика некоторых государств.
> Nearsighted—that's the only word for it—describes the policy of certain states.

Только and *лишь* can be rendered by "only," "solely" and "merely," depending on context:

> Не менее ста конструктивных инициатив выдвинуто нами *только* с этой трибуны.
> From this rostrum alone we have put forward/made more than one hundred/some one hundred constructive initiatives.

Or, if the interpreter has been closely following Russian word order:

> No less than one hundred initiatives have been put forward by our side from this rostrum alone/solely/just from this rostrum.

Or:

> *Только* в этом году у ливийских берегов было проведено 5 крупномасштабных маневров.
> This year alone more than five large-scale maneuvers were carried out on Libyan shores.

> *Лишь* совместной резолюцией можно найти выход из этого тупика.
> Only by a joint resolution/only through a joint resolution can we get out of this deadlock.
> Only a joint resolution can extricate us from this impasse.

И только in a time expression does not necessarily mean "only:"[16]

> *И только* после того, как он несколько дней сидел за книгами, он натолкнулся на замечательную повесть.
> It was not until he had read for several days that he came upon a wonderful/striking/ outstanding story.
> Only after he had read for several days did he come upon…/Only after several days of reading…

Or:

> *И только* она его поняла/*лишь* она его поняла.
> She was the only one who understood/to understand him.

Conjunctions, prepositions, and participles are constant reminders to the interpreter of the need to think of how things are said in English, to think idiomatically rather than automatically when crossing language boundaries.

CHAPTER IX

7,362 MISSILES IN ALLAWALA, SOUTHERN PATAGONIA: NUMERALS AND NAMES

> Наиболее типичными ошибками переводчика являются искажения сложных числительных,…искажение незнакомых имен собственных.[1]

Numerals pose a constant problem for interpreters. The memory's ability to retain more than a limited number of figures is limited by the physiological capacity of the human brain, and complex figures can cause difficulty even for interpreters with excellent short-term memory.[2] Regardless of how well they have mastered a foreign language, most people count and do math problems in their native tongue. Only a limited number of genuine bilinguals—such as people who have learned math using both languages—can manipulate figures with equal ease in either idiom. During World War II suspected spies were ordered to solve dozens of math problems out loud in the hope they would break down and under the pressure of the figures reveal their native language and true nationality.

Numbers often have no semantic reference point. Whether a speaker will say that 415 or 416 schools have been built in an underdeveloped country is anybody's guess, and the "zone of contagion" through which words in close proximity affect each other's meaning does not work for numerals. Nor is there the possibility of using *вероятность прогнозирования*.

When faced with a written text in a foreign language, most people will automatically sound out figures to themselves in their native tongue or, in the case of many bilinguals, the one in which they first studied arithmetic and mathematics. A Russian teacher pointed out this problem in training interpreters:

> Неумение передавать в переводе цифры и фактуалии отчасти объясняется тем, что в процессе обучения иностранному языку наши студенты имеют дело чаще всего не со звуковой, а с визуальной формой восприятия и воспроизведения этих элементов. В письменной речи (и переводе) проблема передачи цифр вообще отсутствует, а передача имен собственных значительно облегчена.[3]

The way to learn to interpret figures, therefore, is by listening rather than reading. Of course, if the speaker is reeling off reams of statistics, having a text makes life much simpler. But the speaker may make changes in the figures, and the interpreter must listen intently rather than burying himself in the text. And often there is no text or reference point:

> Переводчик, не предполагающий, какого порядка цифры будут упоминаться оратором, вынужден воспринимать их пословно[4]

as a leading Russian interpreter has pointed out.

Figures present a double danger to the interpreter. First, he may get them wrong. Second, if he spends too much time trying to grasp a number, he may miss a crucial part or most of the entire sentence. *The way to interpret the number quickly and correctly is to write it down.* Nearly all interpreters do this with any numeral larger than two digits, and for a long list of numbers many write down one or two-digit figures as well. The enormous difficulty of dealing with numerals has led some commentators to suggest a radical solution—omission.[5] This, however, is not always advisable, for like most things in life, numerals vary in importance. Whether 3,493 or 3,494 foreign students were enrolled last year in the University of Southern Patagonia may not be critical to world history. But the number of missiles destroyed or inspected, or the number of millions allocated to a government budget is not something the interpreter can pass over in silence—or fudge. In military and political negotiations figures must be exact.

In some cases the interpreter may be helped by the semantic context provided by the words surrounding the numeral. If the interpreter is not sure he has correctly understood the number of students in Southern Patagonia he may take a stab at "some 3,000 students," "3,000+ students," "more than 3,000 students," or "some 3,000-odd students." On hearing "On December twenty-something we shall leave," the interpreter may say "towards the end of December." The goal is to listen intelligently, using semantic context whenever possible. A speaker listing the number of clinics or schools his country has built is emphasizing that there are a "great," "large," or "considerable" number of these establishments, while the delegate discussing the number of vicious murders perpetrated in his homeland will probably—unless he is asking for law enforcement help—emphasize that these are "few" or "small" in number. This semantic approach can greatly aid the interpreter when he misses a figure. For example:

> Some two hundred clinics were built (The speaker said 208).
>
> More than a million dollars/well over a million dollars were contributed to the fund. (The speaker said $1,110,842.69)
>
> There were hundreds of/several hundred victims. (Speaker: Было (mumble) uh-uh сот жертв)
>
> During the five-year plan labor productivity at this plant rose considerably/noticeably/greatly. (Speaker: За пятилетку производительность труда на этом предприятии повысилась на 37,6%—interpreter does not hear the 7.6 part of the figure).
> Or: productivity rose by more than 30%.[6]

A Canadian interpreter has nicely summed up this technique, noting that these sacrifices of detail which an interpreter can (sometimes!) get away with would horrify translators:

> If you fail to note down all the figures in a series of numbers, don't worry unduly. What really matters is the order of magnitude. If the treasurer says, "Revenues have gone up from $19,732.55 in 1979 to $21,033.41 in 1980," you will probably convey his message well enough if you translate it as, "Revenues have increased by over a thousand in the past year."[7]

The verbs *составлять, исчисляться* and *приходиться* are frequently used in connection with figures, and the interpreter should have several options ready and waiting:

Ущерб *составил* 60 миллиардов долларов.
The damage amounted to/ran to/totalled 60 billion dollars.

Десятками *исчисляется* количество фирм, которые осуществляют такие деловые операции.
There are dozens of firms which work on such deals/carry out such operations.

Почти половина всех школьников *приходится* на сельские районы
Rural areas account for almost half of all the schoolchildren.

На них *приходится* почти 10% британского экспорта.
They account for almost 10% of Britain's exports.[8]

It is important for the interpreter to listen to an entire figure before starting in, as he has no way of knowing if it will turn out to be a two, three or four digit number. Particularly dangerous is the approximative construction, e.g. *Там было восемь-десять человек* (There were eight to ten/between eight and ten people there) which is very easily confused with *восемьдесят* (80), when the speaker is talking quickly and/or swallows the soft sign.

Here are two examples of simplification of complex figures in formal statements:

Ущерб, нанесенный никарагуанской экономике этой войной, уже превысил два миллиарда долларов, а её жертвами стали 16,562 никарагуанца.
Losses to the Nicaraguan economy caused by this war/resulting from this war (or simply: from this war—*нанесенный* does not have to be translated) have already exceeded/surpassed 2 billion dollars—and this war has killed/claimed the lives of more than 16,000 Nicaraguans.

Or:

За годы необъявленной войны террористами сожжено в ДРА около двух тысяч школ, 136 больниц и 547 мечетей, выведены из строя сотни мостов. Жертвами бандитов стали 2510 учителей и 1000 служителей культа.

In a sentence containing several numerals in oblique cases, it is important to make the instrumental *террористами* the nominative subject: "During the years of undeclared war the terrorists in the Democratic Republic of Afghanistan…" This creates a simpler beginning and a more elegant sentence. The participle then becomes an active verb: "The terrorists burned…" Even in the original Russian text *двух тысяч* is written out in words, as nowadays many native Russian speakers stumble over oblique cases of numerals. Seeing the words helps prevent the delegate from hesitating while searching for the right case after *около*.

During the undeclared war terrorists in the Democratic Republic of Afghanistan burned down some 2,000 schools, more than 130 hospitals and some 5,000 mosques. The bandits killed more than 2,000 teachers and 1,000 clergymen.

Geographical and proper names can be as difficult to grasp as numerals. In one study four proper names were rendered incorrectly by 80% to 100% of the interpreters in the sample.[9] If the speaker is referring to NATO countries, the interpreter obviously should know which nations are being named. But mention of a small country's minister of transportation or of a tiny organization's president can leave the interpreter completely in the dark. Without a text he can only go by what he hears: *"Переводчик, не знающий часто упоминаемых на том или ином форуме фамилий и сокращений, вынужден воспринимать их на звуковой основе."*[10] The interpreter can try to repeat phonetically what he is hearing, or can avoid the problem by referring to the person's title: "As the minister said," "The president declared." It is useful to have titles written out, as *зам. начальник отдела* (deputy director of a department) can be difficult to catch on the fly. If he misses a town's name, the interpreter can say "a certain city;" if names are not clear, or mumbled, "several representatives of this party," or "Mr. Ivanov and his colleagues."[11] It is therefore extremely important that the interpreter be given the list of a meeting's speakers or delegates, and background papers containing relevant names.

Care must be taken with the declensional endings of proper names. This is easy enough when translating Russian names, as the interpreter is unlikely to say "Mr. Ivanovym," but such declensional endings should not be carelessly tacked on to foreign names, e.g. "with Mr. Kim Il Sunghom" or the policy of "Presidenta Clintona." Russian names should not be rendered by English equivalents, e.g. Mr. Nikolai Petrov, not Nicholas Petrov. The Russian custom of giving the initial of the first name followed by the full last name sounds strange in English and should be avoided:

> Лидеры двух великих государств – Генеральный Секретарь ЦК КПСС М.С. Горбачев и президент Р. Рейган – показали пример плодотворного диалога в интересах доверия и мира.
>
> The leaders of two great nations/states/countries/powers, General Secretary of the Central Committee of the CPSU Mikhail (Sergeevich if time allows) Gorbachev and President Ronald Reagan set an example of fruitful dialogue promoting trust and peace/the cause of peace.

Russian geographical names with adjectival endings should rendered by the appropriate nominal forms in English:

> ...Успешно развиваются Братско-Усть-Улимский, Курский, Чимкентско-Джамбульский, Западно-Сибирский и другие промышленные комплексы. Продолжается строительство Камского автозавода, Токтогульской ГЭС, Байкало-Амурской железнодорожной магистрали...
>
> We continue to successfully develop Bratsk-Ust-Ilimsk, Kursk, Chimkent-Dzhambul, West-Siberian and other industrial centers. Construction continues of the Kama automobile plant (Kama motorworks), Toktogul Hydropower Station and the Baikal-Amur railway...[12]

When commonly accepted English equivalents exist for Russian place names these should be used, e.g. Moscow (not Moskva), Siberia (not Sibir'), the Urals, etc.

Names of countries and national movements should be memorized. *Движение неприсоединения,* for example, is *the* nonaligned movement, not *a* nonaligned movement. Even in a written text, names of political parties and movements can be confusing. Take the following (note that the name of the movement is not capitalized):

> Выделение 100 млн. долларов бандам самосовцев является свидетельством расширения линии на свержение правительства этой страны.

"The allocation of 100 million dollars to bands of"—the Russian genitive plural ending and what looks like the root *сам* can rattle an interpreter unfamiliar with the subject matter, the Somosistas.

Names of countries must be rendered accurately, and distinctions in names can be politically highly significant. *Южная Африка* is South Africa (*ЮАР, Южно-Африканская республика*—the Republic of South Africa), while *юг Африки* refers to southern Africa or the southern part of Africa. The interpreter should familiarize himself with names of major international organizations: *Международный валютный фонд* (World Monetary Fund), *Всемирный банк* (the World Bank), etc.

Abbreviations can drive interpreters to distraction. Many organizations have their own intricately abbreviated jargon which can only be learned through intensive perusal of documents and sweating through meetings. The interpreter should, however, master a basic series of Russian acronyms. (We will not deal here with the Soviet love of compound abbreviations—e.g. *профсельмашторг,* etc.). Some of the most common ones, though, such as *исполком* (executive committee) or *Госдеп* (State Department) should be part of the interpreter's "automatic baggage," which he pulls out instinctively when needed.

If the interpreter cannot make sense out of an abbreviation or acronym he should simply repeat the Russian letters or syllables—which some listeners may understand— rather than falling silent or inventing something totally wrong. He should know such commonly used acronyms as ОБСЕ (*Организация по безопасности и сотрудничеству в Европе* – the OSCE—Organization on Security and Cooperation in Europe), or *ООП (Организация освобождения Палестины*—the Palestine Liberation Organization). Acronyms come and go with news events. While the treaty was being negotiated and signed the papers were full of *ОСВ (ограничение стратегических вооружений),* the SALT *(*Strategic Arms Limitation Treaty). Now there is much discussion of *СНВ (стратегические наступательные вооружения*— strategic offensive weapons (i.e. the START or strategic arms reduction talks and agreements). It is the interpreter's duty to keep up with constantly changing terms in those fields in which he works.[13]

CHAPTER X

MORTGAGING A SENTENCE: SYNTAX

The syntax of a Russian sentence is a minefield which the interpreter must hope to cross unscathed: "As you start a sentence you are taking a leap in the dark, you are mortgaging your grammatical future. Great nimbleness is called for to guide the mind through this syntactical maze," writes one observer.[1] While the translator can calmly rearrange the components of a sentence, since the interpreter must start without knowing where the speaker's syntax may take him, he should exercise maximum restraint before jumping in. He needs to attempt to "see ahead" and plan out the sentence insofar as possible. The enormous differences between Russian and English syntax ironically mean that Russian spoken too quickly may be easier to interpret than Russian spoken too slowly, since at higher speed bigger—and more complete—syntactic segments sail into view.

The literary scholar Edmund Wilson wrote that "The syntax of the Russian language is so different from ours that the translator, if he wants to be read smoothly, must always do a great deal of paraphrasing."[2] The interpreter must rearrange rather than paraphrase, for failure to do so will produce some very awkward English. As the Russian specialist on syntax Cherniakhovskaia has noted, when the interpreter deals only with lexical and grammatical correspondences and ignores syntactic difficulties, the result is *"переводческий язык: все слова на месте, в грамматическом построении фразы как будто нет ошибок, и тем не менее, так не говорят..."*[3] A few such examples:

> NATO nations will meet in Vienna to deal with this on March 6. The discussion there should be more objective and realistic as a result.

> At the time my views clashed with the official position and this resulted in the 70s and 80s in the persecution of myself and my family.

> We have an organization capable of defending on the highest level the rights of our membership.[4]

This is a clear case of how *"на качестве перевода может отразиться 'давление системы' родного языка."*[5] An awareness of the structural differences between the two languages can help the interpreter avoid the strong pressure of Russian syntax.

> It has been found—and this is highly significant—that Russian syntax has a very strong influence even on the untrained *native speaker* of the language of the translation. Hence the need for training the English-speaking translator [or interpreter-LV] to translate into his own language.[6]

The order in which words reach a listener is of more than grammatical importance, as linguists are well aware:

> It is reasonable to expect that presentation order in speech influences the percepts that are conveyed by determining the order in which they are constructed. Since languages and styles differ in syntactic orders they also differ in certain aspects of the concepts they can convey.[7]

Russian word order is generally described as fairly free and English word order as fixed. Russian syntax, however, is governed by a set of rules which allow for considerable variation depending on the emphasis, emotion, tone, and style of the speaker. The interpreter must know the basic principles of Russian syntax in order to grasp the differentiations which arise in dealing with a non-neutral word order which stresses the semantic importance of one or another part of a sentence. English fixed word order has less possibilities for the kinds of inversion allowed by Russian case endings,[8] for Russian often begins a sentence with a complement, verb, or object, revealing the subject only several words—or from the interpreter's point of view, minutes—later.

Case forms also erect syntactic hurdles. How is the interpreter to handle a sentence which begins with a dative, accusative or prepositional rather than a nominative subject? While he cannot wait for the reluctant subject, even if the structure of the sentence is not fully clear he cannot remain silent. Case endings may seem ambiguous: in a sentences such as *отношение описывает уравнение* knowledge of the subject matter would be helpful in deciding between nominative and accusative.[9] The interpreter must be sensitive to the relationship between shifting intonational centers and syntactic inversion, and to differences in emphasis caused by shifts in word order. While theoretically a single Russian sentence may have five or six possible English syntactic variants,[10] time pressure means that in fact there are only two or three realistic options for the interpreter. While he cannot stop to tinker with a complicated sentence and risk losing the speaker's next utterance, he must pay careful attention to the original Russian word order.

For example, a shift in the position of the particle *не,* which makes it follow rather than precede the verb, radically changes its meaning:

> Он не может прийти (He can't/is not able to come).
> Он может не прийти (He might not come—that is a possibility).
> Я не ходил в гости (I didn't go visiting).
> Я ходил не в гости (but somewhere else).[11]

The extra second spent listening pays off in producing an idiomatic rendering of such phrases as *богатые витаминами фрукты* or *известный всему миру писатель.* If the interpreter has already started in with "Rich in vitamins," he can repeat the phrase: "Rich in vitamins—these fruits rich in vitamins are…" or: "World-famous, this writer" + verb, etc. Placing a Russian adverb directly after rather than before the verb stresses the quality conveyed by the adverb:

Он замечательно рисует.	He draws beautifully.
Он рисует замечательно.	He draws *beautifully* (intonational emphasis.)
	Or: His drawings are really beautiful/ exquisite/he really draws beautifully (intensifier.)[12]

Even in a highly inflected language such as Russian, a shift in parataxis can change the meaning rather than the emphasis of a sentence. Compare:

Задание начальника – начертить план.
Задание – начертить план начальника.[13]

In dealing with Russian word order the interpreter must show great flexibility, a willingness to substitute verbs for nouns, nouns for verbs, switch actives and passives, insert impersonal constructions, omit words and reorder the parts of a sentence, while simultaneously listening to the speaker and continuing to interpret. This requires considerable short-term memory effort—so much, in fact, that at least one eminent Russian expert sees reordering and restructuring as a nearly impossible task:

> Changing the word order, which translators do in written texts to retain the correct emphasis, is often impossible because of the interpreter's need to remember the initial segment of the sentence until he has finished restructuring the whole. This creates the danger of overwhelming and overloading the simultaneous interpreter's short-term (operative) memory.[14]

When he has a written text the interpreter he can avoid such overload and possible confusion by numbering words or phrases in the order in which they are to be uttered in English:

> 1   4   3   2
> В настоящее время в политической жизни Афганистана происходят важные перемены.
> At the present time important changes are occurring in the political life of Afghanistan.

Or:

> Мы с такой уверенностью призываем к переменам также потому,
> 1   2   4   5   3
> что в нашей стране происходит революционная по своему характеру перестройка.
>
> We are calling for changes with such confidence because our country is undergoing a *perestroika* (restructuring) which is revolutionary in nature.

The difference between Russian and English word order is often explained in terms of *тема* (theme) and *рема* (rheme). The *тема,* containing "old" or "familiar" information with a minimum semantic load, generally corresponds to the predicate in Russian and stands in initial position in a sentence, while the *рема,* containing "new," or "unfamiliar" information and conveying the major semantic load or message of the sentence, generally corresponds to the subject in Russian and is located towards the end of the utterance. In English this division into theme and rheme (sometimes called functional sentence perspective) is generally reversed; the subject expressing the theme is located in initial position, and the predicate/rheme in final position.[15] For example:

В комнату вошла молодая девушка.	A young girl came into the room.
Вспыхнула война.	War broke out.

В журнале было опубликовано более десяти статей на эту интересную тему.
The magazine published more than a dozen articles on this interesting subject.

This difference in sentence structure led an American observer to note that "In Russian the most important word often takes the final position in a sentence, and ideally, the interpreter should not begin his English version until he's heard the whole Russian sentence."[16]

Since he cannot possibly wait for the whole sentence, the interpreter must quickly and efficiently deal with the basic *тема-рема* structural difference. Great variation of basic word order is possible in Russian, since depending on emphasis, tone, intonation, etc., almost any secondary part of the sentence can take initial position. An adverbial modifier is often found in the theme/initial position:

> За окном бушевал теплый южный ветер.
> Под звуки скрипки танцевали пары.

Or an expression of time or place can take the initial position:

> Рано утром на реке тронулся лед.
> На этой улице быстро темнело.
> С тех пор прошло много лет.

The object may serve as theme:

> Музыку к этому кинофильму написал очень известный композитор.
> Проблемами долголетия занимается ряд институтов Академии наук.

Or the verb may be in initial position and the subject at the end:

> Помог мне в это тяжелое время мой брат.[17]
> Начала работать крупнейшая в Европе ГЭС.

All of these sentences sound extremely awkward in literal translation into English. Take a much longer phrase:

> Согласно поступившему вчера сообщению, в среду в Париже скончался в госпитале генерал Пьер Кониг, бывший после освобождения Франции в 1944 году министром обороны и военным губернатором Парижа.[18]

These syntactic differences also make themselves felt in English-Russian interpretation. The word order of many English noun-subject-*тема* verb-predicate-*рема* constructions must be changed when they are translated into Russian:

> An airline crash killed 78 people.
> В результате авиационной катастрофы погибло 78 человек.
>
> The fog stopped the traffic.
> Из-за тумана остановилось движение транспорта.
>
> The split in the Democratic Party elected Lincoln.
> Благодаря расколу в демократической партии к власти пришел Линкольн.[19]

In translation, the initial Russian *тема* prepositional phrase or descriptive clause can become the English subject, and the Russian subject then becomes the English object. A reflexive verb may become active, as in rendering of *из-за тумана остановился транспорт* as "the fog stopped the traffic." Or:

> Во время опроса выяснилось, что...
> The survey showed/demonstrated/revealed that...

If time allows, time and place expressions, which tend to be in initial position in Russian, should be placed after the verb:

На следующей неделе в Париже состоится встреча глав профсоюзов.
A meeting of heads of trade unions will take place in Paris next week.

Or the interpreter can make the verb transitive and retain the original word order:

Next week Paris will host a meeting…

As a general rule, the interpreter should try to make Russian phrases in oblique cases and in initial position into the English subject:

В результате несчастных случаев на строительной площадке погибло
восемь человек.
Industrial accidents at this construction site have killed eight people.[20]

When the Russian object of the action becomes the subject of the English sentence, the predicate is expressed by a passive construction:

Толкали его.
He was pushed.

Первые шаги в этой области предприняла ЮНЕСКО.
The first steps in this field were taken by UNESCO.

Ему дали деньги.
He was given money.

Мне предложили другую должность
I was offered another job.

Послали за врачом.
The doctor was sent for.

Impersonal constructions can also be replaced by passives:

Говорят, что он хороший актер.
He is said to be a good actor.

Её считают способной учительницей.
She is considered a good teacher.

Нам внушают, что наша система лучше.
We have been led to believe/told that our system is better.[21]

Or a noun can replace the verb:

Готовились праздновать новый год.
Preparations were under way/begun for celebrating New Year.

Either "it" or a personal pronoun can replace an infinitive in an impersonal construction:[22]

Радоваться нам надо, а не плакать.
We should be happy and not cry/instead of crying.

Не надо так говорить.
You mustn't say that/You shouldn't talk like that.

Что делать?
What should we/you do?

The basic rule for Russian-English syntactic transformations, as Cherniakhovskaia has pointed out, is that the first meaningful syntagma *смысловая группа,* which was an object in an oblique case in Russian, becomes the subject in English:

Своими проектами он предвосхищал наступление космической эры.
His projects anticipated the coming of the space age.[23]

While the verb in such transformations does not necessarily switch mood, in the following example a passive-active transformation is needed:

Им было сказано несколько слов.
He said a few words. ("A few" is more idiomatic than "several.")

Or an intransitive verb may become transitive, as in the following example in which a personal subject replaces an impersonal one:

В этом году было построено тридцать школ.
This year the town/city built thirty schools.

The relative flexibility of Russian word order is particularly evident in colloquial speech. Here the general rule of *тема*—old information followed by *рема*—new information is often broken, for the word or phrase in initial position may be the rheme or something else the speaker wishes to emphasize. This information may also be emphasized through voice stress or intonation:

А почему идешь ты ?
А ты почему идешь?
А почему ты идешь?
А ты идешь почему?
А ты почему идешь?
А почему ты идешь?

A Russian adjective placed in initial position for emphasis may require an intensifier in English along with a change in word order:

А прекрасный ты спекла торт!
What a fantastic cake you baked!

Видела я первые его шаги.
I saw him take his very first steps.[24]

Голодная я!
Am I starving!/Because I'm hungry, that's why!

Невероятная это была история.
It was an absolutely unbelievable story.

The separation of related Russian words which the speaker wishes to stress may create a double intonational center:

Замечательный у тебя муж!
What a wonderful husband you have!

Очень сильно девочка ушиблась вчера.
She really got badly bruised yesterday.

Триста ты мне должен долларов, дорогой!
That's three hundred you still owe me, kiddo!

Intonational emphasis on an initial word which is not in usual position shows that the speaker is stressing it:

Нож дай мне. (It's the *knife* I want—not the fork)

Учительница она. (She's a *teacher*/and not a doctor/She's a teacher, after all, and that explains a lot)

94

Such inversion of normal word order is particularly common in colloquial interrogative sentences:

> Он к вам приходит когда̀?
> When is it he's coming to see you?

> А говорит он ей что̀?
> So what is he telling her?

Inversion is also common when proper names are stressed:

> Ваня, мне кажется, не пришел.
> I don't think Vanya came.[25]

In formal statements and discussions sentences frequently begin with a noun in an oblique case. Transforming the initial object or prepositional clause into the subject and making the appropriate change in the verb is usually the safest way for the interpreter to construct a grammatical and easily understandable English sentence.

В + prepositional occurs very often in initial position:

> В выступлении президента было подчеркнуто, что никакие ссылки на
> терроризм не дают американской администрации права выступать в роли
> международного судьи.
> The president's statement emphasized that no references to/invoking of terrorism
> can/give the American Administration the right to act as/take on the role of an
> international judge.

The prepositional construction becomes the subject, the passive participial construction becomes an active verb, and the double negative *никакие...не* becomes a "no...can" construction.

This type of oblique-subject/passive-active flip works very well for the common phrase *в печати:*

> 6 июля в афганской печати был опубликован закон о политических
> партиях.
> On July 6 the Afghan press published the law on political parties.

The same kind of inversion works for a reflexive verb:

> В международной прессе сообщалось...
> The international press reported...

Such constructions sound much more idiomatic than "in the press was published the law" or "in the press it was reported that."

To produce an English-sounding sentence the verb may also need rephrasing:

> В работе конференции принимали участие рабочие всех отраслей.
> The work of the conference involved/included workers from all industries/fields/
> areas.

This is much easier than trying to flip the entire sentence into

> Workers from all areas were involved in the work of the conference

since such a restructuring requires the interpreter to retain the entire sentence in his head while he is rearranging its components. Or:

> В французской ноте выражался решительный протест против этих
> действий.
> The French note strongly/vigorously protested/contained a strong protest against
> such actions.

The change in the verb avoids an awkward sentence such as "In the French note was expressed a vigorous protest."[26]

B + locative is very frequent in references to documents:

> В принятой вчера резолюции…
> The resolution adopted/passed yesterday stated…

> В этом докладе много материалов на данную тему.
> This report contains a lot of materials on this subject.

> В этих листках зло писали о порядках на фабрике.
> These leaflets harshly criticized the system at that factory.[27]

If the interpreter is willing to risk omitting an initial *в результате,* he may have to do some tricky reordering of sentence components:[28]

> В результате войны погибло много людей.
> The war killed/claimed the lives of a lot of people.

> В результате забастовки заводы были закрыты.
> The strike closed down the factories.

The same type of transformation works with *на* + prepositional:

> На встрече договорились…
> The meeting reached an agreement…

> На рисунке хорошо видны детали.
> The picture gives a good view of these details.

The same transformation of an oblique subject to nominative subject works with *о* + prepositional:

> Об этом говорилось уже много раз.
> This has been discussed/mentioned/referred to/addressed/spoken to/spoken about/ raised/dealt with many times.

In some cases a Russian active verb may be changed to an English passive to turn the oblique case into the subject:

> О конструктивной роли, которую могли бы сыграть средства массовой информации следует напомнить.
> The constructive role which the mass media could play should be recalled.

> О причинах нынешней напряженности мы уже имели возможность сказать на заседаниях этого комитета.
> The reasons for the present tension have already been addressed/are a subject we have already addressed at meetings of this committee.

This reordering avoids such awkward openings as "About the constructive role" or "concerning the reasons for" which lead into extremely clumsy sentences.

In a sentence beginning with an accusative the interpreter may opt for what Cherniakhovskaia calls a *глагол широкой семантики* or a *бытийный глагол:*[29]

> Крайне опасный характер теперь приобретает терроризм.
> Extremely dangerous now is terrorism.
> Of particular danger now is terrorism.

To avoid committing himself to a rigid sentence structure at the beginning of a long sentence the interpreter can stall for time by using the very useful words "something," "that," or "what" with a *бытийный* verb:

Something which is extremely dangerous is terrorism.
What is extremely dangerous…
That which is extremely dangerous is…

The same technique can be used in the following example in which the sentence begins with an instrumental:

Бесспорными являются тяжелые последствия усилий ЮАР в этой области
для безопасности соседних государств.

If the interpreter wants to take the risk he can hold *бесспорными* until the end of the phrase:

The dangerous/serious/onerous consequences of South Africa's efforts/steps in this area/sphere for the security of neighboring states seem indisputable/clear.

Or he can use the verb "to be" and one of the above devices:

What is unquestionable/Something which is unquestionable is the serious consequences of South Africa's steps in this area for the security of neighboring states.

How the interpreter handles such syntactic problems may depend on whether he has a text. Without one he may opt for that solution which leaves open the greatest number of possibilities for rendering whatever constructions may appear later in the sentence, while with a text he can structure more tightly. For example:

Вполне обоснованным представляется вывод, сделанный Генеральным Секретарем в его недавнем докладе о положении на Ближнем Востоке, о том, что…

With no text a safe beginning would be:

What is fully justified is the conclusion…

Something that would seem fully justified is the conclusion drawn by the Secretary General in his recent report that…

With a text the interpreter can invert the sentence:

The conclusion made by the Secretary General in his recent report on the situation in the Middle East is/seems fully justified, namely, that…

A dative case in initial position can also be turned into a subject:

Этой политике «превентивных» ударов должен быть положен конец.
This policy of preventive strikes must be stopped/halted.

По адресу правления совета высказывалось одобрение.
The board of the council was commended.

This kind of flip is virtually automatic with pronouns in the dative in impersonal constructions:

Ему было холодно.   He was cold.
Ей спать хотелось.   She felt sleepy.

An identical transformation occurs with accusative pronouns:

Их беспокоит, что он все еще не приехал.
They are worried because he hasn't yet arrived.

Literal translations of constructions with *от* + genitive are particularly awkward, e.g. "On this depended," "from this remained." Here too, changing the oblique object to a nominative subject is a useful device:

> От пожара уцелело всего несколько домов.
> Only a few houses escaped the fire.

Or the verb can be changed to make the sentence read

> The fire spared only a few houses

thus preserving the original word order.[30]

От + genitive + verb is particularly common—and difficult—with the verb *зависеть*:

> *От понимания* того, что является причиной сползания человечества к ядерной бездне, *зависит* и ответ на вопрос, можно ли остановить этот страшный процесс.

A literal rendering is very clumsy: "On the understanding of what is the reason for... depends..." When the genitive phrase becomes the subject, the English sentence sounds more idiomatic:

> Understanding the reason for mankind's drift towards the nuclear abyss/nuclear disaster...

"И" can be rendered as "in fact" or "indeed:"

> Understanding the reason for mankind's drift towards nuclear disaster indeed/in fact...

"Depends on" is then replaced by "determines:"

> ...indeed determines the answer to the question (as to) whether it is possible to stop this frightening/horrendous/fatal process.

Or "determines" may be replaced by "is decisive," as in the following example:

> *От того*, сумеет ли мир избежать ядерной катастрофы, *зависит* решение всех насущных проблем и само существование человеческой цивилизации.
> The world's ability to avoid nuclear catastrophe is decisive for/is critical for the resolution of all other urgent/crucial problems and for the very survival of human civilization.

Or:

> Whether or not the world can avoid nuclear catastrophe—this will determine/this is what will determine the resolution...

От + the participle *зависящее* also requires reworking:

> Мы намерены и впредь делать все *от* нас *зависящее* для развития дружественных связей с этими странами.
> We intend to continue to do all in our power/all that we can/everything possible to develop friendly ties/contacts with these countries.

"Everything that depends on us" would be awkward. The noun *развитие* is better translated as the verb "to develop," and this is shorter—four syllables for "to develop" vs. seven for "for the development of."

The verb *обуславливаться,* which is closely related in meaning to *зависеть*, also requires syntactic reworking. The reflexive ending tends to make interpreters say "is determined by" and leads to awkward constructions:

> Для нас нет ничего магического в нынешнем количестве ракет СС-20. Их уровень прямо *обуславливается* военно-стратегической обстановкой в этом регионе.
>
> Their level directly depends/hinges on the military-strategic situation in this region.

The verb used to render *обусловлено* can be active or passive:

> Острота этой проблемы *обусловлена* прежде всего сложной обстановкой в данной стране.
>
> The urgency of this problem is primarily determined by/comes from/results from/is a result of the complex situation in that country.

Russian clauses beginning with a participle cause some of the most difficult and frequent syntactic problems. Whenever possible, it is worth the interpreter's while to wait for a few seconds to see where the sentence is going:

> *Представленный* комитету *доклад* верно освещает последние изменения в этой области.
>
> The report submitted/presented to the committee correctly covers/points out/points to/ lists the most recent changes in this field/area/sphere.

Here only one word separates the participle from the noun it modifies. But in the following—and unfortunately all too typical—lengthy sentence, the interpreter cannot wait for the noun before beginning to speak:

> *Выдвинутая* в заявлении Президента от 15 февраля *программа* освобождения человечества к 2000 году от ядерного и иного оружия массового уничтожения рассматривает выделение средств на цели социального и экономического развития в качестве важнейшей сопутствующей меры соглашений по ограничению вооружений и разоружению.

Starting with the participle is asking for trouble. "Proposed in the" does not work at all. In this type of sentence the interpreter can start with "that," "what" or "something" and add a qualifier as soon as he hears the noun:

> That/something which was proposed in the president's statement of February 15, namely/I mean/that is the program for freeing/ delivering mankind by the year 2000 from nuclear and other weapons of mass destruction, provides for the allocation of resources for social and economic development as a most important collateral/additional/accompanying measure for arms limitation and disarmament agreements.

The interpreter who feels adventuresome may try to make *в заявлении* the subject as in the examples discussed above, but this is a bit risky:

> What the president's statement of February 15, 1986 proposed, namely the program for…

In these cases, waiting a few seconds is always helpful, since automatically saying "something which" or "that which" may lead to trouble:

> *Рожденное* этой революцией *государство* рабочих и крестьян положило начало эпохе социальной справедливости…

Waiting a few seconds will allow the interpreter to say

> Born of this revolution, the state of workers and peasants ushered in an era of social justice…

Or:

> The state of workers and peasants which was born of this revolution ushered in an era of social justice…

99

If the flow of a sentence is easily predictable *по вероятности прогнозирования* or by common sense, the interpreter may either risk turning the participle into a nominal construction or can restructure the sentence:

> Интересы этих народов требуют, чтобы были *приняты* безотлагательные *меры* по оздоровлению обстановки в регионе.
>
> The interests of these peoples requires the taking of immediate measures/measures that can be taken/ to improve the situation in the region.

Or

> В полной мере здесь должны быть *использованы каналы* Всемирной кампании за разоружение.
>
> Full use should be made here of the opportunities provided by the World Disarmament Campaign.

Some sentences which are stuffed with syntactical problems can be simplified and shortened by dropping the participle. This requires both logic and good nerves:

> Нам также представляется правильным *принятый* Комитетом *подход* к выработке общих рекомендаций, согласно которому акцент будет делаться на качестве *разрабатываемых* им *рекомендаций*.
>
> We also believe that the Committee's approach to drawing up recommendations is correct, namely that stress will be placed on the quality of the recommendations it produces/draws up/makes/comes up with.

The initial dative pronoun has become the subject, the verb has become active, and both passive participles have been dropped without damage to the meaning. A cumbersome participial clause may be pared down to a single adjective:

> Такой *ориентированный* на деловой результат *подход* даст возможность добиться необходимой активизации роли нашей комиссии.
>
> Such a determined/vigorous/single-minded approach will provide/allow for the required/needed stepping up/intensification of the role of our committee.

Active participles present similar problems:

> *Потерпевшая* в последнее время сокрушительные поражения *контрреволюция* перешла к кровавому террору против гражданского населения.

Rather than the awkward "That, which recently endured a crushing defeat, namely," the interpreter can make a slight switch in word order and say

> Recently, crushing defeats of the counterrevolutionaries led to acts of bloodshed and terror directed against civilians.

In some complex sentences which tax short-term memory, the interpreter may be forced to scribble down a word or two to retain for use later in the sentence:

> Сейчас в Афганистане решаются накопившиеся за предыдущие годы национальные проблемы.
>
> Now Afghanistan (locative becomes the subject) is resolving those national problems which have accumulated/piled up (participle retained in memory or jotted down) over the past/preceding years.

The ultimate decision on whether to rely on memory and hold back the participle, to drop it, or to use "that" or "something" depends on the structure of the sentence, the interpreter's memory, experience, skill, and willingness to gamble in each individual case.

Present and past active participles can describe events which have been completed, have just begun, or are currently in process:

> Россия придает большое значение недавно начавшимся по её инициативе русско-американским переговорам.
>
> Russia attaches great significance to the recent start—on its initiative—of Russian-American negotiations.

Or:

> Russia attaches great significance to the Russian-American negotiations in Geneva recently begun on its initiative.

A meeting which "recently ended a few days ago" can be shortened:

> Как заявил в ходе закончившейся несколько дней тому назад встречи на высшем уровне в Вашингтоне Президент...
>
> As was stated/declared (since the subject is not yet clear *заявил* needs an impersonal/ passive construction) during the recent summit meeting in Washington by the President...

Происходящий can often be dropped, or rendered as "current" or "present" rather than "going on" or "occurring:"

> Сегодня мы хотели бы подчеркнуть, что *происходящие* в этом районе события являются наглядным подтверждением одного из выводов съезда...
>
> Today we wish to emphasize that the events/present events in this region are clear proof/ evidence of one of the conclusions of the Congress...

Or:

> Наша делегация считает весьма полезным *проходящее* на этой сессии Комитета *обсуждение*..
>
> Our delegation finds extremely useful the discussion during this session of the Committee...

If the interpreter has time, of course, he can invert the sentence: "Our delegation considers the discussion to be very useful."

Postnominal forms of *который* in oblique cases can cause syntactic difficulties, as in the following translation from the Russian press:

> No one has met with foreign journalists to explain the situation in Prague about which there have been various rumors and fabrications.[31]

Or take the following example:

> Осуществление положений конвенции следует рассматривать как часть усилий по выполнению решений конференций, приоритетный характер *которых* признан нашей организацией.
>
> Implementation of the provisions of the convention should be considered as part of the efforts to implement/carry out the decisions of the conference, and their high priority is recognized by our organization.

Inserting "and" after *которых* will avoid the awkward phrase "priority character of which." If the interpreter has already said "priority character," however, he can add "is recognized by our organization." Or:

> Ваши глубокие знания будут способствовать конструктивному регулированию актуальных проблем, нерешенность *которых* ставит под угрозу качество жизни человечества.
>
> Your vast knowledge will promote a constructive settlement to urgent problems—and the lack of a solution to these is threatening the quality of human life.

Or the interpreter could give a less literal rendering, omitting the rather obvious "lack of solution" and condense: "a constructive answer to those pressing problems which are threatening human life."

Yet another construction provides a useful way out of syntactic difficulties. In translation of a Russian sentence such as *было много споров* English requires that the subject be in initial position while the rhematic group of words of the Russian subject remain in final rheme position. The construction "there is" allows the subject to move to final position without violating the grammar norms of English:

> There were many arguments/discussions/disputes.[32]

"There is" works particularly well for Russian sentences starting with verbs indicating need or necessity:

> Требует своего совершенствования процедура рассмотрения документов.
> There is a need to improve the procedure for consideration of documents.
>
> Необходимо всемерно повышать…
> There is a need to raise in every way/it is essential to raise in every way…[33]
>
> Необходимо более тесное международное сотрудничество…
> There is a need for closer international cooperation…
> What is needed is closer international cooperation…[34]

"There is" is particularly effective if the interpreter does not want to insert a subject or make the verb passive, e.g.

> Надо это сделать.   There is a need to do this.
>   vs.
>   We need to do this. (inserted subject)
>   This should be done. (passive verb)[35]

"There is" also works for expressions of indefinite quantity:

> В библиотеке мало хороших книг.
> There are few good books in the library.
>
> В магазине достаточно продуктов.
> There is enough food in the store.[36]

The same construction works with negation:[37]

> В городе нет ни одной библиотеки.
> There is not a single library in the city/The city does not have a library (prepositional case becomes subject).
>
> Некому заступиться за нас.
> There is no one to stand up for us.
>
> Нам нечего здесь делать.
> There is nothing for us to do here/We have no business here.

In impersonal sentences "it is" can serve as the English theme-subject:

> Проводить тренировку лучше днем или вечером.
> It is best to do these exercises in the afternoon or evening.
>
> Легче попасть в беду, чем выпутаться из неё.
> It is easier to get into trouble than out of it.[38]

In dealing with the huge problems posed by Russian syntax the interpreter must (to use an old Soviet metaphor) make use of his entire arsenal of devices. He must be careful not to jump in too fast and find himself bogged down in a hopelessly awkward sentence. The interpreter should acquire the habit of numbering words and phrases in a text in the order in which he wishes to say them in English, and if necessary divide excessively lengthy sentences into two or even three short ones. Oblique initial objects should be turned into subjects.

No matter how good an interpreter's choice of words, poor syntax can make him unintelligible. Written translation is an extremely useful training device for the simultaneous interpreter, since the restructuring of various syntactic patterns opens up choices and possibilities which can be put to good use in the high-pressure conditions of the booth.

CHAPTER XI

HIGH AND LOW: THE PROBLEM OF STYLE

To some extent, stylistics is the icing on the interpreter's cake, for producing exact stylistic equivalents in addition to listening, absorbing, finding correct lexical items and restructuring sentences, may be asking too much. As he gains experience, however, the interpreter will have more time to devote to reproducing the speaker's stylistic level, be it literary, formal-bureaucratic, neutral-scientific or colloquial. Russian written statements tend to fit into categories of style much more neatly than English texts, although in the last few years since the collapse of the Soviet system the boundaries between *научно-популярный, литературный, разговорный* styles have become much more fluid.[1] One commentator wrote that *"Переводчик должен владеть по крайне мере двумя нормами каждого из языков, на которые он переводит – литературной и разговорной...подходя к ним как к двум самостоятельным системам средств выражения, и знать правила переключения кода или, другими словами, ситуационную закрепленность каждой из норм."*[2]

It is hard enough under time pressure to come up with a correct word, let alone a stylistically happy one. Yet opting for a high-flown instead of a colloquial word may do a speaker a great disservice, and the choice of a Latin or Anglo-Saxon root can determine the entire stylistic tone of a phrase. A written, formal speech at a large meeting requires a very different tone from statements made at an informal, small working group where "normal" colloquial Russian is spoken. With the advent of *гласность* and *перестройка* the predictable prepared speeches at international conferences have become less clichéd and frequently contain colloquialisms and stylistic "curve balls" which can rattle an overly complacent interpreter. Today English is exerting a strong influence on both spoken and written Russian, and English borrowings have become part and parcel of the language of finance, computers, and the media. These words, too, are not always instantly recognizable. In the context of a Russian sentence, it may take a minute to grasp *брифинговать* or *имидж-билдинг*.

The difference between literary, written Russian and the colloquial spoken language is generally far greater than the gap between written and spoken English. To say of a Russian *Он говорит, как пишет* is not a compliment. It means that the party in question speaks pompously and bookishly. As the Russian linguist L.V. Shcherba noted, *"Литературный язык может настолько отличаться от разговорного, что приходится иногда говорить о двух разных языках."*[3] This has somewhat improved since perestroika, and the Russian spoken at conferences today sounds a good deal more like a spoken language. There are still, however, repetitions, long lists of adjectives, and the occasional sentence lumbering along under a heavy burden of participial clauses. Intonation, which will be dealt with later, is also extremely important in colloquial speech.

Spoken colloquial Russian is characterized by ellipses and inverted syntax. Words are frequently omitted, resulting in "wrong" case endings and verbal government. For example:

> Следующая сойдёте? (Вы не сойдёте на следующей остановке?)
> Пушкинская не скажете? (Вы не скажете, где Пушкинская улица?)
> Ванну чистить есть у вас? (Есть ли у вас чем чистить ванну?)
> Я обедать – пошли вместе. (Я пойду обедать.)
> Вы бы покороче. (Вы бы рассказывали покороче.)[4]

Negation is frequently used in colloquial questions: *Не подскажете, как к театру проехать?* instead of *Скажите мне, как проехать к театру.* Or *Не позвонить ему?* instead of *Пожалуйста, позвони ему.* Such questions must not be rendered by a negative in English. A literal translation of *Не подскажете, сколько времени?* would sound rather odd.

Even in fairly formal written prose, however, English tends to be less stylistically high-flown than Russian. In two Soviet experiments translations from Russian into English done by native speakers of Russian were corrected by native speakers of English, who consistently made the style more natural and less formal. For example:

> Он увидел страну в тисках блокады. Он узнал о голоде и тяготах, выпавших на долю людей.

Translator:
> He saw the country in the clenches [*sic* - LV] of the blockade. He learned of the famine and hardships that had befallen the people.

Editor:
> He saw the country being strangled by the blockade, the famine and hardships the people were suffering.

> Названия стран должны располагаться в алфавитном порядке и писаться с прописной буквы.

Translator:
> The names of the countries should be written with a capital letter and put into alphabetical order.

Editor:
> The names of the countries should be alphabetized and capitalized.[5]

Compression and condensation should not, however, result in changes in stylistic levels. *Российские предложения, направление на ликвидацию ядерного оружия* can be shortened to "Russian proposals for the elimination of nuclear weapons/to eliminate nuclear weapons," but "to scrap" or "to get rid of" is unnecessarily colloquial for this subject matter. The interpreter should remember to maintain the stylistic level during the condensation process:

> Да, события вокруг аварии в Чернобыле ещё раз отчётливо подтвердили: существуют две политические морали, две линии поведения в вопросах, имеющих для человечества поистине жизненное значение.
> Yes, Chernobyl once again demonstrated the existence of two political moralities, two types of conduct in matters/on issues truly vital/of vital importance to mankind.[6]

The interpreter must take care not to excessively lower—or raise—the stylistic level in rendering Russian idioms and colloquial expressions. A weapon which *в одном ряду с такими жестокими способами ведения войны, как применение бактериологического оружия* could be a weapon which

> is similar to/is tantamount to/can be compared to/is comparable to/goes along the same lines as/is on a par with...

"Is comparable to" or "is similar to" are the most neutral equivalents, while "on a par with" or "going along the same lines as" sound more colloquial.

In some cases English provides direct equivalents for Russian colloquial or idiomatic expressions:

> Мы выступаем плечом к плечу с другими государствами.
> We are acting shoulder-to-shoulder with other states.

> Наша страна готова идти рука об руку со всеми государствами.
> Our country is ready/willing to work hand-in-hand with other states.

It is context determines the choice of an English equivalent. Take the fairly neutral Russian *один* in the following sentence:

> Ответ будет один: это невозможно допустить.

Since the speaker is being categorical, the interpreter might say

> The answer is utterly clear/unequivocal.

Sometimes a Russian phrase which sounds colloquial to the English ear may require a neutral translation:

> Мы призываем все государства работать *не покладая рук.*
> We call on all states to work unceasingly/tirelessly.

Or:

> Невозможно представить, чтобы дело *пошло на лад,* если параллельно не будут приниматься меры по укреплению политических гарантий безопасности государств.
> It is impossible to imagine/think that this situation will improve/work out/take a turn for the better unless measures are simultaneously/also/at the same time taken to strengthen the political security of states.

It is not absolutely necessary to translate the image contained in a fixed idiomatic expression:

> Как известно, на одну доску ставятся террористы из Анголы и Мозамбика, Афганистана и Никарагуа, Лаоса и Камбоджи.
> Everyone is well aware that no distinction is made between terrorists from…
> Terrorists from… are considered as equals.

> Наш призыв не всем на Западе приходится по душе.
> Not everyone in the West finds our appeal to his liking.
> Many in the West do not respond to our appeal.

The expression "go for" would be too colloquial here. A similar expression, *не по нутру,* however, has a colloquial tinge:

> Апрельская революция 1978 года в этой стране пришлась *не по нутру* империалистическим силам.
> The April 1978 revolution went against the grain of/was not to the taste/liking of the imperialist forces.

The interpreter should be careful not to go too far in using English colloquialisms. "Rubbed the wrong way" would be inappropriate. Or take:

> Это дело не сдвинется с мертвой точки.
> This (matter) will not even get started/move from A to B/begin/get off square one.

Strictly American idioms such as "get to first base" should be avoided, as these may confuse non-native speakers of English and cause misunderstanding if the Russian speaker is later told he has been referring to baseball games. Context determines how colorful an expression the interpreter should use:

> Но ведь таких переговоров нет – и не по нашей вине – и нельзя сидеть сложа руки.
>
> But as long as there are no such negotiations—and for this we are not to blame— we cannot stand idly by.

Russian sits while English stands. "We cannot sit and twiddle our thumbs" would retain the hand imagery.

If the interpreter is not 100% clear as to the speaker's precise intent and tone, a neutral expression is preferable to a highly colored one:

> Мы задаем им встречный вопрос: а вы готовы пустить на слом сотни ракет и самолетов, тысячи ядерных боезарядов??
>
> We counter with a question: But are you ready/Are you really ready to

Most neutral:	do away with/put an end to
Semi-neutral:	destroy/eliminate
More colored:	wreck/dump
Most colored:	consign to the garbage heap/smash to bits hundreds of missiles and airplanes, thousands of nuclear warheads?

Though a colloquialism in one language may have an exact equivalent in another language, the frequency of usage may vary considerably. Take the following:

> *Ни в грош не ставят* эти права, и среди них первейшее право человека – право на жизнь, те, кто являются приверженцами гонки вооружений.

Neutral:	They set no store by
	They care nothing for
Colloquial:	They couldn't care less about
Too colloquial/vulgar:	They don't give a damn about
Equivalent but archaic in English:	They don't give a brass farthing for
	They don't give a tinker's dam for

Equivalence is one thing and usage another. "A tinker's dam" sounds archaic while *в грош не ставить* does not. Sometimes, though, Russian and English colloquialisms coincide:

> *Это играет на руку* тем, кто выступает с претензиями на право объявлять правительства «законными» или «незаконными.»
>
> This plays into the hands (plural in English) of those who arrogate themselves/ claim the right to declare governments "legitimate" or "illegal."

Many Russian "hand" and "leg" expressions do not have such direct equivalents and can be rendered neutrally:

> Развитие позитивных процессов было подорвано с легкой руки НАТО.
>
> The development of positive processes was thwarted/undermined with some assistance from/with a bit of help from NATO.

Or, if the interpreter insists on retaining the image:

> …with a helping hand from NATO.

Or:

> Предпринимается откровенная попытка поставить все с ног на голову.
>
> There is an open policy of/An open attempt is being made to turn everything upside down/topsy-turvy/to upset everything.

Sometimes an extremely colloquial phrase creeps into an otherwise neutral or even formal statement:

108

> Нравственно разложить, запутать, сбить, как у нас говорят, с панталыку можно лишь утаиванием правды, ложью.
>
> Moral corruption, confusion, driving someone/people crazy/nuts/wild/bats can only be done by hushing up/covering up the truth, by lying/lies.

(Though *ложь* in Russian has no plural, it must often be translated by the English plural "lies.")

A slight change may be needed in an English equivalent:

> Мир давно перешел уже ту черту, за которой гонка вооружений стала поистине безумной.
>
> The world has long gone past/beyond the point/crossed the threshold beyond which the arms race has become genuinely insane.

"Point" or "threshold"—but not "line"—preserve the idiom.

> Международное сообщество не должно вводиться в заблуждение *туманными* оговорками о свободной торговле.
>
> The international community should not be misled/deceived/confused by vague comments about free trade.

"Foggy" does not work, though "fuzzy" might.

To preserve an image an adjective may be changed and a verb switched from active to passive:

> Высокая нота тревоги по поводу обстановки в Центральной Америке прозвучала в декларации министров иностранных дел контадорской группы.
>
> A resounding note of alarm was heard concerning/regarding the situation in Central America in the declaration of the Ministers of Foreign Affairs of the Contadora group.

Elevated language with Church Slavonic roots can be rendered on an appropriate stylistic level by using words with Latin roots:

> Ни для кого не секрет, что обреченные историей расисты, находящиеся и в своей стране, и в регионе в абсолютном меньшинстве, не смогли бы творить преступные деяния без опоры на эти круги.
>
> It is perfectly clear to everyone/it is no secret to anyone that the racists doomed by history, who both in their country and in the region are in the absolute minority, could not have perpetrated these evil deeds without relying on/without support from these quarters/ sectors/circles.

"Low" colloquial Russian language can be rendered on an suitable stylistic level by giving preference to Anglo-Saxon roots:

> Администрация США периодически обращается с подстрекательскими посланиями к афганской контрреволюции. В Белом доме с помпой принимают её главарей. В декабре прошлого года в госдепартаменте было организовано провокационное сборище, на котором с участием предводителей бандитского отребья, окопавшегося в военных лагерях на территории Пакистана, обсуждались вопросы активизации военной, финансовой и политической помощи наемным бандам.
>
> The US Administration periodically sends inflammatory messages to the Afghan counter-revolutionaries. The White House *(locative becomes subject)* received its ringleaders with solemn ceremony/pomp/rolled out the red carpet for its ringleaders. Last December *(no "in" necessary in English)* the State Department organized a provocation/an inflammatory get-together at which, with the (participation of the) top brass/top dogs of this collection of thugs/riffraff/bandit-like riffraff/rabble who had dug into/entrenched themselves on the territory of Pakistan, issues/questions were discussed of how to/ways to step up/increase/ give more assistance to the mercenary bands.

The interpreter should have at his fingertips—or more precisely, at the tip of his tongue—a series of synonyms for certain words which crop up constantly, words describing Good and Bad Things, people, places and concepts. Here is a very short list of some such positives and negatives:[7]

достоверный	meaningful/reliable/excellent/credible/ dependable	concepts, measures
хороший	good/ positive	
справедливый	equitable/fair/good/satisfactory	settlement
дружественный	friendly/constructive/cordial/amicable/ viable	relations
настоящий	genuine/positive/tireless/indefatigable	efforts
честный	honest/frank/straightforward/candid/open	exchange of views
прочный	durable/lasting/guaranteed/permanent/ assured/genuine	peace
устойчивый	stable/lasting/enduring/sustainable	(this is the adjective used in the expression "sustainable development")
огромный	huge/enormous/colossal/vast/significant/ considerable	progress, sums
значительный	significant/meaningful/important/vital/ central/critical/crucial	issues, problems, far-reaching questions
грубый	crude/glaring/outrageous/flagrant/massive	violations
мрачный	gloomy/sinister/dark/somber/black	signs, days

Depending on the stylistic level of the text, the English words "absolute, utter, total, hopeless, out and out, blatant, arrant, unrelieved, dyed-in-the-wool, inveterate, hardened, hardcore, outright" can be used to translate the following list. The interpreter should try to expand his range of synonyms to convey the nuances of:

абсолютный	исконный	непримиримый	стойкий
завзятый	истинный	образцовый	стопроцентный
заклятый	круглый	отпетый	страстный
закоренелый	матерый	отъявленный	твердолобый
заскорузлый	махровый	подлинный	чистокровный
заядлый	настоящий	полный	чистопробный
злостный	неисправный	совершенный	явный
			ярый[8]

The interpreter should constantly be on the alert for more synonyms to expand his repertory and stylistic range. A few examples for such mindstretching:[9]

foreshadow/herald/augur/bode/prefigure/be a harbinger of/be an omen of/point to

rekindle/revive/restore/renew

watershed/key/pivotal/historical/epoch-making/crucial

countless/myriad/numberless/infinite

set great store by/cherish/hold dear/prize/value/embrace/espouse/be dedicated to/ be devoted to

vouch for/attest to/guarantee/back/stand behind/support

abide by/observe/comply with/obey/live up to

trailblazing/path-breaking/pioneering/innovative/breaking new ground/charting a new course/ opening a new chapter

gist/crux/linchpin/heart/core/nub/essence/point

common knowledge/open secret/hardly news/cat out of the bag

in line with/in tune with/consonant with/in keeping with/in accordance with

reportedly/allegedly/said to be/supposedly

well versed in/steeped in/familiar with/conversant with/up on

reach common ground/see eye to eye/accommodate each other/strike a deal/bargain/reach a meeting of the minds

deftly/skillfully/nimbly/agilely/aptly/cleverly

fit into/dovetail with/tally with/mesh/agree/match with/befit

earmark/allocate/assign/budget/set aside

thumbnail sketch/overview/survey/rundown/capsule description

stamp/emblem/imprint/mark/brand/label/insignia

stress/underscore/emphasize/highlight/bring out/underline/give weight/importance to/ be borne out/corroborated by/attested to/demonstrated/proven/shown

brave/gallant/courageous/valiant/fearless/stouthearted[10]

foremost/paramount/key/number one/overriding/top/main/chief

straightforward/truthful/candid/honest/blunt/abrupt/brash/curt/harsh[11]

polar/diametrical/total/absolute (e.g. opposites)

bid/quest/drive/campaign/mass effort

crowded agenda/heavy workload

stray from/deviate from

debunk/discredit/shoot down/scotch/scratch/junk/shatter

topple/overthrow/bring down/unseat

take away from/detract from/diminish/sully/tarnish/smear/blacken

hurt/hit/strike/be detrimental to/violate/encroach on

ignite/touch off/spark/trigger/prompt/lead to/engender/spawn

breed/give birth to/give rise to/set off/launch/start/initiate/open

play into the hands of/be grist for the mill of/fuel/fan the flames of

run short of/deplete/consume/use up/exhaust/drain

overtax/overburden/wear out/run down

go awry/be wide off the mark/miss

unmoved by/cold to/insensitive to/indifferent to

cut/sever/break off/end

strip/deprive/rob/pillage

unmask/expose/bare/reveal/bring to light

rue/regret/deplore/lament/bewail

doctor/alter/tamper with

trump up/fabricate/concoct/make up

inveigh against/bitterly attack/assault

ease/lighten/mitigate/allay

at odds/at loggerheads/pitted against/vying with/locked in/struggle

run down/sell short/belittle/disparage/denigrate/cast aspersions on

juggle/play with/manipulate/pad

upbraid/criticize/reproach/reprimand/take to task/rebuke/reprove/haul over the coals

thwart/foil/dash/bring to naught/nullify

ward off/avert/prevent/head off

fade/slip/weaken/falter

wrest from/seize/grab/take by force/capture

drop/delete/discard/eliminate/throw out/omit

foist on/thrust on/impose

contravene/run counter to/contradict/fly in the face of

wreck/undo/scuttle/torpedo/do in

willfully/on purpose/deliberately/knowingly

void/strike down/repeal/cancel/abolish
hamstring/hamper/impede/obstruct/harass/persecute
dog/plague/bedevil/beset/befall
sparse/scant/paltry/meager/scanty/limited/restricted
tricky/sensitive/delicate/ticklish
drastic/radical/severe/draconian
picayune/petty/piddling
gross/blatant/glaring/flagrant/egregious
hazy/muddy/vague/ill-defined/unclear/nebulous
awkward/clumsy/gauche/inelegant
brazen/shameless/raw/naked/unabashed/impudent
unutterable/unspeakable/beyond words
baleful/sinister/ominous
callous/heartless/ruthless/mean/vicious/brutal
stiff/stringent/exacting/demanding
stubborn/intransigent/intractable/persistent/unyielding/unbending/chronic
to no avail/futile/hopeless/in vain/unpromising
incontrovertible/unquestionable/unimpeachable/unassailable
appalling/loathsome/obnoxious/abominable/odious/vile/despicable/terrible/
    horrendous/inhumane/ghastly/execrable/heinous/monstrous/repugnant/frightful/
    abhorrent/revolting/disgusting/nauseating
shocked/appalled/aghast/dismayed/alarmed/put off/horrified/frightened/terrified
sham/bogus/rigged/fake/trumped up/fabricated/contrived/falsified/phony/forged
onus/burden/responsibility/load
dearth/shortage/lack/scarcity
ordeal/plight/trials/travail
fulminations/thunder/criticism/denunciation/ultimatum
uproar/hullabaloo/ruckus/brouhaha/furor/outrage/riot
hoax/ruse/ploy/maneuver/gimmick/charade
powder keg/time bomb/cauldron/crucible

Sayings and proverbs *(поговорки* and *пословицы)* sometimes seem to have been created expressly to plague the interpreter, for they raise a whole set of stylistic problems.[12] Though a Russian study calmly asserts that "In translating Russian idioms a simultaneous interpreter can always manage to arrange a metaphor rhythmically,"[13] it seems unlikely that the author of those words ever faced a microphone in a conference booth. Since they do not have time to consult reference works or colleagues, interpreters suffer from this *богатство русского языка* even more than translators. When a Russian speaker says *И у нас есть пословица,* quite a few Russian-English interpreters freeze in terror or throw helpless glances at their boothmates.

Proverbs are so difficult because they reduce an abstract concept to a pithy, colorful and concrete form, and often involve word-play and national cultural traditions. If a Russian proverb has no English equivalent the interpreter may provide a literal translation in the hope that listeners will accept this as one more example of quaint Russian customs and the mysterious Russian soul, e.g. *Баба с возу, кобыле легче.* "If a woman gets off the cart it's easier on the horse." If time allows the interpreter can add an explanation—"Or, as we say in English, good riddance/one less headache/one less problem/thing to think about." In cases such as *Покажу я вам кузькину мать* paraphrase is imperative. (An interpreter was once overheard mumbling something about introducing a delegate to the mother of Comrade Kuskin). "I'll *show* you" with intonational emphasis on the verb will get the point across. Or *мотать себе на ус* could be rephrased as "make a mental note of it" or "don't forget that."

Ironically enough, those proverbs and sayings which seem to have perfect English equivalents contain particularly dangerous pitfalls. The interpreter who seizes on "a pig in a poke" as the perfect translation for *купить кота в мешке* may bitterly regret his flash of brilliance if the speaker's cat then proceeds to meow or arch its back—or climb a tree. All theories of *вероятность прогнозирования* notwithstanding, a speaker's development of a metaphor cannot be accurately predicted. "Only the grave will/can straighten out a hunchback" is a far safer rendering for *горбатого могила исправит* than the English equivalents "The leopard cannot change his spots" or "You can't make a silk purse out of a sow's ear." It would indeed be a superhuman feat to then transform the hunchback into a leopard or a grave into a porcine ear. The translation of the common expression *меж двух огней* as "between the devil and the deep blue sea" or of *после дождика в четверг* by "till hell freezes over" is ill-advised because the English theological implications do not come across in the Russian idioms. If another speaker then picks up on the images used in the interpretation and refers to the devil or hell, the Russian speaker may well retort that he never said anything of the sort. The same is true for such idioms as *глуп как пробка*—silly as a goose, *волчий закон*—law of the jungle, or *пьет как сапожник*—he drinks like a fish. Since these expressions are short, the interpreter can say "he drinks like a fish—or as we say in Russian, like a shoemaker." Or a reference to *морской волк* may be rendered as "a sea dog—in Russian, a sea wolf."

For a longer proverb the safest solution is translation of the general meaning. If there is sufficient time the interpreter can give both the literal translation and the English equivalent—e.g. "They want us to buy a cat in a bag or, as we say in English, a pig in a poke." The interpreter should be careful not to make distinctly Russian proverbs sound specifically American—or any other nationality. Kornei Chukovsky warned of this problem in translating foreign proverbs into Russian:

> Для подмены иностранных пословиц русскими нужно брать только такие из них, которые ни в иностранном, ни в русском фольклоре не окрашены ни историческим, ни национально-бытовым колоритом.[14]

Thus Sancho Panza should not be saying *Вот тебе, бабушка, и Юрьев день*, or *пропал, как швед под Полтавой*.[15]

In the worst of all possible worlds—when the interpreter has not understood a single word of the Russian proverb—he can simply say "And in my country we have a proverb appropriate to this occasion." Full stop.

An attempt to list every Russian proverb ever used by Russian delegates at international meetings would be foolhardy. What follows is a highly selective list of idiomatic expressions, proverbs and sayings which have been cropping up with increasing frequency. Speakers often come up with their own variations, adding, subtracting, replacing or inventing parts of these sayings. Familiarity with a few of these popular expressions can save the interpreter moments of breathless panic.

Idioms

больное место, больной вопрос	a sore spot, touchy subject
бросать камешки в чей-либо огород	to make a dig at someone, to allude to someone with implied criticism
Это камешки в мой огород?	Was that aimed at me?
бе́з году неделя	for a short time
бить баклуши	waste time, twiddle one's thumbs
бить ключо́м	go on full speed ahead, full swing
биться как рыба об лед	to try desperately
бросать тень на	cast aspersions, slurs
валить с больной головы на здоровую	shift the blame (unfairly)
ви́лами на воде пи́сано	unclear, undecided, still up in the air
Васька слушает да ест	(from Krylov's fable) listen to advice but then go ahead and do one's own thing; blithely ignore criticism
валять дурака	play the fool, fool around
в ус не дуть	not give a damn
выводить на чистую воду	show someone's true colors, expose, unmask
выходить сухим из воды	emerge unscathed (from difficulty)
га́мбургский счет	objective, unbiased evaluation of a person or his work
(показать), где раки зиму́ют	to "show" someone, to do someone in
глядеть как баран на новые ворота	stare as though seeing for the first time
греть руки	make a profit off someone, benefit from something
да́ром не пройдет	won't get away with it
дать ма́ху	make a blunder, let slip
делать из му́хи слона	to make a mountain out of a molehill
дело в шляпе	it's in the bag
демья́нова уха	too much of a good thing
доверяй но проверяй	trust but verify
ждать у моря погоды	sit around and wait indefinitely
закинуть удочку	put out a feeler, test the waters
идти в Кано́ссу	repent, express abject regret, apologize
искать вчерашний день	go on a wild goose chase
как гром среди ясного неба	like a bolt from the blue
как сыр в масле	living in clover
китайская грамота	it's Greek to me
кот в мешке (купить)	a pig in a poke
кривить душой	pretend
легок на помине	speak of the devil
лезть в бутылку	fly off the handle
лезть из кожи вон	go out of one's way, bend over backwards
ложка дегтя в бочке меда	rotten apple spoils the barrel, fly in the ointment
марты́шкин труд	futile work
медвежья услуга	to render someone a disservice
меж двух огней	between the devil and the deep blue sea
мо́лотом и накова́льней	between the hammer and the anvil

114

Сци́ллой и Хари́бдой	Scylla and Charybdis
моло́чные ре́ки, кисе́льные берега́	land of milk and honey
на худо́й конец	if worse comes to worst
не в службу, а в дружбу	do a favor, as a friend
не в своей тарелке	ill at ease, out of sorts, out of place
не лы́ком ши́ты	not born yesterday, no worse than
не поминай ли́хом	don't think ill of someone
не откладывать в долгий ящик	not put off indefinitely
непочатый край	open field for work, a great deal to do
несо́лоно хлеба́вши	empty-handed
не́чего греха́ таить	it's no secret
ни к селу ни к го́роду	neither here nor there
носиться, как с пи́саной то́рбой	care for as for the apple of one's eye
остаться с но́сом	be left holding the bag
откуда ноги растут	where something is coming from, what's behind it
очки втирать (очковтира́тельство)	pull the wool over someone's eyes, window dressing
(ему) палец в рот не клади	he can take care of himself
перековать мечи́ на ора́ла	beat swords into plowshares
переливать из пусто́го в поро́жнее	engage in a futile exercise
печь как блины	churn out, crank out
после дождика в четверг	when pigs fly
принимать за чистую монету	take at face value
разбитое корыто	left with the ruins
разводить руками	give up
родиться в сорочке	born with a silver spoon, under a lucky star
рубить с плеча	act rashly, straightforwardly, not mince words
рыльце в пуху	guilt is evident
с грехо́м попола́м	with great difficulty
с жиру беситься	to act out of boredom/to have nothing better to do
семь пятниц на неделе	confused
сесть в лужу	put one's foot into it, get into a mess, have egg on one's face
сказка про белого бычка	one and the same thing, repetition of something
с корабля на бал	to dash/rush from one place to another
с легкой руки	thanks to someone's ability
смотреть сквозь пальцы на	turn a blind eye to, wink at
(как) собака на сене	like a dog in a manger
(где) собака зары́та	that's the crux, the rub
собаку съел	to know inside out
с пятого на десятое	randomly, inconsistently
стреляный воробей, тертый калач	old salt, experienced old hand
сыр-бор загорелся	much ado about nothing
то и дело	now and again
точить лясы	babble
три́шкин кафтан	patchwork
тянуть ля́мку	toil away
убить двух зайцев	kill two birds with one stone
ум за разум заходит	at a loss, at wits' end
фи́лькина грамота	worthless piece of paper
чужими руками жар загребать	someone else does the dirty work
этот номер не пройдет	that won't cut any ice

Proverbs

Ба́ба с во́за – кобы́ле легче *horse*	One less problem
Без меня меня женили	I wasn't asked about that
Береже́ного Бог береже́т	The Lord helps those who help themselves
Быть бычку на вере́вочке	Bear responsibility for one's deeds
В огороде бузина́, а в Киеве дя́дька	Apples and oranges
Я про Фому́, а ты про Ере́му	
Волков боятся – в лес не ходить	It takes courage to start
В тихом омуте че́рти водятся	Still waters run deep
В Тулу со своим самоваром не ездят	Don't carry coals to Newcastle
Голь на вы́думки хитра́	Necessity is the mother of invention
Где тонко – там и рвется	A chain is only as strong as its weakest link
Горбатого могила исправит	The leopard cannot change his spots
Долг платежом красен	One good turn deserves another
До свадьбы заживет	He'll manage
Дружба дружбой, а служба службой	Friendship is one thing, work another
Дуракам закон не писан	There is no law for fools
За би́того двух неби́тых дают	Experience is worth it
За здо́рово живешь	For nothing
И на стару́ху бывает проруха	Even an experienced person can err/ Everyone makes mistakes
Как аукнется – так и откликнется	People react in kind to the way they are treated/get what they deserve
Кашу маслом не испортишь	You can't spoil a good thing/You can't have too much of a good thing
Клин кли́ном вышибает	Fight fire with fire/One nail drives out another
Лес ру́бят – ще́пки летя́т	To feel the consequences of others' actions/You can't make an omelet without breaking eggs
Лиха́ беда начало	The first step is the hardest
На безрыбье и рак – рыба	Something is better than nothing
Наводить тень на плетень	To confuse, mess up an issue
На воре шапка горит	If the shoe fits, wear it/A guilty mind betrays itself
Назвался гру́здем – полезай в ку́зов	If you undertook something, do it/see it through
Нашла коса́ на камень	To meet one's match
Не было у бабы хлопо́т, так купила баба порося́	To ask for trouble
Не плюй в коло́дец – пригоди́тся воды́ напиться	Actions can boomerang
Не пойман – не вор	Innocent till proven guilty
Овчинка выделки не стоит	The game isn't worth the candle
Одна ласточка весны не делает	One swallow doesn't make a summer
От добра́ добра́ не ищут	Leave well enough alone
Первый блин комом *(lump ball)*	Things don't work the first time
После драки кулаками не машут	What's done is done
Раз на раз не приходится	You can't expect perfection every time
Рука руку моет	You scratch my back, I'll scratch yours
Рыбак рыбака видит из далека	Birds of a feather flock together/Like draws like/Takes one to know one
Свет кли́ном (не) сошелся	There are other possibilities—that's not all there is to it
С волками жить – по волчьи выть	Run with the pack

Своя рубашка к телу ближе	Everyone is out for himself
Семь раз отмерь, один – отрежь	Look before you leap
Снявши голову, по волосам не плачут	Big things count, not little ones
Соловья баснями не кормят	Talk is cheap – time to eat
С паршивой овцы хоть шерсти клок	Everything is good for something
Тише едешь – дальше будешь	Slow and steady wins the race
У семи нянек дитя без глазу	Many commanders sink the ship/Everyone's business is nobody's business
Утро вечера мудренее	Sleep on it
Хрен редьки не слаще	One is just as bad as the other
Цыплят по осени считают	Don't count your chickens before they are hatched
Человек человеку – волк	Dog eat dog
Чем дальше в лес – тем больше дров	The deeper one gets into something, the more involved it becomes
Чем черт не шутит	Seriously/play it safe/anything is possible
Чья бы корова мычала, а твоя бы молчала	The pot shouldn't call the kettle black
Шила в мешке не утаишь	You can't hide the obvious
Яблоко от яблони недалеко падает/ катится	Like father, like son/a chip off the old block

дрова = firewood

117

CHAPTER XII

LISTEN, SPEAK, LISTEN:
INTONATION, DELIVERY AND TRAINING

The interpreter has to worry about two kinds of intonation: the speaker's and his own. Russian intonation is not just a matter of emphasis, stress, and emotion. A change in an IK (intonational construction) can completely transform the meaning of a sentence. "In oral speech, in colloquial speech in particular, apart from word order, a major role in giving shape to the functional sentence perspective is played by intonation."[1] Though misunderstanding the speaker's intonational stress can lead to mistranslation, blindly reproducing that intonation in another language is also dangerous, since Russian and English intonational patterns are extremely different. The interpreter who unconsciously or consciously begins to mimic the rise and fall of Russian intonational patterns in English may sound jerky and singsong, as if he is making fun of the speaker. He must transform Russian intonation into English intonation in the same way that he transforms the lexical components of a Russian sentence into English. The interpreter must grasp both the speaker's intonational idiosyncrasies – of which there are a wide variety in Russian – and the standard intonational patterns of Russian speech. In summary, these are:[2]

IK-1	Declarative statements:	Он врач.
IK-2	Question with an interrogative word or emphatic sentence:	Куда он пошел?
		Это *мой* карандаш.
IK-3	Question without interrogative word or for emphasis:	Это *ваш* карандаш?
		Завтра он едет в Москву.
IK-4	Interrogative with *A*	А когда он приедет?
IK-5	High emotional intensity:	Как они поют!
IK-6	Intensity of state or condition, particularly in everyday situations:	Какие вкусные конфеты!
IK-7	Negative intensity:	Какой он врач!

IK-2 and IK-3 do not necessarily imply an interrogative sentence:

  2   3
А! Ты приехала!   Oh! (I see that you've arrived!) You're here!

  2
Как, ты приехала?   How come you're here?/How did you get here? (Speaker is surprised)

The Russian-English interpreter should not be concerned with how to produce these IK's, but rather with the semantic differences between them which determine his intonational cadences in English. For example:

Он живет в Ленинграде. (1)
Он живет в Ленинграде. (3)

The first sentence is a simple declarative: He lives in Leningrad. The second, with IK-3, stresses that he lives in *Leningrad,* and not in some other city. The interpreter can convey this through voice stress on the word *Leningrad.* Similarly:

Они живут на *шестом* этаже. (2)
They live on the *sixth* floor./It's the *sixth* floor they're on.

Or:

        (3-4)   (1)
Это не английский текст, а французский.
This isn't the *English* text – it's/no, it's the French one.

        (2)   (1)
Это французский текст, а не английский.
This is the *French* text – not the English one.

Particular care should be taken not to imitate IK-3 or IK-6 in English, as this will result in a very squeaky linguistic product:

    1   6   1
Говорит Москва. Московское время – тринадцать часов.
         3   3   1
Дайте мне стакан чаю, бутерброд с ветчиной и персик.
 6   6   6
Идите, не торопитесь, не беспокойтесь.

The use of IK-3 intonational stress can change the meaning of a sentence:

     3
Он там был?   Was he *there?*   (was he there or not?)
3
Он там был?   Was *he* there?   (or someone else?)

Or:

     3
Завтра он едет в город?   Is it *tomorrow* that he's going to town?
          3
Завтра он едет в город?   Tomorrow *he's* going (not someone else)
             3
Завтра он едет в город.   Tomorrow he's going to *town* (not somewhere else)
  2   3
Завтра он едет в город.   *It's tomorrow* that he's going to town (emphatic on when)

The difference between IK-3 and IK-4 can indicate major differences in meaning:

Когда она поступила в аспирантуру?
   – В 1992 году.
А защитилась? (3) – В 1994 году   Did she defend/*ever defend* her thesis? Yes, in 1994.

А защитилась? (4) В 1994.   And *when* did she defend? In 1994.

Иван в среду позвонил. А не во вторник? (3)   I thought it was on Tuesday.
Во вторник он не сможет приехать.
   – А не во вторник? (4)   Can he make it another day?

120

Bryzgunova gives an excellent example of how a shift from an IK-1, 3, or 4 to IK-2 totally changes the meaning of a sentence:[3]

1- 3-4   3-4   1

Товарищ Николаев, директор этого завода, в цехе.

2   3-4   1

Товарищ Николаев! Директор этого завода в цехе..

Shifting an IK-2 from one word to another can also change the meaning of a sentence:

2	
Лучше учись!	You need to study harder!
2	
Лучше учись!	Studying is better than anything else for you!

A very slight intonational difference can make a request considerably more polite:

2	
Напишите это предложение!	Write that sentence down!
3	
Напишите это предложение!	Please write that sentence down.

A question such as *Вы знаете его?* has three different shades of meaning depending on the IK used:

2	
Вы знаете его?	You/do/ know him/don't you? (Speaker is sure of a positive answer)
3	
Вы знаете его?	Do you know him? (Neutral question)
4	
Вы знаете его?	Are you acquainted with him/do you know him? (More formal than the neutral IK-3, IK-4 implies here both surprise and a questioning of what the speaker has said) How come you know him?/You really know him?

The intonational differences between IK-3 and IK-1 are the most striking, for here intonation distinguishes a declarative from an interrogative sentence:

3	
Им музей понравился?	Did they like the museum?
1	
Им музей понравился.	They liked the museum.
3	
Завтра вы уезжаете?	Are you leaving tomorrow?
1	
Завтра вы уезжаете.	You're leaving tomorrow.

An American student once got into serious trouble on a crowded Moscow bus by using IK-1 instead of IK-3 when saying *Вы выходите сейчас?* to the person standing next to him, for the Russian took the utterance as a formal order to leave the premises and responded none too positively.

The distinction between IK-2 and IK-3 is also critical, for the former can indicate an order and the latter an inquiry:

2
Не разговаривать!   Be quiet!
3
Не разговаривать?   Should I/we be/keep quiet?

IK-3 may also indicate great surprise on the part of the speaker:

3   3
Иван это сказал? Это невозможно! Другой мог бы – но он?

Ivan really said that? That's impossible! Someone else might have – but not he!
(but he – no way!)

IK-7 also conveys the notion of a negative reaction or the impossibility of an action:

7
Идти в кино? Какое кино! Мне нужно работать!!
Go to the movies? No way/You must be kidding/Out of question! I've got to work!

7
Ты ходишь к этому врачу? Какой он врач! Он же шарлатан!
You go to that doctor? What kind of a doctor is he?/You call that a doctor?/He's a terrible doctor/He's a charlatan/quack.

The interpreter should be very sure of his IK-s, however, before committing himself to a statement as strong as "He's a terrible doctor." Similarly: *Где ему учиться?* (7) is very different from *Где ему учиться?* (2) The IK-2 can indicate a neutral question: Where should he study? The IK-7 means "What good will it do him to study?/He's a hopeless case." *Сколько он работает!* (7) is not an expression of admiration of how much work he is doing, but an exclamation: "He's not doing any work at all!"

An utterance such as *какой парк* could have three different IK's:

2
Какой парк?   Which park?
5/6
Какой парк!   What a wonderful park! What a great park!
7
Какой парк!   You call that a park? What an awful park! That thing isn't a park/can't be called a park!/Some park!

Or take the following with IK-2, 5, and 7:

Он читает стихи.   Какие стихи? (2)   What poems?
Свои собственные.   Какие стихи! (5)   What fantastic poems!
                   Какие стихи! (7)   Unbelievably bad poems!/You call *that* poetry!/Some poetry!/Fine poetry!

IK-5 and 6 can act as intensifiers:

Какая (6) погода!   What wonderful weather!
Он так (5) устал!   He's absolutely exhausted.
Жарко (6) здесь!   It's horribly hot here/It's boiling here.
Яблоки! (6)   What wonderful apples!
А мы в музее (6) были!   What a great museum we went to!

A genitive plural noun used with IK-6 implies a great quantity of something:

Шуток было! (6)	There were so many jokes!

Compare:

Сколько студентов? (3)	How many students are there?
Сколько студентов! (6)	How many students there are!

IK-3 or 6 used with a nominative plural can imply intensity of quality:

    3/6   3/6

Цветы! Цветы у тебя очень\такие красивые!	What beautiful flowers you have there!

Compare with IK-6 and the genitive plural indicating quantity:

    6   6

Цветов! Цветов там столько!	How many flowers there are!

IK-6 can imply positive or negative intensity:

Где (2) он живет?	Where does he live?
Где (6) он живет!	That place he lives in…That awful place… You can't *imagine* that place where he lives.
Где(6) он живет!	I'll tell you where he lives!

Similarly, IK-7 can express positive or negative intensity of emotion, depending on context:

Какая (5) голова! Вот (3) радость для родителей!	
Не говори! (7)	Sure!/And how!/Absolutely!
Смотри! Такой молодой, (3) а уже пьет!(2)	
Не говори! (7)	I know—it's terrible!/How awful!

IK-6 expresses intense emotion—e.g. approval, vs. IK-1 with its statement of fact:

Иван загорел. (1)	Ivan's got a suntan.
Иван загорел! (6)	Ivan's got a great suntan!
Загорел Иван! (6)	What a great tan he's got!
Хорошо. (1)	Right/Good/OK.
Хорошо! (6)	That's great!

To avoid misunderstanding or *contresens,* the interpreter should be thoroughly familiar with basic Russian intonational patterns and should not let Russian intonational constructions influence his interpretation into English.

In working on delivery, the interpreter should concentrate on articulating grammatical segments and chunks which are easy for the listener to absorb. Insofar as possible, the subject and verb should be kept close together, prepositions and their objects should not be unduly separated, and verbal noise such as "uh-uh," heavy breathing, and coughing should be avoided. It is much easier for the listener to understand "These are the ways/to resolve this set of problems/within the next ten years/as we see it," than "These are/the ways to/resolve this set—uh-uh—of problems within the—cough—next ten years as we see it." Staccato, rapid-fire, machine gun-monotonous delivery should be avoided. The interpreter must pace himself to the speaker, and even if he is nervous, his voice should convey a sense of calm and control. In a situation in which the speaker is making no sense at all, however, a hint from the booth—through the interpreter's tone of voice—that something is wrong can be useful.

The interpreter must manage to strike a balance between sounding overly authoritative and excessively weak. No matter how boring or obnoxious he finds the subject—or the speaker—he must not let personal feelings influence his delivery. (This is easier said than done.) It is his job to convey the speaker's true tone and meaning. "Really" can express surprise, boredom, or disgust. Above all, no matter how fast the speaker is going, the interpreter should finish his sentences.

Unless he has made a genuine *contresens,* the interpreter should avoid correcting himself. There is no reason to repeat a phrase just because he has found a perfect—instead of an adequate—adjective, since this makes for a very jerky translation and causes the listener to lose confidence. In front of the microphone, the interpreter cannot afford to be a perfectionist. He must fight the temptation to say nothing because he is still vainly searching for the single word which will not come to mind. If he feels that he has lost a critical word or phrase the interpreter can summarize an entire sentence rather than blindly spouting out a literal translation of half of it. He should chop excessively long sentences into digestible units, listen carefully for nouns and verbs, and cut back on strings of adjectives.

While he is speaking the interpreter must simultaneously listen to his own voice and concentrate on the speaker. He must avoid shouting (a tendency of nervous interpreters), and pitch his voice level so that it does not cover the speaker's. Some interpreters prefer to use only one earphone so that they can listen to themselves with the other ear; others prefer the security of two headphones. While listening to himself the interpreter should not get so carried away that he involuntarily begins analyzing his own interpretation and thus slows himself down. Amateur interpreters in particular tend to act both as interpreter and as listener to their own translations.[4]

An interpreter who has been working for a long stretch, particularly if he is translating a very rapid speaker, may encounter a phenomenon known as "automatic pilot." Like a pilot flying a plane on automatic pilot rather than by manual controls, the interpreter may rattle on mechanically, as though someone or something is speaking through him. Automatic pilot can lead to sloppiness and the failure to monitor oneself. This is different from quality interpretation at top speed, in which energy is entirely concentrated on processing the material as fast as possible, devoting maximum attention to vocabulary and grammar and allotting a minimum of time to stylistic niceties and intonation.

Sadly, despite an excellent—or even native—knowledge of languages and a real desire to work in the profession, some people will never be good interpreters. Memory problems, inability to code switch, perfectionism and "translatoritis," (excessive searching for a precise term at the expense of an entire sentence), a fondness for literal translation, stage fright, speech defects, a strong regional or foreign accent, stuttering, hoarseness and hearing problems are clear obstacles to success in this profession. Many students of the piano would not have profited from lessons with Vladimir Horowitz, but gifted musicians certainly would have. While interpreter training is not particularly helpful for people with no talent, it can greatly benefit those who have a flair for code switching and an excellent knowledge of source and target languages. While in the US training possibilities for Russian-language interpreters are limited (a full-time professional-level simultaneous interpretation training program exists only at Monterey), there are excellent schools in Geneva, Paris, and London, and today American programs are forming and expanding. The Moscow International School of Translation and Interpreting (MISTI) and the Moscow Linguistic University have excellent programs in the theory of translation and interpretation and in interpretation into Russian, taught by highly qualified professionals, but the native speaker of English may hesitate at doing Russian-English interpretation with a teacher who is a native speaker of Russian and has acquired English as a second language. For beginning interpreters and for those who wish advanced Russian language training, however, both these places can be highly recommended.

The only way to learn to interpret is by interpreting. The value of written translation tests in determining a candidate's talent for interpreting has been hotly debated: "Written translation should not be part of an interpretation aptitude test,"[5] writes one educator. "It is only when a satisfactory translating base has been established that a test in interpreting should be given,"[6] writes another. While translation tests do show whether or not a candidate has mastered the basic grammatical structures and vocabulary of a language, they do not reveal speech defects, voice problems, ability to keep up and deal with syntax and intonation, and what can only be described as a flair or a knack for the job. Interpreting at sight from written texts is a useful exercise for learning to cope with vocabulary and syntactical problems, but it is no substitute for the immediacy of live voices and tapes.

Just as only an actor can truly teach acting, only an interpreter can truly understand all the problems interpreters face.

> Strangely enough, while nobody would claim that medicine should be taught by someone who has never seen an ill person, or music by somebody who has never been to a concert, there are, still now, quite a number of schools pretending to train interpreters where there is not one conference interpreter among the faculty... only one who has lived it all and seen it all, and often suffered under adverse conditions, can teach conference interpreting. It is granted that he should moreover have a gift for training and be familiarized with modern teaching methods.[7]

An interpretation school is not a language school. While the interpreter will pick up a good deal of specialized vocabulary during training, he must arrive with his languages mastered. The teacher must make the student do the interpreting and not do it for him—a great temptation for an experienced conference interpreter. The student should be forced to abandon literal interpretation and to restructure the Russian original in English. It is the role of the teacher to:

> заставить обучаемых отказаться от гипнотического влияния оригинала и от связанного с ним стремления к буквальному переводу и научить их добиваться адекватности в переводе (conceptual fidelity), т.е. устанавливать функционально-смысловые соответствия.[8]

Exercises for the beginner can start with shadowing, repeating what he has heard in successively larger chunks, first in the original Russian and then in English. The pauses between chunks can vary, speed can be changed, and the student asked to practice a deliberate lag, a useful technique to keep him from jumping in too soon.[9] Or the teacher can read out a short paragraph and ask the student to give back a summary. This comes close to consecutive interpretation, but it is good memory training, and the pressure to rephrase helps get the student away from literal translation.

Paraphrasing the main points of a paragraph or sentence is a very useful exercise. Once in the booth the student should start by doing short pieces and recording his interpretation. Ideally, he should interpret without a text, and afterwards see the original Russian. This will allow him to grasp the sentence as a whole and see what he has omitted. Text in hand, he should review his tape and then do the piece over without the text. In the best of all possible worlds he will do all this under the supervision of an experienced Russian-English interpreter.

There are numerous training devices which the aspiring interpreter can practice on his own with Russian tapes. If he cannot obtain audio or video tapes of Russian radio and TV programs (some of these are now commercially available), he can have a native speaker record Russian newspaper articles or speeches at varying speeds. With these he can practice

Lag:	Deliberately waiting until the end of a sentence or a break in the sentence before starting to interpret.
Accents:	Practice listening to Georgian, Ukrainian and other non-native accents in Russian.
Tense:	Practice concentrating on correct English tenses.
Active and passive verbs	Concentrating on Russian actives and passives and various ways of rendering them in English.
Prepositions:	Concentrating on the correct use of prepositions in English.
Negation:	Changing Russian negative constructions to English positive ones.
Numbers:	Doing a text with many digits; practice writing them down.
Condensation:	Practicing making the interpretation as succinct as possible. The interpreter should practice with a tape to see what can safely be left out, reduced, or shortened.
Synonyms:	The interpreter should do a short text, and then try to repeat it using as few words as possible of those he used the first time.[10]
Divided attention:	Interpret a text while simultaneously working on a crossword puzzle, playing solitaire, or writing numbers backwards from 100. While at first this may seem impossible, it will become easier and is a good exercise in the kind of intense and yet divided concentration needed to follow a speaker's Russian while keeping an eye on the English translation of his text.
Proper names:	Concentrate on names of people and places in a text filled with such items.
Anticipation:	Stop tape in mid-sentence and try to finish it using syntactical, grammatical and lexical *вероятностное прогнозирование*. Do the same exercise filling in the missing beginning of a sentence.

126

Closing:	The student must fill in a test or tape on which every tenth or so word is missing.[11]
Speed:	Alternate very fast and very slow speeches.
Delivery:	Concentrate on intonation, breathing, smooth segments. The student should record himself, listen to the tape, and then repeat the interpretation, concentrating on problems with delivery.
Flowers:	Student should practice greetings, thanks, condolences, and basic conference terminology until these become internalized and nearly automatic reflexes.
Putting parts back into the whole:	Do an entire speech putting together all the above elements: tense, prepositions, anticipation, lag, proper speed, smooth delivery. This should be done after doing the individual exercises on tense, prepositions, etc.
Written translation:	This is a useful exercise which forces the interpreter to take the time to think about syntax, grammar, and awkward turns of phrase. Back translation is also useful. Take an English speech which has been translated into Russian and put it back into English. Then compare with the original.

For the advanced student, longer Russian radio and TV programs or films can be very useful. These include news programs, documentaries, political commentary, lectures, scientific programs and feature films, which are useful for practicing interpretation of dialogue. The visual information contained in films gives the student a great many more cues than does an oral tape.[12] Simultaneous interpretation of films, however, is murderously difficult. Most professional interpreters will insist on seeing a roll-in or film segment in advance before attempting simultaneous interpretation. As an exercise, though, interpretation of film material can be quite useful.

Above all, the student interpreter should be concerned with making sense. As one interpreter beautifully put it,

> Could the Foreign Minister of Zimbabwe be praising apartheid? Could anybody congratulate the delegation of Mexico for an earthquake?[13]

If such a *contresens* has been committed, it is then the interpreter's job to extricate himself as gracefully as possible:

> What do you do if you have already congratulated them and only now you realize your mistake? Well, why not congratulate them for the spirit with which their people and government had faced the terrible earthquake? If sense is in our minds, it will somehow manage to come out of our lips.[14]

The would-be Russian-English interpreter should keep up with the Russian press, which is producing a daily stream of new vocabulary and expressions. He should read widely – about the Russian political system, economic reforms, banking and finance, taxation, labor legislation, crime, education, religion, science, computers, space, medicine, ecology. The mass media, sports, and the arts can be just as important as political vocabulary – or more important – depending on the delegation or the conference with which the interpreter is working. And the interpreter must keep working on his English; he needs to read widely, think about synonyms, and keep up with new terms. "The dictum *Humani nil a me alienum puto* (nothing human is alien to me) is perhaps more applicable to interpreters than to any other profession."[15]

CHAPTER XIII

CONFERENCE TERMINOLOGY

While conference terminology and parliamentary procedure cannot be covered in a few pages, certain terms recur at even the most informal of meetings and are vital to the interpreter. Giving the floor, presenting a proposal, accepting or rejecting recommendations are part of most group proceedings. What follows is a highly selective list of basic terms and some examples of their use.[1]

заседание	meeting (formal)
открытое заседание	public, open meeting
закрытое заседание	closed, private meeting
пленарное заседание (coll. пленарка)	plenary meeting
встреча на высшем уровне	summit meeting
съезд	convention/conference
конференция	conference
правление	board of governors
совет директоров	board of directors
комитет	committee, commission
комиссия	subcommittee, subcommission
специальный комитет	ad hoc committee
редакционный комитет	drafting/editorial committee
круглый стол	round table
рабочая группа	working group/party
собраться/заседать	to meet/hold a meeting
собрать заседание	to call/convene a meeting
учредить/создать комитет	to establish/found/set up a committee
назначить представителя	to appoint a representative
поручить комитету	to charge/entrust a committee with something
торжественное открытие	formal opening/ceremony/session
заключительное заседание	final/closing meeting
совместное заседание	joint meeting
постоянный комитет	main standing committee
зарегистрироваться на конгрессе	register at a congress
принимающая страна	host country
приглашающая страна	inviting country
составить/выработать программу работы	draw up the program of work
крайний срок/срок подачи	deadline
заблаговременно	in sufficient time/early enough/in good time
штаб-квартира	headquarters
официальные языки	official languages
рабочие языки	working languages
условия назначения	terms and conditions of appointment
сверхурочная работа	overtime

су́точные	per diem
командиро́вочные	travel, subsistence allowance
конституция	constitution
устав	charter
Заключительный акт	Final Act
пакт	covenant, pact
догово́р	treaty
соглашение/договоре́нность	agreement
декларация, заявление	declaration
двусторо́нний, многосторо́нний	bilateral, multilateral
кодекс	code
правила процедуры	rules of procedure
предвари́тельная пове́стка дня	provisional agenda
включить в повестку дня	to include on the agenda
быть в повестке дня	to appear on the agenda
пункт повестки дня	agenda item
прочие вопросы, разное	other matters/other business/ miscellaneous
расписание	timetable/schedule
резолюция	resolution
проект резолюции, доклада	draft (resolution, report)
решение	decision
доклад	report
совместный (доклад, резолюция)	joint
основной доклад	keynote address
вступи́тельное слово/речь	opening address
заключительное слово	closing/concluding remarks
рабочий документ	working paper/document
тезисы доклада	abstract
обзор	survey, review
выступление/сообщение/заявление	statement
конспект/резюме́/сводка	abstract, summary
вести протоко́л	to take the minutes
стенографический/полный отчет	verbatim record
машинопи́сное бюро	typing pool
список ораторов	list of speakers
поправка	amendment
добавление	addition
вставка	insertion
исключение/изъятие	deletion
подгота́вливать, разрабатывать,	produce, prepare, draw up, draft
редактировать документ	edit a document
рассматривать (документ)	consider
первоначальный текст	original text
догова́ривающие сто́роны	contracting parties
быть участником конвенции	be a party to a convention
присоединиться к конвенции	adhere/accede to a convention
присоединение	accession
с огово́рками	with reservations
безогово́рочно	without reservations, unconditionally
войти, вступить в силу	to enter into force
осуществлять конвенцию	apply, implement, put into effect a convention
выполнять, осуществлять положения конвенции	to implement provisions

130

нарушать положения (конвенции)	violate provisions (of a convention)
глава делегации	head of delegation
Полномочный представитель	plenipotentiary representative
с правом голоса	with a right to vote
наблюдатель	observer
заместитель	deputy
ревизор	auditor
должным образом уполномоченный	duly authorized
присутствовать	to attend/be present
членство	membership
состав (делегации, конференции)	composition/membership of a delegation, conference
действовать в качестве...	to act as...
полномочия, верительные грамоты	credentials
должность	post/job/position
должностные лица	officials
председатель	chairman, president
Госпожа председатель	Madam Chairman/Chairwoman
заместитель председателя	vice-chairman, vice-president
докладчик	rapporteur
срок полмномочий	term of office
занимать должность	be in office
Генеральный секретарь	Secretary General (UN and international organizations); General Secretary (Communist Party)
казначей	treasurer
сотрудники	staff/associates
зал заседаний	conference hall
трибуна	rostrum
поставить вопрос на голосование	put a question to a vote
приступить к голосованию	proceed to a vote
голосовать	vote
воздержаться	abstain
голос за	affirmative vote, in favor
голос против	negative vote, opposed
равенство голосов	a tie vote
единодушное голосование	unanimous vote
тайное голосование	secret ballot
поименное голосование	roll call vote
избирательный бюллетень	paper ballot
требуемое большинство	required majority
выступить по мотивам голосования	to explain one's vote
выставить свою кандидатуру	to put forward/propose one's candidacy
предложить кандидатуру	to nominate
отложить, отсрочить (голосование, заседание)	to defer, postpone
наложить вето	to veto
заседание обявляется открытым	the meeting is called to order
комитет заседает	the committee is meeting
объявить дискуссию открытой	declare the discussion open
возобновить заседание, прения	resume meeting, debate
общие прения	general debate
перейти к существу вопроса	come to the substance of the matter

131

предоставить слово	to call upon/give the floor to/ recognize
слово предоставляется делегату...	
просить слово	to ask for the floor
дать слово	to give the floor to
получить слово	to get, have the floor
выступать	to take the floor/speak
Кто еще хотел бы выступить?	Are there any other speakers/Would anyone else like (to take) the floor/ Are there any further contributions?
оставить за собой право ответить позже	reserve one's right to answer at a later stage
Комитету представлен доклад...	The Committee has a report before it/A report has been presented/ submitted to the Committee
произнести речь, выступить	to make/deliver a speech
Первым выступит профессор Иванов	Professor Ivanov is the/our first speaker/ The first speaker is Professor Ivanov
высказать замечание	to make a remark/comment
Мое правительство поручило мне...	My government has instructed me...
сделать заявление в личном порядке	to make a statement in a personal capacity
выступая в качестве ...	I speak in my capacity as...
принимать во внимание	to take into consideration
возражать	to object
возражение	objection
ссылаться на (статью, документ)	to invoke/refer to an article, document
в порядке уточнения	on a point of clarification
принимать, одобрить предложение, доклад	to adopt/approve a proposal/report
внести предложение, резолюцию	to make a proposal/submit a motion/ to move
внести поправку	to make an amendment
выступить по порядку ведения заседания	to raise a point of order
высказаться за, против предложения	to speak for/against a proposal
снять предложение	to withdraw a proposal
закрыть заседание	to close/adjourn a meeting

Some drafting/document terms

принимает/утверждает	adopts (e.g. program of action)
признаёт, что	acknowledges that
утверждает, заявляет, подчеркивает, что	affirms that
призывет/обращается с призывом к	appeals to
назначает (кем)	appoints Mr. X as
выражая признательность	appreciating
заверяет народ и правительство в своем глубоком сочувствии	assures the people and government of its deep sympathy
сознавая	aware of
учитывая, принимая во внимание	bearing in mind/considering
считает/полагает, что	believes/considers that
по-прежнему считая, что	continuing to believe that

озабо́ченный/будучи озабо́ченным тем, что	concerned about
осуждает	condemns
поздравляет	congratulates
будучи убеждён в том, что	convinced that
объявляет, заявляет, провозглашает, что	declares, states, proclaims that
выражает глубокое сожаление	deeply deplores/regrets that
с сожалением отмечает, что	regrets/notes with regret
констатирует, что	determines that
обращает внимание на	draws attention to
подчёркивает	emphasizes/stresses/underlines
поощряет, поддерживает	encourages/supports
одобря́ет	endorses (i.e. proposal)
создаёт, учреждает	establishes (an organization)
выражает свое удовлетворение, признательность, благодарность, озабоченность, сочуствие, сожаление, решимость	expresses its satisfaction, appreciation, gratitude, concern, sympathy, regret, determination
выражает мнение, что	expresses the view that
принимает (приняв) к сведению	notes (having noted)
настаивает на том, чтобы	insists that
настоятельно призывает	urgently requests
руково́дствуясь	inspired by/guided by
предлагает/просит/призывает	proposes, invites, calls on
ожидает с интересом, надеется	looks forward to
вновь подчеркивает, вновь заявляет	reaffirms
просит/предлагает/поручает	requests

Sample procedure at a meeting:[2]

103-е заседание подкомитета объявляется открытым.
I declare open/I call to order the 103rd meeting of the subcommittee.

Первым пунктом повестки дня является рассмотрение доклада.
The first item on the agenda is consideration of the draft report.

Желает ли кто-либо из членов подкомитета высказать замечания по проекту доклада?
Do any of the members of the subcommittee wish to comment on the draft report?

Я предоставляю слово уважаемому представителю…
I give the floor to the distinguished representative of…

Я благодарю уважаемого представителя…
I thank the distinguished representative of…

Если нет других замечаний, то я буду считать, что подкомитет утверждает доклад.
If there are no other comments, I shall take it/shall consider that the subcommittee approves the report.

Решение принимается.
It is so decided.

Наше следующее заседание состоится…
Our next meeting will be…

Заседание объявляется закрытым.
The meeting is adjourned.

Утверждение повестки дня
Adoption of the agenda:

ПРЕДСЕДАТЕЛЬ: Предварительная повестка дня сегодняшнего заседания содéржится в документе 123. Если не будет возражений, то я буду считать, что повестка дня утверждается.

.....

Повестка дня утверждается.

THE PRESIDENT: The provisional agenda for this meeting is contained in document 123. Unless I hear any objection, I shall consider the agenda adopted.

.....

The agenda is adopted.

ПРЕДСЕДАТЕЛЬ: Первым оратором в моем списке знáчится представитель Франции, которому я предоставляю слово.

.....

Я благодарю представителя Франции за его заявление (из за любезные слова, сказанные в мой адрес).

THE PRESIDENT: The first speaker inscribed on my list is the representative of France to whom I give the floor.

.....

I thank the representative of France for his statement (and for his kind words addressed to me).

ПРЕДСЕДАТЕЛЬ: Кто за мое предложение, прошу голосовáть нажáтием зеленой кнопки. Кто против – нажáтием красной кнопки. Кто воздержался – нажáтием желтой кнопки.
Результаты голосовáния следующие:
за _____; против _____;
воздержались _____.
Мое предложение принимается/не принимается.

THE PRESIDENT: Those in favor of my proposal, please signify by pressing the green button. Those against, the red button. And those abstaining, the yellow button.
The result of the vote is as follows: In favor _____;
Against _____; Abstentions _____.
My proposal is/is not adopted.

Закрытие заседания
Closure of the meeting:

ПРЕДСЕДАТЕЛЬ:	В моем списке больше нет ораторов. Таким образом, наш комитет завершил данный этап рассмотрения этого пункта повестки дня. Заседание закрывается.
THE PRESIDENT:	There are no further speakers inscribed on my list. Our committee has thus concluded the present stage of its consideration of the item on the agenda. The meeting is adjourned.

Flowers

Most speeches contain some kind of introduction or thanks to the chairperson. Also common are expressions of gratitude to a preceding chairman, president or outgoing official, condolences, and expressions of sympathy. The interpreter must have an array of stock phrases with which to handle these "flowers," as they are known. Generally, these expressions come at the beginning or end of a speech, and are relatively predictable. No one ever says that his predecessor or the person introducing him is a mean-spirited moron. Skill, knowledge, expertise, wisdom, diplomatic and human qualities are the order of the day. Work will be successful or crowned with success. A disaster is always terrible, death untimely or sudden.

The opening of a speech is not always a flower, however, and the interpreter must be prepared for a delegate who launches in saying *мы констатируем с удовольствием* or *мы отмечаем с сожалением* one or another event. Or the delegate may simply express thanks for being given the opportunity to speak:

Господин председатель,

уважаемые дамы и господа,

Прежде всего, разрешите поблагодарить за предоставленную мне возможность выступить на этом заседании.

Mr. Chairman, ladies and gentlemen (*distinguished can usually be omitted*), first of all permit/allow me to thank you for (giving me) this opportunity (*much better than possibility*) to speak at this meeting.

Прежде всего, от имени…а,

мне хотелось бы поздравить вас, господин X, по поводу занятия Вами поста председателя…

Позвольте приветствовать вас на высоком посту председателя…
поздравить вас с избранием на этот ответственный пост.
Поздравляю вас с избранием…

First of all, on behalf of (not in the name of!)…
I should like to/permit me to/congratulate you on your election…
as chairman
to the post of chairman
to chair
to this lofty/responsible/high/important post/position/office

Примите поздравления делегации Х... а по случаю (единодушного) избрания

Примите наши горячие поздравления по случаю вашего избрания председателем этой сессии и пожелания успехов в вашей ответственной работе.

Мы хотели бы выразить искреннее удовлетворение по поводу того, что вновь видим Вас
на посту...
в кресле...
Мы с удовлетворением видим Вас...

Please accept the congratulations of the delegation of ... on your (unanimous) election
as/to the post of
Please accept our warmest congratulations
and allow us to wish you every success/success/all success

We should like to express/convey/voice/state our sincere satisfaction at seeing you once again elected/appointed in the chair

Пользуясь случаем, хотелось бы также выразить глубокую признательность представителю Х...а

Мы хотели бы также отдать должное Х...у за его умелое руководство и квалифицированное руководство этой сессией...

I should first (and foremost) like to take advantage of this opportunity to express profound gratitude to the representative of...

We should also like to pay a (well deserved) tribute to X on his skillful and expert/able/competent guidance/leadership of the work of this session.

Хотелось бы также отдать должное вашему предшественнику

We also wish to pay a tribute to/congratulate your predecessor

Мы с удовлетворением отмечаем, что Вы успешно используете свой богатый государственный и дипломатический опыт, руководя работой комитета...

We note with satisfaction that you are putting to good use your governmental and diplomatic experience in guiding the work...

Мы уверены в том, что под Вашим компетентным/умелым/искусным/квалифицированным/руководством комитет успешно справится с стоящими перед ним задачами.

We are confident that under your skilled/capable/competent/able leadership the committee will successfully cope with/face/deal with the responsible/important/ significant tasks/problems/items before it/facing it/on its agenda.

Разрешите нам выразить уверенность, что ваша деятельность будет способствовать плодотворной работе этой сессии комитета.

Allow us to express our confidence that your guidance/activity/actions will promote/advance the fruitful work of this session of the committee.

Мы убеждены, что Ваши глубокие знания, богатый опыт, неизменная преданность делу мира и справедливости будут и впредь отданы служению интересам комитета.

We are convinced/we know that your vast knowledge, wealth of experience, tireless/unflagging/unswerving dedication to the cause of peace and justice will continue to serve the interests of the committee.

Мне выпала сегодня большая честь приветствовать Вас/открыть это заседание.

Today I have the/it is my great honor to welcome you/open this meeting.

Выражаем свою неизменную готовность сотрудничать с вами.

We should like to express our continuing readiness to cooperate with you.

От имени руководства конференции, благодарю всех участников, которые содействовали ее успешному проведению.

On behalf of the conference organizers I should like to thank all those participants/delegates who contributed to the success of this session/meeting/made this meeting a success.

Even these standard clichés have a great number of variations in English. Here are a few examples:

I cannot sufficiently thank you
I cannot say how glad/pleased/gratified/happy I am
I cannot hope adequately to express
I can scarcely find fitting words
I don't know how else to express
I find it difficult to put into words
Words are not adequate to express
Words cannot/are unable to convey/express my feelings
Words fail me
It affords me deep satisfaction to
I am deeply/very honored
You have done me great honor
I consider myself privileged/I am thankful for the privilege
I feel it a proud privilege
It is a great honor for me to
I have great/much/enormous/vast pride (and/or) pleasure in
It is my pleasant duty to
I welcome this opportunity to/appreciate this opportunity
I wish/desire/want/would wish/would like/intend/rise to
I beg/take leave to/take the liberty to/of
Let me
Permit me
Allow me
May I be allowed/permitted/given leave/granted permission to
If I may be allowed to/If you will allow me to
I think/believe/consider/feel/trust/deem/regard/assume/suppose/presume/take it/ surmise/claim/submit/contend/hold/affirm/assert/guess/am under the impression that
I think we all feel/we all will agree/I am sure everyone will agree/I may take it for granted that/No one will dispute
I must say/am bound to say/feel obliged to/cannot but/cannot fail to/must take this opportunity/occasion to say/cannot but say/would be remiss if I did not say/ express

*   *   *

An anniversary or date can be noted, marked, or celebrated:

Примечательно, что в этом году наш комитет отметил свое тридцатилетие.

It is noteworthy that this year our committee marked/celebrated/observed its thirtieth anniversary.

Condolences

Condolences require special effort on the interpreter's part. Confusing a name or uttering congratulations instead of expressing sympathy is a serious offense. Condolences nearly always come at the beginning of a statement, and in rare cases towards the end.

There are two main types of condolences, on natural disasters and deaths. Disasters include floods, earthquakes or volcanic eruptions, mudslides, and avalanches. There are also politically caused disastrous situations: a bombing, surprise attack or raid, hijackings. The death of a leader can be natural or violent, a result of illness, bombs, a coup d'état or sabotage.

Examples:

Делегация Украины выражает глубокое соболезнование правительству и народу Мексики в связи со стихийным бедствием, сильным землетрясением, повлекшим многочисленные человеческие жертвы и большие разрушения.

The delegation of Ukraine expresses its deepest [not deep] sympathy/ sincere [not profound] condolences to the government and people of Mexico on/in connection with the natural disaster, the major/violent earthquake which has resulted in/ caused great loss of life/numerous casualties and destruction of property/considerable damage.

Прежде чем перейти к повестке дня сегодняшнего утреннего заседания, позвольте мне от имени всех членов комитета выразить наше самое искреннее соболезнование правительству и народу Х-а в связи с трагической гибелью людей и серьезным материальным ущербом в результате недавних стихийных бедствий, обрушившихся на эту страну.

Before taking up the items on our agenda for this morning, may I, on behalf of all the members of the committee, extend our deepest sympathy to the Government and people of X on the tragic loss of life and extensive material damage caused by the recent natural disasters which have struck this country.

May I also express the hope that the international community will show its solidarity and respond promptly and generously to any requests for help.

Expressing condolences is a "sad duty." A delegate will often ask that his condolences be expressed/conveyed/transmitted to the government, people and/or bereaved family of a leader. Death is often *преждевременная* (untimely) or *скоропостижная* (sudden). Someone may have died *скончался)* or passed away *(ушел из жизни)*. If the death occurred in an accident or natural disaster the person *погиб* (perished) rather than *умер*. A loss *(утрата)* can be *невосполнимая* (tragic/terrible):

Мы понесли тяжелую/невосполнимую утрату.
We have suffered a terrible/tragic/irrevocable loss.

Example:

Я должен выполнить печальную обязанность и известить нашу Ассамблею о безвременной кончине Главы государства Республики Х Его Превосходительства Н.Н. Известие о кончине Н.Н.-а, всегда стоявшего за дело мира и взаимопонимания – то есть за дело нашей организации – вызвало у меня чувство глубокой скорби. От нашего имени я прошу представителя Х...а передать наши соболезнования правительству и народу X..а и семье покойного. Прошу членов нашей Ассамблеи встать и почтить память Н.Н.-а минутой молчания.

It is my sad duty to inform our Assembly of the untimely death of the Head of State of the Republic of X, His Excellency N.N. It is with deep sorrow that I have learned of the death of N.N., who always stood for the cause of peace and understanding and for self-determination and development, that is, for the cause of our organization. On behalf of all of us I request the representative of X to convey our condolences to the government and people of X and to the bereaved family. I now invite members of this Assembly to stand/rise and observe a minute of silence in tribute to the memory of N.N.

In answer a delegation may voice its thanks for expressions of sympathy:

Наша делегация искренне благодарна всем представителям, высказавшим во время сессии Комиссии сочувствие.

Our delegation is sincerely/deeply/most grateful/expresses its profound appreciation to all those representatives/speakers who have expressed/voiced/conveyed their sympathy during this session of the Commission.

PART II

SELECTED PRACTICE TEXTS AND VOCABULARY

Practice texts are adapted from United Nations published documents (General Assembly, Security Council, and various committee speeches), excerpts from the Russian press, and speeches at various Russian-American conferences. Sources for the Vocabulary section include:

Англо-русский словарь по основам компьютерной грамотности (Москва, издательство «Компьютер», 1993).

Англо-русский словарь по средствам массовой информации (Москва: Московская международная школа переводчиков, 1993).

Акишина, А.А, Формаковская, Н.И. *Русский речевой этикет* (Москва, Русский язык, 1983).

Денисова, М.А. *Народное образование в СССР: Лингвострановедческий словарь* (Москва: Русский язык, 1978).

Крупнов, В.Н. *Русско-английский словарь активной деловой лексики* (Москва: Дело, 1997).

Милославская, Светлана. *Народное образование*: серия «Становление СССР» (Москва, Русский язык, 1980).

Миньяр-Белоручев, Р.К. *Последовательный перевод* (Москва: Воениздат, 1969).

Пособие по развитию навыков устной речи, под ред. В.И. Матвеевой (Москва: Высшая школа, 1972).

Пособие по развитию навыков устной речи для иностранцев, изучающих русский язык, под ред. В.М. Матвеевой, Р.Е. Назаряна (Ленинград: Издательство Ленинградского университета, 1972).

Словарь биржевой лексики на шести языках (Москва: МаксОР, 1992).

Справочник по разговорной речи, (Slavic Workshop, Indiana University, Bloomington, Indiana, 1964).

Стороженко, Вячеслав. *Беседы о советской экономике* (Москва: Русский язык, 1980).

Чернявская, Т.Н. *Художественная культура СССР: Лингвострановедческий словарь* (Москва: Русский язык, 1984).

Burton, C.R. *Russian Composition and Conversation* (Illinois: Passport Books, 1990).

DeBeer, Shane R. *Dictionary of Business and Legal Terms, Russian-English/English-Russian* (New York: Hippocrene Books, Inc., 1995).

English-Russian Comprehensive Law Dictionary (Moscow: Sovetnik, 1993).

English-Russian Dictionary for a Christian Translator (Moscow: Association for Spiritual Renewal, 1997).

Gherasiova, Natalia. *Talking Business in Russian* (Moscow: Russkii Iazyk, 1982).

Khavronina, S. *Russian as We Speak It* (Moscow: Progress, n.d.).

Kolakova, K.I., and Shakh-Nazarova, V.S. *I Can Give You a Hand* (Moscow: Mezhdunarodnye otnosheniia, 1976).

Maximov, Andrei. *Maximov's Companion to Who Governs the Russian Federation* (London: Maximov Publications, 1994).

MIP/L and H Business Dictionary, English-Russian (Moscow: Moscow International Publishers and L and H Publishing Co., Copenhagen, 1994).

Sannikov, N.G. *Conference Terminology*: Англо-русский глоссарий-справочник (Москва: Остожье, 1996).

United Nations, Terminology Bulletin No. 344, Volume I. *Environment and Development* (New York: United Nations, 1992).

United Nations, Terminology Bulletin No. 348. *Women's Issues* (New York: United Nations, 1995).

Yudina, G.G. *Learn to Interpret by Interpreting* (Moscow: Institut mezhdunarodnykh otnoshenii, 1962).

Yudina, G.G. *Improve Interpreting Skills* (Москва: Международные отношения, 1976).

Practice Texts

Господин Председатель,

Поскольку я впервые выступаю на этой сессии Комитета, позвольте мне искренне поздравить Вас и Ваших коллег по бюро с избранием на высокие посты и выразить уверенность, что Ваше умелое руководство работой нашего Комитета будет способствовать успешному продвижению мирового общества к достижению поставленных целей.

*   *   *

Ясность в этом вопросе необходима не только ради исторической справедливости. От понимания того, что является причиной сползания человечества к ядерной бездне, зависит и ответ на вопрос, можно ли остановить этот гибельный процесс и как добиться этого.

Мир сегодня в борьбе за то, чтобы каждый народ мог свободно выбрать путь своего развития.

Эта кровавая война унесла 10 миллионов жизней и нанесла неслыханный ущерб народам. Мы будем и впредь бороться за то, чтобы отвести от мира угрозу войны.

Вряд ли кто-нибудь станет отрицать, что завоевание этой страной независимости является сегодня одной из более актуальных международных задач. От того, насколько быстро она будет решена, зависит развитие обстановки в этой стране и за ее пределами.

Здесь речь идет о серьезнейшей проблеме. Мы пока не видим практического решения, но каждый серьезный человек должен обратить внимание на эту сложнейшую проблему.

Мир охвачен большими переменами. Весь он – в движении, в борьбе. В борьбе за то, чтобы каждый народ мог свободно, самостоятельно выбрать путь своего развития и безбоязненно идти по этому пути в условиях цивилизованных отношений в мировом сообществе.

Мы не раз указывали на остроту вопроса, о котором идет речь. Ведь прежде чем заговорили пушки агрессора, развязавших вторую мировую войну, на протяжении многих лет велась пропаганда войны, не прекращались – призывы к тому, чтобы перекроить карту Европы и мира в соответствии с планами агрессоров.

Нынешняя сессия Спецкомитета проходит в обстановке, характеризующейся опасным обострением международной напряженности, усилением угрозы возникновения ядерной войны. Общеизвестно, что причины нынешнего осложнения международной обстановки кроются в политике тех кругов, которые, не считаясь с интересами других государств и народов, пытаются обеспечить себе доминирующие позиции в мире, наращивают в беспрецедентных масштабах вооруженные силы и вооружения, выдвигают доктрины, ориентированные на применение силы, в том числе – что наиболее опасно – путем использования ядерного оружия.

Перед всеми нами стоит актуальная и неотложная задача создать эффективно действующую всеобъемлющую систему международного мира и безопасности, которая обеспечила бы равную безопасность для всех.

А разве сегодня работа на благо укрепления мира менее актуальна, чем вчера? Слов нет, в последние годы удалось продвинуться в этом направлении.

Поэтому мы, конечно, не можем безразлично относиться к продолжающимся дебатам вокруг этого договора, к принципиально важной задаче его сохранения и укрепления.

Самое важное – иметь в виду, что все это единый комплекс. Это делается не потому, что на бумаге легче оперировать с тремя проблемами во взаимосвязи, удобнее подводить какие-то итоги, искать какие-то несовпадающие моменты. Нет, сама жизнь, реальное положение заставляют рассматривать все это в комплексе.

На нынешней сессии Комитета эти страны внесли конкретные, деловые рабочие документы практически по всем вопросам повестки дня.

Радикальные шаги в области ядерного разоружения, говорим мы, должны сочетаться с широким комплексом конкретных мер военной разрядки, укрепления доверия.

Конечно, многое изменилось. Расходы стран-членов НАТО на оборону сократилось на 22 процента. Личный состав вооруженных сил уменьшился почти на четверть. Более чем на 80 процентов сократились запасы ядерного оружия земного базирования в Европе. Большой упор стал делаться на политическую роль альянса. Однако количество не переросло в качество. Идеология НАТО с трудом поддается модернизации. И поэтому, когда Советский Союз как геополитическая реальность «прекратил существование», НАТО, по определению, не смогла держать свой «дранг нах остен».

ОБСЕ целесообразно дополнительно активизироваться на профильных для нее направлениях – таких, например, как правозащитный мониторинг, содействие становлению демократических институтов, наблюдение за выборами.

Рассчитываем, что Миссия ОБСЕ в Боснии будет и впредь работать в тесном контакте с соответствующими структурами ООН и ее спецучреждений в решении таких насущных задач, как содействие обеспечению прав нацменьшинств, решению проблем беженцев, нормальному функционированию муниципальных органов власти. Обеспечению прав беженцев, включая их имущественные права и личную безопасность, а также мониторингу соблюдения прав нацменьшинств следует уделять первостепенное внимание и в деятельности создаваемой долгосрочной Миссии ОБСЕ в Хорватии, мандат которой будет охватывать всю территорию этой страны.

Углубляющееся партнерство двух организаций проявилось в ходе подготовки и проведения операции Многонациональных сил по охране в Албании по мандату СБ ООН. Успех этой операции – показательный пример необходимости общего руководства со стороны Совета Безопасности за осуществлением ОПМ.

Господин Председатель,

Моя делегация считает, что Комиссия по разоружению может в этом году внести полезный, весомый вклад в решение жгучих проблем разоружения.

Вступление в силу Договора о всеобъемлющем запрещении ядерных испытаний на глобальной основе так же, как и стоящие на повестке дня переговоры о запрещении производства расщепляющихся материалов для целей оружия – это тоже крайне необходимые меры, призванные придать устойчивость всеобщей безопасности в XXI веке.

Радикальное оздоровление международных отношений, построение безъядерного, демилитаризованного, ненасильственного мира требует преодолеть сопротивление тех, кто цепляется за старую политику сил, за отжившие стереотипы в отношениях между государствами.

Человечество находится в преддверии нового тысячелетия и происходящие изменения меняют его облик, смещаются акценты в парадигмах понимания и объяснения мира. Распад биполярного мира дал нам шанс сконцентрировать усилия на решение проблем бедности, здравоохранения, образования, экономического развития, демократии. Однако мы все еще находимся под угрозой локальных и региональных конфликтов, международного терроризма, организованной преступности, незаконной торговли наркотиками и оружием, распространения оружия массового уничтожения, ухудшения состояния окружающей среды. Весь этот негатив человеческой деятельности ставит под угрозу глобальную тенденцию в направлении укрепления мира и прогресса, подрывает хрупкие новые демократии, подтачивает силы развивающихся стран, и, в целом, угрожает нашим общим усилиям, ориентированным на строительство более безопасного и благополучного мира.

Интересы мира и международной безопасности требуют скорейшего достижения всеобъемлющего, справедливого и прочного урегулирования на Ближнем Востоке. Такое урегулирование может быть достигнуто лишь путем совместных усилий с участием всех заинтересованных сторон.

Важной, заслуживающей самого пристального внимания, остается проблема сокращения военных бюджетов.

Мы за всеобщее и полное разоружение.

Они не вправе прибегнуть к нанесению первого удара.

Речь шла о сокращении вооруженных сил и обычных вооружений в Европе.

Солидным шагом для предотвращения нового опасного витка гонки вооружений стало заключение в 1972 между СССР и США соглашения ОСВ-1, а также договора об ограничении подземных ядерных испытаний и о ядерных взрывах в мирных целях.

Они были инициаторами создания всех новых систем оружия – межконтинентальных стратегических бомбардировщиков, атомных ракетных подводных лодок, новых видов боеголовок, и т.д. А потом поступили к развертыванию крылатых ракет.

Переход к обсуждению СНВ-3 до осуществления СНВ-2 должен

подвигнуть Думу к ратификации последнего. Его российским критикам не нравится то, что договор дает Соединенным Штатам некое преимущество. В то время как Россия обязуется ликвидировать все свои стратегические ракеты наземного базирования с кассетными боеголовками, то есть свою главную наступательную ракетно-ядерную мощь, США сохраняют в неприкосновенности свой козырь – аналогичные ракеты, базирующиеся на подводных лодках. Так вот, по СНВ-3 этот класс оружия тоже становится мишенью сокращений.

Несомненно, что историческим событием последнего времени стало заключение Договора о всеобъемлющем запрещении ядерных испытаний (ДВЗЯИ), венчающего 40-летние переговоры по этому важнейшему вопросу. Значение этого Договора не только в том, что он будет эффективно способствовать укреплению режима нераспространения ядерного оружия, станет надежным тормозом его качественного совершенствования и действенным импульсом переговорного процесса в области ядерного разоружения. Универсальность участия в таких договорах как ДВЗЯИ и ДНЯО – необходимый критерий их жизнестойкости и эффективности.

*   *   *

В ряде развитых стран достигнут высокий уровень экономического развития и они обладают большим экономическим потенциалом. Подобный высокий уровень экономического и научно-технического развития может обеспечить решение острых социальных проблем, таких как жилищная и продовольственная, наличие большого числа бездомных, массовая безработица, голод, неграмотность, преступность, наркомания, и т.д. В мире имеются все материальные возможности, которые позволяют осуществить социальные программы с целью полной ликвидации этих тяжелых проблем, которые оборачиваются трагедией десятков миллионов людей в разных странах.

Речь идет о неграмотности, хроническом недоедании и голоде, детской смертности, эпидемиях, поражающих сотни миллионов людей.

Устойчиво высокими темпами росли общественные фонды потребления, расходуемые на нетрудоспособных и социальные нужды: образование, здравоохранение, социальное обеспечение, содержание школ, высших и средних учебных заведений, медицинских и дошкольных учреждений, санаториев и домов отдыха, строительство жилья и др.

Обеспечение пожилых и нетрудоспособных не ограничивалось денежными выплатами. Неуклонно развивалось общественное обслуживание пенсионеров, росло число интернатов и специальных домов для них, улучшались условия для пожилых.

Так, льготы установленные для молодых трудящихся (запрещение привлекать их к ночным и сверхурочным работам, сокращенный рабочий день с оплатой труда как за полный рабочий день, предоставление им оплачиваемых учебных отпусков) делает для предприятий невыгодным принимать на работу молодежь до 18 лет.

В самом деле, конкретное содержание и объем таких прав, как право на социальное обеспечение и страхование, право на жилище, размер и характер льгот, предоставляемых трудящимся женщинам, семьям с детьми и т.д., зависит от той доли национального дохода, которую на эти цели общество может выделить. В нашей стране четыре пятых национального дохода идет на повышение благосостояние народа.

С одной стороны, экономические преобразования в странах с переходной экономикой открыли перед женщинами новые горизонты, дали возможности по-новому реализовать себя, а с другой – социальные издержки рыночных реформ более всего сказываются именно на женщинах: усиливается феминизация бедности, растет женская безработица, ухудшается здоровье женщин.

Нас беспокоят негативные демографические процессы: снижение рождаемости, низкие показатели ожидаемой продолжительности жизни (в среднем 66,9%), высокие цифры смертности населения, особенно в трудоспособном возрасте, негативные тенденции в репродуктивном здоровье. Говоря о нравственном состоянии общества, следует отметить факты жестокого обращения в семье и насилия в отношении женщин.

Особое место в Конвенции занимает раздел содействия обеспечению равных прав и равного обращения на рынке труда. Раздел концепции предусматривает разработку региональных программ развития малого и семейного бизнеса, экономического стимулирования в виде временного освобождения от налогов, льготного кредитования, укрепления системы правовых норм, государственной поддержки научных разработок в области гендерных исследований, осуществления постоянного мониторинга женщин на рынке труда, разработка критериев оценки влияния экологических факторов и условий труда на здоровье женщин, создание условий для обеспечений занятости женщин.

До последнего времени был известен только один способ не умереть от СПИДа: не заразиться вирусом иммунодефицитного человека. Соответственно единственный по-настоящему эффективный способ борьбы с самой эпидемией – образовательные кампании. Самые впечатляющие результаты дают просветительские программы, с середины 80-х проводящиеся в американских городах и предназначенные для мужчин-гомосексуалов: уже к концу прошлого десятилетия количество новых инфекций среди геев стало падать, в то время как в других слоях населения оно неуклонно росло. За последние 15 лет в странах Запада и Юго-Восточной Азии придуманы просветительские кампании для самых разных групп: наркоманов, проституток, студентов, богатых «секс-туристов». Объединяет все кампании одна предпосылка: если человеку объяснить, как избежать смертельной опасности,он начнет себя беречь. В общем, кампании бывают эффективны ровно настолько, насколько верным оказывается это предположение. Но только в двух городах в России созданы программы по обмену шприцов. И необходимо вспомнить механизм развития этой болезни. Как известно, она вызывается особым вирусом иммунодефицита человека (ВИЧ), принадлежащим к группе так называемых ретровирусов.

*   *   *

Православное широкое, народное, массовое – это долгие пышные богослужения, водосвятные молебны, крестины и отпевания, постоянное поминание умерших, почитание чудотворных икон, паломничество к гробницам святых угодников Божиих. Это православие почти умещается в храме, почти совпадает с религиозным обиходом и бытовым укладом.

Вселенское и национальное, духовное и плотское, умозрение и аскеза, храм и пустыня, взятые в их различии и единстве – таково восточное греко-православие.

*   *   *

В России практикующий психолог до недавних пор не нуждался в каких-либо документах, помимо диплома, подтверждающих его профессиональную деятельность. Если он работал (и работает) в учреждении соответствующего профиля, например, психоневрологическом диспансере или психиатрической больнице, ответственность за его деятельность берет на себя его начальство. Вопрос о лицензировании встает, когда речь идет о частной практике. Как правило, российские психотерапевты работают без лицензий. Выгоды она не дает никакой, а мороки много: получать ее надо в Министерстве здравоохранения, для чего нужно собрать много бумаг, тратить время, доказывать, что ты не верблюд (профессиональный спор между психиатрами и психологами относительно того, может ли человек без медицинского образования заниматься лечением, пусть даже немедикаментозным, пока не завершен). Кроме того, обладание лицензией чревато сложными, подчас мучительными отношениями с налоговой инспекцией (система налогообложения частнопрактикующих лиц не вполне отлажена, приходится ходить по инстанциям, стоять в очереди).

На рынке труда грядут перемены, спрос на специалистов разных профессий меняется так же быстро, как и экономический ландшафт. У работодателей больше не в чести ушлые посредники и хитроумные бухгалтеры, умеющие главным образом виртуозно уклоняться от налогов.

Работодатели нанимают, обучают и переманивают друг у друга профессионалов сферы обращения (все, что не связано непосредственно с производством) – услуги, торговля, финансы) и управленцев, имеющих хорошее образование и прошедших стажировку на Западе. Резкий поворот в сфере обращения легко объяснить: в советской экономике в промышленном производстве было занято 70-80% трудоспособного населения, а на сектор услуг приходилось считанные проценты. Сегодня экономика выходит из порочного круга типа «производства станков для станкостроительной промышленности».

Роста уровня зарплат в частном секторе ждать не приходится. В этом повинно не только снижение темпов инфляции, которая в прошлом году дошла до 21,8%, а в текущем, по оптимистическим прогнозам, опустится до 12-15%, но и большая конкуренция на рынке труда. Преобладание спроса над предложением подтверждает и тот факт, что работодатели стали охотно пользоваться обзорами зарплат, которые регулярно составляются рекрутинговыми агентствами, чтобы, не дай Бог, не переплатить своему сотруднику.

В настоящее время принята система, включающая долгосрочный и среднесрочный перспективные планы, а также текущий план. Предприятия наделяются собственными финансовыми ресурсами, для чего создаются соответствующие фонды. В этом году в распоряжении предприятий и хозяйственных организаций было оставлено 44% полученной прибыли.

С момента внесения правительством в Государственную Думу проекта федерального бюджета 1998 года прошел уже почти месяц. За это время успела угаснуть первая волна праведного оппозиционного гнева, и сейчас государственную смету обсуждают главным образом только специалисты. Предполагается, что на депутатский суд бюджет-98 будет впервые вынесен не ранее первой декады октября.

По данным Счетной палаты РФ, доходная часть бюджета за первое полугодие исполнена на 74% от утвержденного показателя на этот период: доходы федерального бюджета составляют 11,8% от объема валового внутреннего продукта (ВВП) против 15.9%, предусмотренных законом о бюджете на 1997 год. Невыполнение заданий по поступлению налогов было компенсировано некоторым увеличением неналоговых поступлений.

К сожалению, российский топливно-энергетический комплекс остается в критическом состоянии. Производство нефти и газа за последние пять лет упало на 47% и 7% соответственно. В прошлом году, по данным Госкомстата, Россия добыла лишь 293 млн. т. нефти. Прирост добычи природного газа составил всего 1%, нефтяного – 2%. Выпуск бензина сократился на 5%, первичная переработка нефти уменьшилась на 3%. По мнению руководителя Комитета по природным ресурсам и природопользованию разработка нефтегазовых месторождений при помощи иностранных инвесторов окажет влияние и на другие отрасли российской экономики, в первую очередь на машиностроение.

В следующем году в Японии ожидается замедление темпов экономического развития. Однако к концу века ситуация начнет стабилизироваться на фоне ожидаемого роста процентных ставок. В отношении США ОЭСР подняла планку экономического роста на 1997 до 2.2%.

Началось реальное падение доходности по государственным ценным бумагам. Появилась законодательная база, в виде трех основополагающих законов: Гражданского кодекса, федеральных законов об акционерных обществах и о рынке ценных бумаг. Началась борьба за перераспределение контроля над предприятиями, а значит сразу начались нарушения прав акционеров. В самом законе «О рынке ценных бумаг» была заложена определенная система сдержек и противовесов.

* * *

Ежедневно примерно около 60 тонн отходов в этом районе исчезает, минуя городские свалки. Это может означать только одно – незаконное, тайное их захоронение.

О состояние дел в этой области говорит тот простой факт, что главными проблемами этой страны в области охраны среды сегодня являются не выбросы загрязняющих веществ, не нехватка заповедных и других охраняемых территорий, не загрязнение водоемов, а шум и запахи.

Этот канал планировался как элемент проекта по переброске части стока северных рек в Волгу.

Наступило резкое нарушение экологического равновесия всего района. В воде неудержимо прогрессирует концентрация токсических веществ.

Конференция подтвердила, что социально-экономическое развитие и охрана окружающей среды тесно взаимосвязаны и взаимообусловлены. В рамках эффективной политики они должны рассматриваться совместно. Она свидетельствовала также о том, что новые экологические угрозы: повреждение озонового слоя, изменение глобального климата, сокращение запасов пресной воды, обезлесивание, сокращение биологического разнообразия, заражения окружающей среды промышленными и радиоактивными отходами, наступление пустынь, сокращение плодородных земель и другие стали более острыми и их решение не терпит отлагательства.

* * *

На орбите масса этого корабля с полезной нагрузкой превышает 210 тонн. Новый корабль имеет свою собственную систему управления, включающую бортовой компьютер.

Компьютер отвечает за ориентацию станции. Идет зарядка аккумуляторов – комплекс должен быть повернут так, чтобы солнечные батареи имели максимальную освещенность. Ведется эксперимент по изучению вспышки сверхновой звезды – и станция принимает положение, при котором телескопы направлены в нужную точку пространства.

За 15 лет, с 1971 по 1986 год, семь наших долговременных орбитальных станций работали в космосе. Семь «Салютов», первые из которых летали на орбите месяц – полгода. Потом срок их жизни в космосе увеличился до двух – четырех лет. И венец этой программы – запуск в 1986 фонду «Мира».

Был накоплен гигантский опыт, который, естественно, захотели перенять национальные космические агентства европейских стран и США. НАСА даже приняло нашу схему строительства орбитальной станции XXI века, для которой мы соберем и доставим на орбиту первые модули и подготовим для них первые космические экипажи. К сожалению, работы над этим проектом омрачаются драматическими событиями, которые происходят на «Мире».

*   *   *

Можно представить себе Internet как развивающуюся паутину неупорядоченных, взаимно пересекающихся сетей – спутниковых, оптоволоконных, телефонных и радиорелейных каналов, соединяющихся миллионы компьютеров во всем мире.

Бумажная пресса должна теперь конкурировать не только с другими привычными масс-медиа, но и с электронной почтой, а также с сайтами необозримой Повсеместно Протянутой Паутиной (WWW). По последним статистическим данным, средний сотрудник крупной корпорации получает и отправляет за день на первый взгляд немыслимое количество сообщений – 177! Это – безумный коктейль из разговоров по проводимому и сотовому телефону, электронной почты, посланий на пейджер, факсов и бумажных записочек.

Проблемы с электропитанием постоянно угрожают работе сети. Если Вы хотите защитить свое оборудование и своих пользователей от сбоев системы и пореже обращаться к сервисной службе, Вам необходимое самое надежное в мире средство...

SELECTED VOCABULARY

Interpreting

синхронный перевод (СП)	simultaneous interpretation
последовательный перевод	consecutive interpretation
синхронный переводчик/переводчица, синхронист	simultaneous interpreter
линейный переводчик	escort interpreter
исходный язык	original language
переводящий язык	target language
буквализм	literal translation
кабина, будка	booth
включить, выключить микрофон	turn the microphone on/off
канал	channel
наушники	headset, earphones
запись	notes
аудиотехник, звукотехник	sound engineer
двухступенчатая система	relay system
краткосрочная память	short-term memory
вероятностное прогнозирование	probability prediction

Russian and American Political Systems

СНГ (Содружество Независимых Государств)	CIS (Commonwealth of Independent States)
Российская Федерация	Russian Federation
республика (автономная)	Republic (autonomous)
область	oblast' (region)
район	region (also city district)
округ	national territory/territorial district
край	territory, region, district
город федерального подчинения	federal city
Президент	President
Канцелярия Президента	President's Office
Генеральный Секретарь (Генсек)	General Secretary (formerly of Soviet Communist Party, now used for leading official of the United Nations and of other international organizations)
председатель	president, chairman
заместитель председателя (зампред)	deputy chairman, vice-chairman, vice-premier
министр, замминистра	minister, deputy minister
Премьер-министр, председатель правительства	Prime Minister, Premier
Съезд Народных Депутатов	Congress of People's Deputies
Федеральное Собрание	Federal Assembly
Совет Федерации	Federation Council (upper house of Parliament)
Государственная Дума	State Duma (lower house of Parliament)
созвать Думу	to convene the Duma
распустить Думу	to disband the Duma
депутатская неприкосновенность	immunity of the deputies
фракция	faction

КПРФ (Коммунистическая партия российской федерации)	CPRF (Communist Party of the Russian Federation)
ЛДПР (Либерально-демократическая партия России)	RLDP (Russian Liberal-Democratic Party)
Наш дом – Россия	Our Home is Russia
Аграрная депутатская группа	Agrarian Deputy Group
Депутатская группа «Народовластие»	The "People's Power" Deputy Group
Яблоко	Yabloko
райсовет	Regional Council
горсовет	City Council
Горисполком (Городской исполнительный комитет)	City Executive Committee
народный суд	People's court
народные заседатели	People's assessors
Верховный суд	Supreme Court
Конституционный суд	Constitutional Court
Высший арбитражный суд	Court of Final Arbitration
Прокуратура	Public Prosecutor's office
Генеральная прокуратура	Prosecutor General's Office
прокурор	Public Prosecutor
Госплан (Госкомитет по планированию)	State Planning Committee
Министерство высшего и среднего образования	Ministry of Higher and Secondary Education
Министерство тяжелой промышленности	Ministry of Heavy Industry
Министерство обороны (МО)	Ministry of Defense
Министерство иностранных дел (МИД)	Ministry of Foreign Affairs
Министерство связи	Ministry of Communications
Министерство внутренних дел	Ministry of the Interior, of Internal Affairs
Министерство охраны окружающей среды и природных ресурсов	Ministry for Environmental Protection and Natural Resources
Федеральная служба безопасности (ФСБ)	State Security Service
государственные деятели	statesmen/government officials
мэр	mayor
мэрия	mayor's office
Госсекретарь	Secretary of State (US)
палата представителей	Congress (US)
сенат	Senate
законодательные органы	legislative bodies
исполнительные власти	the executive branch, executive authorities
судебные власти	the judiciary, judicial branch, authorities
центральная избирательная комиссия	Central electoral commission
всеобщее избирательное право	universal suffrage
баллотироваться	to run for office
переизбираться	to run for office again
лидировать	to be in the lead, to play a leading role
финишировать	to finish, end up
избиратели	voters
избирательный округ	electoral district
повторное голосование	runoff election
повторные выборы	repeat elections
досрочные выборы	early elections
выдвижение кандидатов	nomination of candidates
предвыборная кампания	electoral campaign
урна	ballot box
бюллетень	ballot

сдержки и противовесы	checks and balances
вести переговоры	to conduct negotiations
присоединение к договору	accession to a treaty
наложить санкции	impose sanctions
снять санкции	lift sanctions
приостановить санкции	suspend sanctions
МОП (Меморандум о понимании)	MOU (Memorandum of Understanding)
большая семерка	G-7
ОБСЕ (Организация по безопасности и сотрудничеству в Европе)	OSCE (Organization for Security and Cooperation in Europe)
ЕС (Европейский Союз)	EU (European Union)

Disarmament

противостояние	confrontation
всеобщее и полное разоружение	general and complete disarmament
ВС (военные силы)	armed forces
ВВС (военно-воздушные силы)	air forces
ВМФ (военно-морской флот)	naval forces
морская пехота	marines
сухопутные войска	land forces
пехота	infantry
полк	regiment
взвод	platoon
рота	company
личный состав	personnel
"звездные войны"	"star wars"
СОИ (Стратегическая оборонная инициатива)	SDI (Strategic Defense Initiative)
развертывание/размещение/дислокация	deployment
на местах	on site
контроль/проверка	verification
поддающийся контролю	verifiable
пробная инспекция	trial inspection
проверка по запросу/по требованию	challenge inspection
обязательство	commitment, obligation
устрашение	deterrence
сдержанность	restraint
соблюдение	compliance
нарушение	violation
гарантии	safeguards
демонтаж	dismantling
Международное агентство по атомной энергии (МАГАТЭ)	International Atomic Energy Agency (IAEA)
Договор о частном запрещении ядерных испытаний	Limited Test-Ban Treaty
нераспространение	nonproliferation
ядерный взрыв	nuclear explosion
испытания ядерного оружия	nuclear tests
полигóн	testing ground/site
РЛС (радиолокационная станция)	radar
упреждающий (превентивный) удар	preventive/preemptive strike
ответный удар	counter/retaliatory strike
оружия массового уничтожения (поражения) (ОМУ/ ОМР)	weapons of mass destruction
взаимное гарантированное уничтожение	mutual assured destruction (MAD)

154

истреби́тель	fighter plane
бомбардиро́вщик	bomber
эсми́нец	destroyer
тра́льщик	minesweeper
авиано́сец	aircraft carrier
разве́дывательный самолет	reconnaissance aircraft
линко́р	battleship/warship
подводная лодка	submarine
противопехотная (наземная) мина (ППМ)	antipersonnel (land) mine (APM)
ловушка	booby trap mine
сапер	deminer
разминирование	demining
обезвредить мину	defuse a mine
снаряд	shell
обстрел	shelling
миномет	mortar
стрелковые оружия	light arms
боеприпасы	munitions
бронетранспортер (БТР)	armored personnel carrier (APC)
химическое оружие	chemical weapons
биологическое оружие	biological weapons
боевые действия	hostilities
прекращение огня	ceasefire
расправа	retaliation
перемирие	truce
комендантский час	curfew
чрезвычайное положение	martial law
СНВ (стратеги́ческие наступа́тельные вооруже́ния)	Strategic Offensive Weapons
ПРО (противораке́тная оборо́на)	ABM (Anti-Ballistic Missile)
зенитный	anti-aircraft
Недискриминационная конвенция о запрещении производства расщепляющихся ядерных материалов	Cut-off Treaty (ban on production of fissile material for nuclear or other explosive devices)
Обычные военные силы в Европе (ОВСЕ)	Conventional Forces in Europe (CFE)
Договор о/переговоры по ОСВ (ограниче-ние стратегических вооружений)	SALT (Strategic Arms Limitation Treaty/ Talks)
Сокращение стратегических вооружений	START (Strategic Arms Reduction Treaty/Talks)
Договор по нераспространению ядерного оружия (ДНЯО)	Treaty on the Nonproliferation of Nuclear Weapons (NPT)
Договор о всеобъемлющем запрете на ядерные испытания (ДВЗЯИ)	Comprehensive Nuclear Test Ban Treaty
МБР (межконтинентальная баллистическая раке́та)	ICBM (Intercontinental Ballistic Missile)
МБР оснащенная РГЧ (разделяющаяся головная часть индивидуального наведения)	MIRVed ICBM (multiple independently targetable reentry vehicle)
РСД-РМД (ракеты средней дальности-ракеты меньшей дальности)	medium-shorter range missiles
ОТР (оперативно-тактические ракеты)	shorter-range missiles
крыла́тая ракета	cruise missiles
забрасываемый вес	throw weight
боеголо́вка	warhead
заря́д	warhead, device
шахта	silo

155

средство доставки	delivery system
пусковая установка	launcher
диверсия	sabotage
терракт	act of terrorism
штаб-квартира	headquarters
объединенный комитет начальников штаба	joint chiefs of staff
операция по поддержанию мира (РКО)	(ОПМ) peacekeeping operation
коллективные миротворческие силы (КМС)	collective peacekeeping force (CPKF)
миротворчество	peacemaking
миростроительство	peacebuilding
принуждение к миру	peace enforcement
меры по укреплению доверия	confidence building measures

Social System

благосостояние	welfare, well-being,
соцстра́х (социальное страхование, система социальной защиты)	social security, social safety net
заработная плата (зарплата)	salary, wages
месячный оклад	monthly salary
гонорар	honorarium/royalty
плата	pay, fee
денежные пособия	allowances, benefits, payments
льготы	benefits
подохо́дный налог	income tax
безработица	unemployment
за́нятость (полная занятость)	employment (full employment)
биржа труда	labor market
распределение на работу	job assignment system
повреме́нная, сде́льная оплата труда	piece work
почасови́к	contract, part-time employee
оплачиваемый отпуск	paid leave
декретный отпуск	maternity leave
больничный лист/бюллетень	sick leave
выходить на пенсию	to retire (on pension)
пенсионер	retiree, pensioner
пенсии по случаю потери кормильца, инвалидности, нетрудоспособности	pension for loss of breadwinner, disability pension
средняя продолжи́тельность жизни	average life expectancy
профсоюз	trade union
рабочее, трудовое законодательство	labor legislation
охрана труда	labor protection
меры безопасности труда	labor safety regulations
техника безопасности	labor safety devices
работа на вредном производстве	hazardous occupation
производственные травмы и профессиональные заболевания	industrial injuries and occupational diseases
коллективный договор	collective bargaining agreement
арендный подряд	leasing contract
семейный подряд	family contract
установление производственных норм	quota setting
материальная заинтересованность/ материальные стимулы	material/financial incentives
премия	bonus
стаж	seniority, work record
повышение	promotion

156

взыска́ние, нагоня́й, вы́говор	reprimand
увольнение	dismissal/firing
смена	shift
иждиве́нцы	dependents
квалифицированные кадры	skilled/trained personnel
бригада, команда	team
завко́м, фабко́м	plant committee
цех	shop
пото́чные линии	production/assembly lines
сме́жная отрасль	related industry
ремонтные работы	repair, overhaul
госприе́мка	quality control
наём	hiring
сверхурочная рабо́та	overtime work
рабочий день	working day
скользящий график	flextime
работа на местах, полевые работы	field work
лобби	lobby, pressure group
неправительственная организация (НПО)	nongovernmental organization (NGO)
некоммерческая организация	nonprofit organization
конференция по объявлению взносов	pledging conference
доброволец	volunteer
работа на общественных началах	volunteer work
пожертвование, дар	donation
сбор средств	fund raising
здравоохранение	health care
черта бедности	poverty line
прожиточный минимум	minimum level subsistence
грамотность, неграмотность	literacy, illiteracy
питание, рациональное питание	nutrition
голод	hunger/famine
недоеда́ние	malnutrition
наркомания, злоупотребление наркотиками	drug abuse
наркоман	drug addict
жилищная проблема	housing problem
трущобы	slums
бездомные, бомжи (без определенного места жительства)	homeless
беженцы	refugees
перемещенные лица	displaced persons
Международный Комитет Красного Креста (МККК)	International Committee of the Red Cross
права человека	human rights
нарушения прав человека	human rights violations
геноцид	genocide
этническая чистка	ethnic cleansing
дедовщина	dangerous hazing by senior personnel (in the army)
престарелый	aged
инвалид	disabled
проблема "отцов и детей"	generation gap
продолжительность жизни	life expectancy
(коэффициент) рождаемости	birth rate
смертность	mortality rate

Women's Issues

гендерные проблемы, вопросы	gender issues
планирование семьи	family planning
беременность	pregnancy
выкидыш	miscarriage
аборт	abortion
кесаровое сечение	cesarian section
преждевременные роды	premature birth
поверженный риску	at risk
противозачаточные средства, контрацепция	contraceptives
презерватив	condom
шеечный колпачок	cervical cap
внутриматочное противозачаточное средство	intrauterine device
плодовитость	fertility
бесплодие	infertility
искусственное оплодотворение	*in vitro* fertilization
искусственное осеменение	artificial insemination
деторождение	child bearing, reproduction
зачатие	conception
зародыш	embryo
роды	delivery, birth, labor
акушерка, повивальная бабка	midwife
отнятие от груди	weaning
рак груди	breast cancer
рак шейки матки	cervical cancer
наделение соответствующими полномочиями	empowerment
сексуальное преследование, домогательство, приставание	sexual harassment
изнасилование	rape
женщины, подвергающиеся избиению	battered women
насилие в семье	domestic violence
обрезание у женщин	female circumcision
гражданский брак	civil marriage
мать одиночка	single mother
внебрачный, незаконнорожденный ребенок	child born out of wedlock, illegitimate child
брак по договоренности	arranged marriage
кормилец	breadwinner
домашняя хозяйка	housewife
развод, расторжение брака	divorce, dissolution of marriage
алименты	alimony
пособия, льготы	benefits
опека над детьми	child custody

Religion

Христианство	Christianity
Православие	Orthodox Christianity
Старообрядцы	Old Believers
Католичество	Catholicism
Протестантство	Protestantism
Пятидесятники	Pentecostals
Еврейство, иудаизм	Judaism
еврейские общины	Jewish communities
Буддизм	Buddhism

Индуизм	Hinduism
Ислам	Islam
Мусульманин	Muslim (n.)
церковь, храм, собор	church, temple, cathedral
синагога	synagogue
мечеть	mosque
благодарение	Thanksgiving
благоговение	devotion, reverence
благочестие	piety
благодать	grace
благословение	blessing
Богоматерь	Mother of God
Непорочное Зачатие	Immaculate Conception
Страшный Суд	Last Judgment
Чистилище	Purgatory
первородный грех	original sin
распятие	crucifixion
Неопалимая купина	burning bush
Ноев ковчег	Noah's Ark
Земля Обетованная	Promised Land
Богословие	theology
Вечная память	eternal memory
Воздаяние	reward
Воплощение	Incarnation
духовенство	clergy
Всемирный Совет Церквей (ВСЦ)	World Council of Churches (WCC)
сан	clerical office, orders
священник	priest
ряса	cassock
раввин	rabbi
муфтий	mufti
духовный отец	spiritual adviser, confessor
эпископ	bishop
настоятель храма	prior, rector, Father Superior, Abbot
Патриарх	Patriarch
Митрополит	Metropolitan
Папа римский	The Pope
Его Святейшество	His Holiness
призвание	calling, vocation
паломник	pilgrim
обет	vow
служба	religious service
эктения	liturgy
утреня	matins
вечерня	vespers
панихида	requiem
отпевание	burial service
пост	fast
Пасха	Easter
Страстная неделя	Holy Week
Великий пост	Lent
Ветхий Завет	Old Testament
Новый Завет	New Testament
Десять заповедей	Ten Commandments

Евангелие	The Gospels
Священное Писание	Holy Scriptures
Коран	Koran
молитвенник	prayer book
откровение	revelation
искупление	atonement, redemption
искушение	temptation
исповедь	confession
крещение	baptism
креститься	to be baptized
перекреститься	to make the sign of the cross
милосердие	mercy, compassion
проповедь	sermon
причастие	communion
обрезание	circumcision

Education

всеобуч	compulsory secondary education
обязательное обучение	compulsory education
дошкольные учреждения	preschool facilities
ясли	nursery, creche
детский сад	kindergarten, day-care center
ученик	pupil, high-school student
студент	college student
аспирант	graduate student
выпускник	graduate
учитель	high-school teacher
преподаватель	teacher, instructor
ассистент	instructor, teaching fellow
лаборант	departmental/laboratory assistant
ректор	university chancellor/provost
декан	dean
профессор	professor
доцент	assistant professor (approximate equivalent)
научный сотрудник	research associate/researcher
средняя школа	high school
школа с продлённым днем	school with after-school activities program
интернат	boarding school
техникум	technical school
ПТУ (профессионально-техническое)	vocational school
ВУЗ (высшее учебное заведение)	institute of higher learning, college, university
институт	institute
НИИ (научно-исследовательский институт)	scientific research instititute (research institute)
НИОКР (Научно-исследовательские и опытно-конструкторские работы)	R and D (research and development)
юридический институт	law school
медицинский институт	medical school
педагогический институт	teacher's college
дневник	record of marks
отличник	A student
пятерка	A
двойка	D
балл	point (on an exam)

зачет	credit, pass for a course
сдавать экзамен	to take an exam
сдать экзамен	to pass an exam
сессия	exam period
шпаргалка	pony, trot
поступать в университет	to apply to a university
поступить в университет	to be admitted to a university
окончить университет	to be graduated from a university
плата за обучение	tuition
стипендия	scholarship
аудитория	classroom
посещать занятия	go to class, attend class
заóчные курсы	non-matriculated/correspondence courses
курсы повышения квалификации	advanced course/refresher course
записаться на семинар	take/enroll in/register for a seminar
обязательный предмет	required course
факультативный предмет	elective course
специальность	major
кафедра	department
завкафедра	department chairman
факультет	division (e.g. филологический, философский)
дипломная работа	senior thesis
курсовáя работа	term paper
аттестат зрелости	high school diploma
диплом	diploma
научная степень	academic degree
степень бакалавра	B.A.
магистра	M.A.
кандидатская	Candidate; equivalent of American Ph.D.
докторская	Doctorate; Russian highest graduate degree, higher than American Ph.D.
кандидатский минимум	written Ph.D. exams, comprehensives
диссертация	dissertation, thesis Note: *тезис* does not mean dissertation. *Тезисы доклада* is the summary of a report, the main ideas. *Тезис* means a basic assumption, idea.
научный руководитель	thesis adviser
оппонент	discussant at dissertation summary
автореферат	published dissertation summary
учеба без отрыва от производства	part-time study
прогуливать	to play hookey
записаться в библиотеку	to get a library card
читательский билет	library card
открытый доступ	open stacks

Economics, Business and Finance

хозяйство, экономика	economy
плáновое, рýночное хозяйство	planned, market economy
Общий рынок	Common Market
Всемирная Торговая Организация (ВТО)	World Trade Organization (WTO)
Международный валютный фонд (МВФ)	International Monetary Fund (IMF)
Европейский банк реконструкции и развития (ЕБРР)	European Bank for Reconstruction and Development (EBRD), World Bank

Евро	Euro
выполнить/перевыполнить план	to fulfill/overfulfill a plan
при́быльно, выгодно	profitable, advantageous
прибыль	profit
рента́бельность	profitability
спад	recession
производитель	producer
потреби́тель	consumer
потреби́тельские товары	consumer goods
това́ры широкого употребле́ния	mass consumer goods
потребление	consumption
сбереже́ния	savings (e.g. in savings bank account)
экономия, экономить	savings, to save on something/economize
темпы роста	growth rate
спрос и предложение	supply and demand
продажа и закупка	sales and purchase
средства производства	means of production
предпринима́тель	entrepreneur
предприя́тие	enterprise
совме́стное предприя́тие	joint venture/enterprise
малое, среднее предприя́тие	small, medium enterprise
работода́тель	employer
слу́жащий	employee
повышать производительность труда	raise labor productivity
хозрасчёт	cost accounting
себесто́имость	production/prime cost/cost price
соглашение по разделу капитала	product sharing agreement (PSA)
самофинанси́рование	self-financing
самоокупа́ющийся	profitable, self-subsidizing
самоокупа́емость	cost recovery
би́ржа	stock exchange/(Am.) stock market
фондовый рынок	stock market
биржево́й ма́клер	broker
ценные бумаги	securities
акционерное общество	stock company
акция	stock
портфель	portfolio
доля	share
коэффициент	ratio
держатель акций	stockholder
облигация	bond
Государственная казначейская облигация (ГКО)	government, treasury bonds (T-bills)
паевый фонд	unit fund, mutual fund
котироваться	be listed on stock market
котировка	listing
денежная масса	money supply
акционерный капитал	equity capital
чистая стоимость капитала	equity investment
основной капитал	fixed capital
кредитное соглашение	loan agreement
оборотный инструмент	negotiated instrument
бухгалтерский учет	auditing
ревизия, контрольная проверка	audit

учет и отчетность	accounting and reporting
ограниченная ответственность	limited liability
неплатежноспособность, несостоятельность	insolvency
сырье	raw materials
природные ресурсы	natural resources
нефтепровóд	oil pipeline
трубопровóд	pipeline
месторождение	oil field
буровая установка	oil rig
выкачка	pumping
промысловые скважины	oil wells
торговая палата	chamber of commerce
фонды предприятия	factory assets/funds
отчисления	payments
стимул	incentive
конкуренция	competition
конкурент	competitor
конкурентоспосóбный	competitive
рекламный лист	descriptive materials, ad
реклама	publicity, advertising
трудоёмкий	labor intensive
капиталоемкий	capital intensive
руководство, управление, менеджмент	management, administration
рабочая сила	manpower
эксплуатировать	to manage, run (e.g. a firm, hotel)
выпуск, объем (производства)	output
валюта	currency
конвертúруемая, твердая	convertible, hard
свободно конвертируемая валюта (СКВ)	freely convertible currency
утечка капитала	capital flight
вексель, переводные векселя	bill (of exchange)
банкомат	ATM (cash machine)
эмиссия	issue
заём	loan
ссýда	loan
срок погашения	maturity
задолженность	arrears
ипотека	mortgage
залог	collateral
кредитодатель, получатель	lender, borrower
безвозмездная субсидия	grant
процентная ставка	interest rate
учетная ставка	discount rate, bank rate
вклад	deposit
счет	account
издéржки	costs
затраты/расходы	expenditures/expenses
налúчные	cash
накладнýе расходы	overhead
обесценение, амортизация	depreciation
внешняя задолженность	external debt
управление риском	risk management
капиталовложения, инвестиции	capital investment
инвестор, вкладчик	investor

163

поступления	revenue
текучесть кадров	personnel turnover
военно-промышленный комплекс (ВПК)	military-industrial complex
ВНП (валовой национальный продукт)	GNP (Gross National Product)
ВВП (валовой внутренний продукт)	GDP (Gross Domestic Product)
на ду́шу населения	per capita
фонд потребле́ния, накопле́ния	consumption, accumulation fund
торго́вый оборо́т	turnover
товарооборо́т	commodity turnover, circulation
долгосро́чные, среднесро́чные, теку́щие планы	long-term, medium-term, current plans
дефици́тный	scarce, rare
дефицит	shortage, deficit
оптовый, розничный	wholesale, retail
плате́жный баланс	balance of payments
торго́вый баланс	balance of trade
са́льдо	balance
активы	assets
пассивы	liabilities
МВЭС (Министерство внешних экономических связей)	Ministry of Foreign Economic Ties
Госбанк	State Bank
торгпред	trade representative
торгпредство	trade mission
торговый советник	trade/commercial counselor
прейскура́нт	price list
внутренний рынок	domestic market
пробный заказ	trial order
скидка	discount
пользоваться спросом	to be in demand
сбыт	sales
сделка	deal/transaction
поставить/снабжать	to deliver/supply
поставщи́к	supplier
поставка	delivery
условия доставки	terms of delivery
условия платежа́	terms of payment
фрахт	freight
фрахтование	chartering
страхова́ние	insurance
склад	warehouse/storehouse
груз	cargo
погрузка, разгрузка	loading, unloading
аккредитив	letter of credit
рассрочка платежа	credit terms, installment payment plan
торги, заявка на торгах, предложение, тендер	bid, tender
коносаме́нт	bill of lading
запчасти	spare parts
счет, фактура	bill, invoice
посре́дник	agent, intermediary
подря́дчик	subcontractor
закупить	buy/purchase
закупка	procurement
заказчик	client/customer

погашение креди́тов	repayment of credit
ставка возмещения	rate of reimbursement
брать на себя расхо́ды	cover expenses
по́шлина	tariff
паушáльная сумма	lump sum
КПД (коэффициент полезного действия)	efficiency
забраковать	find/turn out to be defective/substandard
по́рча	damage
понесéнные убытки	losses sustained/incurred
передать дело в арбитрáж	submit dispute to arbitration
экспортировать	to export
экспортные поступления	export earnings
импортировать	to import
запатентовать	to patent
секвестр	budget cuts
Налоговый кодекс	tax code
подоходный налог	income tax
налог на добавленную стоимость (НДС)	value added tax (VAT)
налогооблажение	taxation
подлежит налогооблажению	taxable
подать декларацию	to file taxes
налоговая декларация	tax return
освобожденный от налогов, не облагаемый налогом, не подлежит налогооблажению	tax-exempt
налоговые льготы	tax privileges, tax relief
уклонение от налогов	tax evasion
вычитать, списать с налогов	deduct, write off from taxes
недоимка	non-collected taxes
недоимщик	tax payer in default
сбор налогов	tax collection

The Law

правопорядок	law and order
правоохранительные органы	law enforcement agencies
органы правосудия	judicial bodies
привлечь к ответственности	subject to prosecution
законодательство	legislation
международное, гражданское право	international, civil law
расследование, следствие	investigation
СИЗО (следственный изолятор)	confinement cell
КПЗ (камера предварительного заключения)	preventive detention cell
преступность	crime
преступник	criminal
уголовный, гражданский кодекс	criminal, civil code
КЗоТ (Кодекс законодательства о труде)	labor law
система мест заключения	penitentiary system
ордер на арест, на обыск	arrest, search warrant
задержать	detain
неприкосновенность	immunity
«крыша»	Mafia protection (slang)
разборка	shootout among gang members
кража, грабеж	robbery, theft
хищение	embezzlement
мошенничество	fraud

отмывание денег, средств	money laundering
вор	thief
убийца	murder
изнасилование	rape
вымогательство	extortion
взяточничество	bribery
лжесвидетельство	perjury
взломщик	burglar
телесное повреждение	personal injury, assault
избиение	battery
клевета	slander
подать суд на	to sue
иск	lawsuit
судебное дело	legal case, court case
обвинение	indictment
соучастие, соучастник	complicity, accomplice
смягчающие обстоятельства	attenuating circumstances
отягчающие обстоятельства	aggravating circumstances
умышленный	premeditated
совершеннолетний, несовершеннолетний	of age (adult), minor
свидетель	witness
показание, свидетельство	testimony, evidence
доказательство	proof
улика	piece of evidence
осознанное согласие	informed consent
иск давности	statute of limitations
обратная сила	retroactive
судья	judge
прокурор	prosecutor
истец	plaintiff
ответчик	defendant
подсудимый, обвиняемый	accused, suspect
народный заседатель	people's assessor
присяжный	jury
приговор	sentence
признан виновным, невиновным	found guilty, innocent
апелляция	appeal
под залогом	on bail
отпустить под залогом	to release on bail
смертный приговор, смертная казнь, высшее наказание (вышка)	death sentence, death penalty
казнь	execution
лишение свободы	imprisonment
пожизненное заключение	life imprisonment
заключенный	prisoner
каторжник	convict (noun)
осужден	convicted (past participle of verb)
осуждение	conviction (legal)
условное осуждение	suspended sentence
приговор (вынести)	sentence
рецидив	repeated offense
осознанное согласие	informed consent
самосуд	vigilante justice

Computers and Electronics

More and more Russian computer terms are calques from English, and thus easy to recognize: байт, принтер, он-лайн, etc. An effort has been made here to include terms which differ from the English cognates.

математическое обеспечение	software
компьютерное устройство, аппаратура, оборудование	hardware
установка	installation
жесткий диск	hard disk
гибкий диск, дискет/а	floppy disk
дисковод	disk drive
клавиатура	keyboard
нажатие клавиши	keystroke
модернизация	upgrade
запуск	startup
отключение, установка, выключение	shutdown
загружать	download
регулятор тока	circuit breaker
микросхема	computer chip
схема	circuit, design, drawing
граф-схема	flow chart
полупроводник	semiconductor
обработка данных	data processing
поиск, извлечение данных	data retrieval
сопряжение	interface
обслуживание компьютера	computer maintenance, servicing
обратная связь	feedback
режим	mode
пользователь	user
удобное для пользования	user-friendly
распечатка, печатная копия	hard copy
пароль	password
мышь	mouse
зайчик курсора	cursor bar
нажать, щелкнуть	click
выделить	highlight
точка вставки	insertion point
сохранить	save
дублирование	backup
резервное устройство	backup device
отмена	cancel
удаление, уничтожение	deletion
сбой	malfunction
авария, аварийный отказ	crash
полный отказ системы	system crash
шрифт	font
знак, символ	character
дистанционное управление, доступ	remote control, access
память, запоминающее устройство (ЗУ)	memory, storage
ОЗУ (оперативное запоминающее устройство)	RAM
РВ (реальное время)	real time
выровненный	aligned

167

диалоговой режим	interactive application
совместимость	compatibility
ввод данных	input, entry
выход, вывод	output
сеть	network
бродить, заниматься серфингом	to surf the Internet
цифровой	digital
сотовый телефон	cell phone
видеомагнитофон	VCR
автоответчик	telephone answering machine
система	stereo system

Medical

здравоохране́ние	health care
болен	sick, ill (may be short term)
больной	sick (chronically); patient
мне нужен терапе́вт	I need an internist/general practitioner
идти на прием к врачу	to have a doctor's appointment
я записан к врачу	I have a doctor's appointment
часы приема/приемные часы	office hours
врач принимает	The doctor is seeing patients
он лечится у	he is a patient of/goes to Dr. X
он лечится от	he is being treated for
вылечиться	to be cured
выздороветь	to recover
поправляться	to get better (also to gain weight)
на что вы жалуетесь?	what hurts you/what's your complaint?
поставить диагноз	to diagnose
выписать рецепт	to write out a prescription
прописать лекарство	to prescribe a medicine
врач пошел по вызовам	the doctor made house calls
первая медицинская помощь	first aid/emergency service
скорая (помощь), неотложки	the ambulance
пункт неотложной помощи	emergency treatment center
травмопу́нкт	accident/trauma care center
стациона́р	hospital
диспансе́р	clinic, health center
санаторий	sanatorium
путе́вка в санаторий	voucher for a sanatorium
родильный дом	maternity hospital
он лег в больницу	he was admitted to the hospital
он выписался из больницы	he was discharged from the hospital
участко́вый врач	local/district doctor
хиру́рг	surgeon
медсестра	nurse
поставить пло́мбу	put in a filling
удалить зуб	to extract a tooth
проте́з	denture
офтальмо́лог	ophthalmologist/eye doctor
близору́кий	nearsighted
дальнозо́ркий	farsighted
косо́й	cross-eyed
профилакти́ческие меры	preventive measures
укол	shot
прививка	vaccination

одноразовый шприц	disposable syringe
делать рентгеновский снимок	take an X-ray
градусник	thermometer
(36.6 Celsius = 98.6 Fahrenheit, normal temperature)	
давление	blood pressure
жар	fever
лихорадка	high fever, delirium
охрипнуть	get hoarse, lose one's voice
тошнить	to be nauseous
насморк	head cold
простуда	cold
ангина	sore/strep throat/tonsillitis (*not* angina pectoris)
грипп	flu
желудочный грипп	intestinal flu
воспаление	inflammation
воспаление легких	pneumonia
корь	measles
краснуха	German measles
ветряная оспа (ветрянка)	chicken pox
коклюш	whooping cough
свинка	mumps
брюшной тиф	typhoid
сыпной тиф	typhus
радикулит	sciatica
одышка	shortness of breath
сердечно-сосудистые заболевания	cardio-vascular disease
инфаркт/сердечный приступ	heart attack
кровеносный сосуд	blood vessel
кровотечение	hemorrhage
переливание крови	blood transfusion
клапан	valve
инсульт	stroke
рак	cancer
доброкачественная, злокачественная опухоль	benign/malignant tumor
ткань	tissue
СПИД	AIDS
ВИЧ	HIV
презерватив	condom
лекарства/препараты/медикаменты	medicines
дежурная аптека	on duty drugstore
принимать, пить таблетки, капли	to take pills, drops
снотворное	sleeping pill
успокоительное	tranquilizer
болеутоляющее	painkiller
пирамидон/анальгин	types of aspirin
валидол	cardiac medicine
пластырь	bandaid
марля	gauze
спирт	distilled alcohol
перекись водорода	hydrogen peroxide
перелом	fracture
гипс	cast
пересадка	transplant
шунт, шунтирование	bypass

169

Environment

охра́на окружа́ющей среды	environmental protection
Госкомитет по природе	State Committee on Environmental Protection
Глоба́льный экологи́ческий фонд (ГЭФ)	Global Environment Facility (GEF)
вторичное использование, рекуперация, рециркуляция	recycling, recycled
загря́знение воды, воздуха	water, air pollution
отхо́ды	wastes
вы́ходы/выбросы	emissions
загрязни́тель	pollutant
свалка	dump
захороне́ние, дампинг	dumping
свалка мусора	landfill
токси́ческое вещество	toxic substance
загрязняющее вещество	pollutant
парнико́вый эффект	greenhouse effect
озо́нный слой	ozone layer
озо́нная дыра́	ozone hole
обезле́сивание	deforestation
опусты́нивание	desertification
за́суха	drought
наводнение	flooding
кисло́тные дожди	acid rain
соленость, засоление	salinity
щелочность	alkalinity
осадок, илы, шлак	sludge, slurry
осадки	sediment, precipitation
о́кись углеро́да	carbon monoxide
углеки́слый газ/двуокись углеро́да	carbon dioxide
углеворо́ды	hydrocarbons
способность к биологическому распаду	biodegradability
ископа́емое топливо	fossil fuel
Красная книга	list of endangered species
исчезающий вид	endangered species
переброска рек	diversion of flow of rivers
истощение	depletion
сток, отвод	runoff
уровень водосбора	catchment level
система очистки сточных вод	sewage system
запове́дник	preserve
водоём	reservoir
вечная мерзлота	permafrost
полихлори́рованные бифени́лы	polychlorinated biphenyls

Outer Space

КЛА (космио́ческий летательный аппара́т)	spacecraft
космический корабль	spaceship
неопознанный летающий объект (НЛО)	unidentified flying object (UFO)
космона́вт	astronaut, cosmonaut
космодро́м	space center
скафа́ндр	space suit
ста́ртовая площадка	launching pad
запускать	to launch

170

ракета-носитель	launch vehicle
ракета-ускоритель	booster rocket
ракетная техника	rocketry
многоступенчатая ракета	multistage rocket
прибóрная доска	instrument panel
система ручнóго управления	manual controls
полезный груз	payload
зонд	probe
дистанциóнное зондирование	remote sensing
пилотируемый	manned
беспилóтный	unmanned
центр управления полетом (ЦУП)	mission control
двигательно-тормознáя система	retro-rocket system
взлет	takeoff
ускорение	acceleration
вывести на орбиту	put into orbit
силы притяжéния	gravitational forces
перегрузка	stress
стыковка	docking
траектóрия спуска	descent trajectory
приземлéние	landing

Media

срéдства мáссовои информации (СМИ)	mass media
эфир	air (waves)
эфирное время	air time
пиковое время, время массового просмотра	prime time
передача	broadcast
передавать/транслировать	to broadcast
прямая передача	live broadcast
высокая разрешаемость	high definition
освещение	coverage (i.e. news)
оперативная сводка	situation report
телемóст	spacebridge
канал	channel
ОРТ (Общественное Российское Телевидение)	Russian State Television channel
реклама	commercials
викторина	quiz show
рóлик	roll-in
передáча по спутниковой связи	satellite broadcast
озвучивание	voiceover
монтаж	editing
звукооперáтор, аудиотехник	sound technician
диктор	announcer
ведущий	host, anchor

Art and Museums

выставка	exhibition
экспонáт	exhibit (item on display)
макéт	model
искусство	art
живопись	painting
прикладнóе искусство	applied art
изобразительное искусство	decorative art

худо́жник	painter, artist
скульптор	sculptor
рисунок	drawing
акварель	watercolor
масло (писать маслом)	oil painting
уголь	charcoal
гравюра	engraving, print
офорт	etching
роспись	mural, wall painting
пейзаж	landscape
натюрмо́рт	still life
холст, полотно́	canvas
сле́пок	cast, copy

Theater and Movies

представление	performance
постановка	production
спектакль	show
поставить пьесу	to put on, produce a play
постано́вщик	producer
режиссер	director
состав	cast
артисты	actors
Заслуженный артист	honored artist
Народный артист	people's artist
играть роль	to play a role
трактовка	interpretation
художник-декоратор	set designer
декорации	sets
суфле́р	prompter
дубле́р	understudy
стати́ст	extra
занавес	curtain
за́дник	backdrop
реквизиты/бутафо́рия	props
грим	makeup
репетиция, генера́льная репетиция	rehearsal/dress rehearsal
гриме́рная	actors' dressing rooms
люби́тельский/самодеятельный	amateur (productions)
гастроли	tour (of a theater company)
пьеса идет с аншлагом	the play is sold out
антракт	intermission
вызвать на бис	encores, curtain calls
театральная касса	box office
МХАТ (Московский художественный театр)	Moscow Art Theater
ТЮЗ (Театр юного зрителя)	children's theater
кукольный театр	puppet theater
зрители/публика	audience
лишний билет	an extra ticket
броня, бронь	reserved seats (retained by the theater and not available for immediate sale to public)
сдать пальто в гардероб	to check one's coat
номерок	coat check
билете́р	usher

172

ряд, место	row, seat
партéр	orchestra
амфитеатр	back of orchestra
бельэтаж	mezzanine/dress circle
балкон	first balcony
первый ярус	second balcony
дневной сеанс	matinee

Films

художественный фильм	feature film
полнометражный фильм	full-length film
коротко-/непóлнометражный фильм	short film
мультфильм (мультипликационный фильм)	cartoon
научно-популярный фильм	documentary, scientific documentary
кинохрóника/киножурнал	news film
двухсерийный фильм	two-part film
цветной	color
черно-белый	black and white
сценарист	script writer
сценарий	script
оператор	cameraman
директор картины	associate producer
(режиссер is the director, постанóвщик – producer)	
съемки	shooting, filming
сниматься в фильме	to be in a movie, to shoot a film
поставить по роману, фильм снят по роману…	based on (a novel by X)
кадр	shot, scene, still
просмотр	screening
сеанс	show
éкскурс в прошлое/ход назад	flashback
Кинотеатр повтóрного фильма	movie revival house
фильм идет в этом кинотеатре	The movie is playing/is being shown in that moviehouse/cinema.

Music

дирижёр	conductor
оркестр под управлением дирижёра…	the orchestra is conducted by…
эстрáдная мýзыка	popular music
эстрадный концерт	variety show
танцевальная музыка	dance music
траурная музыка	funeral, solemn music
партитýра	score
партия	part
исполнять партию	sing a (musical) role
подпевать	sing along with, join in a song
напевать	croon, hum
напев	tune, melody
припев	refrain
припевать	hum
хор	chorus, choir
сопрано	soprano
альт	alto
тенор (*мн.* тенорá)	tenor(s)

173

бас	bass
романс	(musical) romance, classical song
ансамбль	performing group, ensemble, company
настраивать (инструмент)	to tune an instrument
камерный оркестр	chamber orchestra
смычко́вые/стру́нные, духовные, медные, уда́рные иструменты	string, wind, brass, percussion instruments
скрипка	violin
виолонче́ль	cello
виола/альт	viola
контраба́с	double bass
флейта	flute
труба́	trombone
кларне́т	clarinet
гобо́й	oboe
фагот	bassoon
труба́	trumpet
валто́рна	French horn
барабан	drum
лита́вры	kettledrum
концерт	concerto (as well as concert)

Sports

спорт	sport(s) (singular and plural), athletics
соревнова́ния	competition
матч	match
состяза́ние	competition, meet
команда	team
сборная (страны)	national team
болеть за команду	to root for a team
боле́льщик	fan
любитель	fan, amateur (amateur vs. professional)
судья	referee
какой счет?	what's the score?
очко́	point
ничья́	tie score
матч законился вничью	the match ended in a tie
побить рекорд по	break a record in/for
промахнуться	miss (the net, basket, etc.)
тре́нер	coach
делать разминку	warm up
плавать кро́лем, бра́ссом	swim the crawl, breast stroke
теннис	tennis
настольный теннис	table tennis, ping-pong
подача	serve
удар слева, справа	forehand, backhand
эстафе́тный бег	relay race
врата́рь	goalie, goalkeeper
шайба	puck
бокс	boxing
борьба	wrestling
велоспорт	cycling
легкая атлетика	track and field
тяжелая атлетика	weightlifting

фехтова́ние	fencing
планери́зм	gliding
кросс	cross-country running
ке́ды, кроссо́вки	running shoes, sneakers
зае́зд	round, lap, heat
гре́бля	rowing
парусный спорт	sailing
лыжный спорт	skiing
фигу́рное катание	figure skating
като́к	rink
шахматы	chess
ход	move (in chess)
объявить шах	check
объявить/поставить мат	mate
ферзь	queen
ладья́	castle
конь	knight
слон	bishop
пе́шка	pawn
коло́да	deck (of cards)
тасова́ть	shuffle
сдавать	to deal
тре́фы	club
бу́бен, бубны	diamond
че́рвы	heart
пи́ки	spade
валет	jack/knave
дама	queen
король	king
туз	ace
джо́кер	joker

Hunting

Now that Russian hunting preserves and fishing facilities are opening up to foreigners the interpreter may suddenly find himself confronted by new quarries and bait…

охота на оленя, дичь, кабана́, лося, изюбра	hunting for deer, game, wild boar, elk, moose
куропа́тка	partridge
те́терев	grouse
пе́репел	quail
вспугнуть перепели́ный вы́водок	flush a covey of quail
браконьерство	poaching
е́герь	game warden
ягдта́ш	game bag
галифе́	hunting breeches
прима́нная птица	decoy
сидеть в заса́де	ambush an animal
загнать зве́ря в засаду	drive an animal to bay
бекаси́нник	snipeshot
крупная дробь	buckshot, coarse lead shot
карте́чь	case shot
ружьё	rifle
оптический прицел	telescopic sight
свежевать оле́ня, кабана́	gut and skin a deer, wild boar
чистить и потрошить рыбу	clean and gut fish

175

Fishing

Сегодня рыба клюёт. А вчера поймал такую ры́бину! Рыба рекордного размера. Сначала рыба клюнула нажи́вку, но не захвати́ла, и сорвалась с крючка́. Но потом опять подплыла, я нама́тывал ле́ску на кату́шку – и кончен бал.

The fish are biting today. Yesterday I caught a great one! A trophy-size fish. First the fish tugged at the bait, but didn't catch on it, and got away. Then I reeled in the line, and that was that.

У меня все, что нужно, вся осна́стка уди́льщика: у́дочка, ле́ска с поплавко́м, грузи́ло, крючо́к с поводко́м. Люблю спортивную рыбалку в открытом море, а также зимнюю рыбалку, или подледный лов. На льду реки или озера делается про́рубь (ло́мом или коловоро́том). Рыба ловится с помощью короткого удилища, в лу́нку опускается блесна, на прочной ле́ске. Опустив блесну́ на дно или на некоторую глубину, блесну́ «дергают» и рыба клюёт.

I have an angler's fishing tackle: rod, line with float, sink, hook with leader. I like deep-sea fishing, and also winter hole fishing, when you make a hole in the ice (using a crowbar or breast drill) and using a short rod you sink a spoon bait to the bottom, bouncing it on the bottom to attract fish, which come up for air and up into the pouch.

Также занимаюсь ловлей спи́ннингом на му́шку и ловлей форе́ли на суху́ю му́шку. Нужно забросить мушку как можно дальше: лучше всего забрасывать по ве́тру. Затем спи́ннинг ставится на тормоз и ле́ску дергают коротким рывко́м, имитируя живую прима́нку, и рыба хватает нажи́вку. Рыба должна хорошо сидеть на крючке, иначе она сорвется с крючка́. Для этого, после того, как рыба захватила и заглотила прима́нку, ее подсека́ют, резко дернув уди́лище, чтобы крючок хорошо зацепился (вонзился).

I also do wet fly fishing and dry trout fishing. You need to cast the fly as far as possible. It is best to cast downwind. You cast the fly with a reel brake and then pull at the line with a sharp tug, imitating a live lure, and the fish strikes the bait. The hook must sit well or the fish will get away. When the fish strikes you want to pull sharply to sink the hook, or the fish will get away.

В море ловить рыбу можно с лодки или ка́тера, стоящего на я́коре. До́нную рыбу ловят на влесну́, которую опускают на дно и поде́ргивают. Хорошо ловится камбала и все придо́нные выды рыб.

Хорошо тра́лить рыбу с медленно движущегося ка́тера. Снасть для трале́ния выглядит как о́стов зонтика без ручки. К концу и середине каждой спины кре́пится прима́нка в виде искусственной рыбки, из хвоста которой торчит крепкий крючок, всего 12-16 прима́нок на одном «зонтике.» Когда медленно движущийся ка́тер тянет – «тралит» – зонтик в воде, хищной жиру́ющей рыбе кажется, что плывет стайка ме́лочи и одна жадно нападает на нее.

Мне нравштся марли́нь, рыба-пару́с, меч-рыба, тарпо́н, форе́ль, осе́тр и щу́ка: ловлю и пресново́дную и морскую рыбу. У меня есть и кле́ти для ловли ома́ров, и бреде́нь: рыба ловится в мотне́. Покупаю рыболовные сна́сти и черве́й из пластмассы для наживки в магазине рыболо́вных принадлежностей около морской станции с причалами. Там все есть – и блесна́, и наживка, и рыболовные крючки́.

Salt-water fishing includes fishing from an anchored boat by bouncing the bait off the bottom for flounder, sole, and all bottom lying fish.

Fishing from a moving boat trolling is fun. There the tackle includes an umbrella secured to the end of a line, which is in the form of an umbrella carcass, with artificial lures secured to the ends and the middle of the spokes. In the water the umbrella with a dozen or so lures, trolled along or pulled by a slow moving boat, looks to the fish like a school of small fry, and they strike voraciously.

I like marlin, sailfish, swordfish, tarpon, trout, sturgeon, and pike; I catch fresh-water and salt-water fish. I have lobster pots (traps) and fishing nets; you catch the fish in the net's central sleeve. I buy my fishing tackle and plastic worms in a bait shop near a marina. They have everything, bait (artificial, live and dead), and fish hooks.

Some Fishy Expressions

нем как рыба	silent as the grave
плавать как рыба	swim like a fish
биться как рыба об лед	struggle desperately, pull the devil by the tail
чувствовать себя как рыба в воде	feel in one's element/totally at home, take to something like a duck to water
ни рыба ни мясо	neither fish nor fowl
ловить рыбку в мутной воде	fish in troubled waters
рыба гниет/тухнет с головы	the fish rots from the head down (trouble starts at the top)
напрашиваться на комплименты	to fish for compliments
что-то здесь не то/это дело плохо пахнет	something's fishy
это туфта́/выдумки	that's a fish story
это из другой оперы	that's another kettle of fish
безчувственный человек	he's a cold fish
не в своей стихии	like a fish out of water
мне не до этого	I have other fish to fry

ESCORTING DELEGATIONS
SELECTED VOCABULARY

Greetings

Здравствуйте, добрый день	Hello
Привет	Hi (informal)
Как дела?	How are you doing/how are you/how are things? (informal - what's up?)
Как жизнь? (разг.)	How's life?
Что нового/слышно?	How are things/you/what's up?
Хорошо/все в порядке/нормально/ничего/ не жалуюсь	Fine, just fine, great, OK
Плохи дела/плохо/неважно	Not so good (not so hot)/Not too well (in answer to how are you)/Could be better
Не ахти́ как	So-so
Лучше не спрашивай/хуже/некуда	Awful/Terrible/Don't ask
Рад вас приветствовать/видеть	I'm so glad/delighted to see you
Очень рад с вами познакомиться	(Very) pleased to meet you
Я приветствую вас от имени…	I welcome you on behalf of (our club, the Department of State, etc.)
Мы с вами уже знакомы	We've already met/been introduced
Сколько лет, сколько зим/тысячу лет не виделись	Haven't seen you in ages
Чем могу служить/быть полезен/помочь?	What can I do for you/How can I help you/be of assistance to you?
Какими судьбами/Как вы-то сюда попали?/ Кого я вижу!	What a surprise!(to see you here)/What brings you here/What are you doing here?
Хорошо, что вы пришли	I'm delighted/glad you've come
Ну, вот и вы!	At last!

Introductions

Давайте познакомимся	Let's introduce ourselves
Я хотел бы с вами познакомиться	I'd like to introduce myself
Моя фамилия Иванов	My name is Ivanov

А как Вас зовут?	And what's your first name?
Разрешите/позвольте вас познакомить	Allow me to/I'd like to introduce you to
Это…	This is…
Разрешите представить вас моему другу	I'd like to introduce you to/I'd like you to meet my friend X
Мне очень приятно/Я очень рад с вами познакомиться	Delighted/very pleased to meet you
Прошу любить и жаловать	He's my good friend/I hope/I'm sure you'll get along
Позвольте представиться	I'd like to/Allow me to introduce myself
Мы с вами уже час говорим, а еще не знакомы	We've been talking for an hour and haven't introduced ourselves/but still don't know your name
Вы ко мне?	Are you looking for me?/Do you want to talk to me?
Не вы ли руководитель (переводчик) группы?	Are you the group leader (interpreter)?

Meeting a visitor

Как вы устроились?	How's the hotel (room)?
Как долетели?	How was the flight?
Все нормально?	Is everything all right?
Какие пожелания?	What would you like (to do)?
Как семья, здоровье?	How's the family/How are you feeling?
Какие впечатления?	How do you like it here?
Ну как, выспались?	Did you get a good night's sleep/Are you rested?
Как добрались?	No trouble getting here?/Was the trip OK?
Не хотелось бы/не хочется ли вам…	Would you like to…
Можно вас попросить…	May I trouble/ask you…

Hotel registration

У вас номер заказан?	Do you have a reservation?
Обратитесь к администратору	Go see the manager
В какой гостинице вы остановились?	At what hotel are you staying?
Номер меня устраивает/не устраивает	The room is fine/won't do
Номер не убран	The room isn't made up
Заполните листок для гостей	Please fill out the registration blank
Номер с удобствами	Room and bath
Он уже выписался	He's already checked out
носильщик	porter, bellhop
камера хранения	luggage room

Telephone conversations

дозвониться	to get through to someone on the phone
рабочий номер	office number
домашний номер	home number
подойти к телефону	to answer/come to the phone
созвониться	to call each other
снять трубку	answer the phone
бросить трубку	hang up on someone/slam the phone
набрать номер	to dial a number
висеть на телефоне	to be stuck on hold
соединять	to connect
разъединять	to disconnect
коммутатор	switchboard

добавочный	extension
ждать гудка	to wait for a beep/dial tone
частые гудки	busy signal
неисправность телефона	out of order
сотовый телефон	cell phone
автоотве́тчик	answering machine
оставить запись/записаться на автоответчике	leave a message on an answering machine

*   *   *

Да/Я вас слушаю	Hello/Good morning/afternoon
Говорит Иванов/Вас беспокоит Иванов	This is Ivanov/Ivanov speaking/May I trouble you for a moment?
Я у телефона	Speaking
Позовите, пожалуйста, Иванова/Можно Иванова?	I'd like to/I need to speak to Ivanov/ May I speak to Ivanov?
Передайте, пожалуйста…	Please tell him/leave a message for him
Он *вышел*	He's stepped out/away from his desk/ for a moment
Он *ушел*	He's left/gone for the day/not here
Его нет	He's out
Вы ошиблись номером/Вы не туда попали	You've got a wrong number

Mail

отправитель	sender
адресат	addressee
обратный адрес	return address
авиапочта	airmail
заказно́е письмо	registered letter
бандероль	registered mail package
опускать/отправлять письмо	to mail/send a letter
почтовый ящик	mailbox
вы́емка писем	mailbox pickup
письмо идет два дня	the letter takes two days
до востребования	poste restante
главпочтамт	central post office
денежный перевод	money transfer/money order
открытка	postcard
наклеить марки	to stick on stamps
поздравительная открытка	greeting card
телеграфный бланк	form for a telegram
простая телеграмма	regular telegram
срочная телеграмма	urgent telegram
отправить/послать факс	to send a fax

Requests

Я прошу вас…	Please (do)…
Я хотел бы попросить вас.	I would like to ask you to…I should like to ask you to…
Вы не могли бы прийти завтра?	Could you manage to/find the time to come tomorrow?
Будьте добры, позвоните ему	Please/kindly/Be so kind as to call him
Не могу ли я вас попросить	Could I (possibly) ask you
Я предлагаю вам	I propose/suggest/offer
Вас не затруднит зайти к Иванову?	Could I ask you to go see Ivanov/Would you have the time to/be able to see Ivanov?

Хорошо было бы…	It would be nice to/I'd (really) like to…
Как вы смотрите на то, чтобы…	What would you think of/How would you like to…

Answers to requests

Хорошо, с удовольствием	Fine/With pleasure/I'd be delighted
Пожалуйста	Sure
Сделаю/будет сделано	I'll do it/Yes, of course
Давайте	Let's/Sure
Не беспокойтесь/Можете быть спокойны/ уверены	Absolutely/You can count on me/No question
Обязательно/конечно	Of course
Ладно	OK
Сейчас	Right away
Я–за!	Sure!/I'm for it!/Great idea!
Договорились	Fine/Agreed
Ну что же/пожалуй/почему бы и нет!	All right/Why not?/I guess so
Придется + infinitive	I guess I should/have to
Не могу/не в моих силах	I can't/I'm unable to
Что-то мне не хочется	I don't really feel like/want to
Что вы!	What!? Absolutely not!
Не может быть и речи!	Out of the question/No way
Вот еще! И не подумаю!	Forget it! No way!
Не приставай!	Get lost!
Очень нужно!	Whatever for!
Кому это надо!	What a bad idea! That's ridiculous!
Ну что вы…	That's all right/Now, now/Really
Ничего, пустяки́	Never mind/It doesn't matter/That's not important

Invitations—Suggestions

Приглашаю Вас на/ Хотелось бы Вас пригласить на…	I'd like to invite you to…
Приходите ко мне в гости	Come visit me/to my house/to see me
Заходите (когда-нибудь)	Do come see me sometime/We must get together (not a formal invitation)
Надо было бы пойти к профессору	It would be a good idea to/Ithink you should go the professor
Как вы относитесь к тому, чтобы пойти к…	How do you feel about/What about/Would you like to go/see…
Не пойти ли нам/Вы не хотите (К Иванову, в кино)	Would you like to go to(see)/What about going to (seeing) Mr. Ivanov, the movies
Входите, пожалуйста, раздевайтесь	Come in, let me take your coat (Not: get undressed!)
Что можно вам предложить/Чем вас угощать?	What would you like to eat (drink)/What may I offer you?

Schedule—Plans

Давайте обсудим программу вашего пребывания в нашем городе	Let's discuss your schedule in our city
У вас завтра (назначена) встреча с…	You've got an appointment tomorrow with…
Машину подадут к 8 часам	The car will pick you up at eight
Иванов зайдет за вами в 7	Ivanov will come by/pick you up/come to get you at 7
Вы будете предоставлены самому себе	You'll have some free time
Будет самостоя́тельный осмотр города	You can see the city/sightsee on your own
Остаток дня и вечер вы можете провести по своему усмотрению	The rest of the day and in the evening you are free/you have free time

У нас ничего не запланировано на завтра	We've left tomorrow free
Можно будет пройтись по магазинам, посетить музеи	You can go shopping or to a museum
Завтра мы осмотрим город	Tomorrow we'll tour the city
Вечером у нас банкет/прием/а ля фуршéт	This evening we have a formal dinner/reception/buffet
Поставьте чемодан за дверью в коридоре	Leave your suitcase outside the room/in the hall
Отъезд в 8:30	We're/You're leaving at 8:30/Departure is at 8:30
Автобус будет в 6, я подойду в 7	The bus will be there at 6 and I'll come/be there around 7
Нужно оформить/подтвердить ваш билет	We need to take care of/confirm your ticket

Agreement—Disagreement

Вы прáвы	Absolutely/Definitely/You're right
Это само собой разумеется	Of course/That's obvious/Absolutely/We take that for granted
Я не против	I agree/I'll go along with that
Допýстим	Possibly/Perhaps/That might be so
Не может быть!	Impossible!
Ничего подобного	Certainly not/nothing of the sort/kind/ absolutely not
Вряд ли	I doubt it/that's unlikely

Apologies

Извините	I'm sorry/excuse me
Простите	I'm very sorry/excuse me/pardon me
Виноват	Sorry/My fault
Я должен извиниться перед вами	I must apologize to you/I owe you an apology
Прошу извинения/прощения за	I apologize for/Please excuse me for
Не хотел вас обидеть	I didn't mean/want to offend you
Я оговорился	I slipped up/said the wrong thing/erred
Я причинил вам столько забот	I've been such a bother/caused you so much trouble/given you such headaches

Answers

Ничего, пожалуйста!	Not at all/Don't mention it/Forget it/Don't worry.
Это мелочь! Ничего страшного!	It's not worth worrying/bothering about/Don't give it another thought/That's peanuts/Forget it

Congratulations (See also "Flowers" section)

От всей души поздравляем вас с днем ждения	Our best wishes/We warmly congratulate you *on* (watch preposition!) your birthday
Поздравляем юбилярa/винóвника торжества	We congratulate the guest of honor/the birthday boy/our friend/colleague/the reason we are here/the man/woman who has brought us together
Поздравляем вас с избранием на пост председателя нашего комитета	We congratulate you on your election as chairman of our committee
Желаем вам всяческих успехов в вашей работе/в благородной деятельности	We wish you great/every/ success in your work/noble undertaking

Condolences - Sympathy

Я вам искренне соболéзную	You have my deepest sympathy
Разрешите выразить вам искренние соболéзнования	I should like to convey/express my deepest sympathy
Я тебе сочувствую	I feel for you

Farewells

До скорой встречи	See you soon/later (depending on if the next meeting is that afternoon or in a month)
Будьте здоровы	All the best/be well
Я с вами не прощаюсь/Мы еще увидимся	See you later
Кланяйтесь/привет всем	Regards to/my best to everyone
Счастливого пути!	Depending on context: I wish you much/every success Bon voyage
Желаем вам счастливого пути/легкой посадки на родной земле	Bon voyage, have a good/ safe trip/flight home
Пока	So long/ciao/bye
Ждем вас с ответным визитом	We'll be expecting you
Ну и теперь мы вас ждем в гости	Now it's your turn to visit us/We are waiting/ expecting your visit
Приезжайте к нам в страну!	Come visit us/our country!

Toasts

Most formal– and many informal – luncheons, dinners and banquets are accompanied by one or more toasts to the hosts, guests, success of their projects, Russian-American friendship, peace, grandchildren, football teams, etc. The interpreter is well advised to bring along a pad and pencil, as toasts are frequently so lengthy as to require consecutive interpretation. He should keep eye contact with the audience, though, as burying himself in his notes will also bury postprandial feelings and good cheer.

Я предлагаю тост за…Хочу предложить/ произнести тост за…	I propose a toast to.
Я хотел бы поднять бокал за/выпить за…	I raise my glass to…
Я поднимаю бокал за…	
Давайте выпьем за…	Let's drink to/Let's toast
вас	Here's to you
ваше здоровье	your health
ваши успехи	your success
хозяйку дома	our hostess
наших гостей	our guests
тех, кто в море	those who are not/cannot be here with us
мир и дружбу между нашими народами!	peace and friendship between/among (depending on how many people are involved) our peoples!
В добрый час!	To the success of (whatever project)/Good luck! (If seeing someone off)/All the best!
С днем рождения!	Happy Birthday!
До дна!	Bottoms up!
На посошок!	One for the road!

Answers to toasts

Благодарю/Спасибо за поздравления и добрые слова…	Thank you/I am grateful for/I appreciate/your congratulations and kind words
Я поднимаю мой бокал за гостеприимных организаторов нашей встречи…	And I wish to raise my glass to the hospitable organizers of our meeting/ conference…
…без которых наша встреча была бы невозможна/ой	who made our meeting possible/brought about our meeting/without whom our meeting would have been impossible

183

Мы хотели бы поблагодарить вас за внимание/за теплый/радушный прием/ за сердечные поздравления

We would like to thank you for your consideration/help/thoughtfulness/for the warm/friendly reception/welcome/for your heartfelt congratulations

Мы надеемся, что наши встречи будут содействовать делу/укреплению/ развитию дружеских связей

We hope that our meetings will advance/ promote/ further the development of/strengthening friendly contacts

От всего сердца/с благодарностью принимаем приглашение

We are most happy/delighted to accept/ We accept with gratitude your invitation

Sample Toasts

1. Господин министр, господин президент, дамы и господа!
Я хотел бы сначала от своего имени и от имени моей делегации сердечно поблагодарить Вас за приглашение на этот прием.

За прошедшие дни мы ощутили большую дружбу и сердечность и смогли убедиться в высоком уровне Ваших научных исследований. Мы приобрели много ценного опыта, который послужит стимулом для нашей работы.

Но самое большое впечатление произвели на нас ваши люди, благодаря трудолюбию, знаниям и умению которых Вы достигли больших успехов в строительстве Вашей страны.

Эти успехи стали возможными лишь потому, что Ваше правительство оказывает беспримерную поддержку науке и образованию. Мы хотели бы от всего сердца поздравить Вас с этими успехами.

Позвольте мне поднять бокал за нашу дальнейшую совместную работу (за наше сотрудничество).

1. Mr. Minister, Mr. President, ladies and gentlemen,
First of all, speaking personally and on behalf of my delegation, I should like to thank you most warmly/sincerely for the invitation to this reception.

In/during/over the past few days we have felt/received/experienced great friendship and warmth, and have seen for ourselves/gotten to know ("become convinced of" is awkward) the high/advanced/sophisticated level of your scientific research. We have gained much valuable experience/learned much which will stimulate/encourage our (own) work.

But we have been most/especially/particularly/above all impressed by your people/for it is their hard work/diligence/willingness to work, knowledge and skill which have led to/resulted in/enabled you to achieve great success in building your country/whose hard work… has led to…/and ("and" is a good device when interpreter does not know what is coming) their hard work which has led to great success in building your country.

Such success/achievements were possible only because of the exemplary manner in which your government supports science and education/because of the outstanding/unique/extraordinary/remarkable support given/shown by your government for science and education. We most warmly/sincerely congratulate you on these outstanding/remarkable achievements/successes.

Allow me to/Permit me to/I should like to raise my glass to/offer/make a toast to your health and to our further joint projects/work/successful cooperation/cooperative projects.

185

2. Уважаемый господин Генеральный секретарь! Дамы и господа!
Мы провели в этой стране пять прекрасных солнечных дней и притом не только в смысле погоды, но и в смысле сердечности и гостеприимства людей. Мы все тронуты этой дружбой, которая так щедро была проявлена к нам.

Наши беседы с Вами, г-н Генеральный секретарь, и Вашими коллегами, а также с многочисленными представителями всех слоев населения привели нас к лучшему пониманию идеалов и политики Вашей страны.
Хотя наше пребывание в Вашей стране было очень кратким, все же мы увидели, каких замечательных успехов добилась Ваша страна в науке, технике, промышленности и повышения благосостояния людей.

Дамы и господа!
От имени всех я благодарю за оказанное нам гостеприимство, а также за торжественный прием в этой стариной ратуше. Прошу Вас поднять бокал за здоровье Генерального секретаря, за дальнейшие научные успехи, за укрепление сотрудничества между нашими народами в духе гуманизма.[1]

2. Mr. General Secretary, ladies and gentlemen,
We have spent five wonderful sunny days in this country, sunny both literally and figuratively, because of the/ thanks to the warmth/cordial welcome and hospitality shown us/we have received ("of people" is awkward). We were all deeply touched/moved by your generous friendship/generous display of friendship/the generous friendship shown us.

Our talks with you, Mr. General Secretary, and with your colleagues, as well as with many people from all walks of life/ many different people ("representatives of all strata of the population" is awkward) have given/ provided us with a better understanding of the ideals and policies of your country. Although our stay in your country /here/in this land has been very brief/ short, we have seen/ were able to see what remarkable/outstanding progress your country has made/ success your country has achieved in science, technology, industry and raising the standard of living/improving the quality of people's lives.

Ladies and gentlemen:
On behalf of all of us I should like to thank you for your hospitality, and also for the elegant/impressive reception in this ancient town hall. I should like to ask you to raise your glasses/to join me in a toast to the health of the General Secretary, to further scientific success/ achievements, and to strengthening cooperation between our peoples in a constructive spirit/in a spirit of humanistic ideals ("in a spirit of humanism" is awkward).

ENDNOTES

Introduction

1. В.Н.Комиссаров, "Советское переводоведение на новом этапе". *Тетради переводчика*, No. 23 (1989), стр. 4.

2. Л.С. Бархударов, "Процесс перевода с лингвистической точки зрения" в книге *Лингвистика и методика в высшей школе* (Москва: Высшая школа, 1967), стр. 26.

3. Henri Charles Barik, "A Study of Simultaneous Interpretation," Diss., University of North Carolina at Chapel Hill 1969, p. 1.

4. Richard W. Brislin, ed., *Translation: Applications and Research* (New York: Gardner Press, 1976), p. 1.

5. Barik, *op. cit.,* p. 1. Or, "interpretation occurs whenever a message originating orally in one language is reformulated and retransmitted orally in a second language." R. Bruce W. Anderson, "Interpreter Roles and Interpretation Situations," in *Language Interpretation and Communication,* ed. David Gerver and H. Wallace Sinaiko (New York and London: Plenum Press, 1977), p. 218.

6. We will not deal here with machine translation. See Barry Hillenbrand, "Trying to Decipher Babel," *Time,* 24 July 1989, p. 62: "Machine translation is only to reduce the work involved in human translation. Machines have enormous trouble with syntax, and obviously cannot cope with intonation."

7. Brian Harris, "Prolegomenon to a Study of the Differences Between Teaching Translation and Teaching Interpreting," in *L'enseignement de l'interprétation et de la traduction,* ed. Jean Delisle (Ottawa: University of Ottawa Press, 1981), pp. 158-159.

8. *Ibid.,* p. 157.

9. Edmond Cary, *La traduction dans le monde moderne* (Geneva: Librairie de l'Université, 1956), p. 146.

10. Nearly all interpreters, including even those who know one of the various shorthand systems, take notes in the form of symbols—e.g., a drawing of a flag for "country," a question mark for "issue" or "problem," a frowning face for "disagreement," an arrow pointing left for "yesterday" and pointing right for "tomorrow." There is apparently a symbolic plane through which the shift occurs from one lexical system to another (cf. the theories of Vygotsky).

11. Gelii Chernov, a leading Soviet interpreter and scholar, gives this definition of simultaneous interpretation: "Синхронный перевод есть вид устного перевода (в отличие от всех видов письменного перевода с листа), осуществляемый переводчиком одновременно с получением речевого сообщения на ИЯ (исходный язык) (в отличие от последовательного перевода)." Г.В. Чернов, *Основы синхронного перевода* (Москва: Высшая школа, 1987), стр. 8.

12. As quoted in *Newsweek*, 14 December 1987, p. 9.

13. Doreen Mangan, "What's New in Language Translation: New Popularity as Markets Become More Global," *The New York Times,* 19 November 1989, p. F 15.

14. Brislin, *op. cit.,* p. 27.

15. Michael Kernan, "Voices in the Midst of History: The Summit Interpreters and Their Subtle, Indispensable Way with Words," *The Washington Post,* 7 December 1987, p. D 8.

16. Marjorie Smith, "My Turn: A Matter of Interpretation," *Newsweek,* 14 December 1987, p. 9.

17. *Ibid.,* p. 9.

18. Alain L. Sanders, "Libertad and Justicia For All," *Time,* 29 May 1989, p. 9.

19. Rep. Claudine Schneider in *Newsletter,* North East Conference on the Teaching of Foreign Languages, No. 26 (September 1989), p. 19.

20. Richard D. Lambert, "The National Foreign Language System," Occasional Papers (NFLC at the Johns Hopkins University: Washington, 1989), pp. 6-7.

21. See Daniel Gile, " An Overview of Conference Interpretation Research and Theory," in *Languages at Crossroads: Proceedings of the 29th Annual Conference,* American Translators Association, Seattle, Washington, 12-16 Oct. 1988 (Medford, N.J.: Learned Information, Inc., 1988), pp. 363-371.

22. Marianne Lederer, *La traduction simultanée: Fondements théoriques.* Diss. Université de Lille III, 1978 (Lille: Service de reproduction des thèses, 1980),   p. 19.

23. See D. Gerver, "A Psychological Approach to Simultaneous Interpretation," *Meta,* 20, No. 2 (1975), 119, and Gile, *Ibid.,* p. 366

24. Б.Н.Климзо, "О переводе некоторых отрицательных конструкций на английский язык." *Тетради переводчика,* No. 23 (1989), стр. 92.

25. *Soviet Translation into English. Summary of General Criticisms* (Moscow Foreign Languages Publishing House: 1952-56), quoted in Ю. Денисенко, "О некоторых приемах 'необусловленной' компрессии при переводе с русского языка на английский (на материалах переводческой печати)" в книге *Теория перевода и научные основы подготовки переводчиков: Материалы всесоюзной научной конференции, ч. 1* (Москва: МГПИИЯ им. Мориса Тореза, 1975), стр. 139.

26. *Moscow News,* English-language edition, 5 February 1989.

27. Г.И. Пядусова, *Пособие по переводу для лиц, говорящих на английском языке* (Москва: Русский язык, 1988).

28. E. Weintraub, M. Lederer, J. De Clarens, "Enseigner l'interprétation," *Etudes de linguistique appliquée,* 12 (October-November 1973), p. 121.

29. David Gerver, "Empirical Studies of Simultaneous Interpretation: A Review and a Model," in Brislin, *op. cit.,* p. 176.

30. See Barik, *op. cit.,* pp. 18-19 and 259-61, and Г.В. Чернов, *Теория и практика синхронного перевода* (Москва: Международные отношения, 1978), стр. 164-165.

31. Gerver, "Empirical Studies of Simultaneous Interpretation," *op. cit.,* p. 176, and R. Pinhas, "Les retombées scientifiques des opérations 'Apollo' sur l'interprétation simultanée," *La Linguistique,* 8 (1972), pp. 143-147.

32. Interview with Natalya Owens in *No Uncertain Terms,* FBIS, vol. 3, No. 4 (1988), 6.

33. А.Д. Швейцер, *Теория перевода: статус, проблемы, аспекты* (Москва: Наука, 1988), стр. 25-26.

34. Ю.М. Катцер, "К вопросу об основах методики обучения письменному переводу с русского языка на иностранный (английский) язык на переводческом факультете." *Вопросы теории и методики преподавания перевода.* Тезисы всесоюзной конференции 12-14 мая 1970 г., ч. II (Москва, 1970), стр. 125.

35. See TAALS Yearbook 1987 (Washington, D.C., 1987), p. 10.

36. Sanders, "Libertad and Justicia For All," p. 65.

37. Quoted in Kernan, "Voices in the Midst of History," p. 8.

38. Hilaire Belloc, *On Translation* (Oxford: The Clarendon Press, 1931), p. 20.

39. Georganne Weller, "Bilingualism and Interpretation: An Under-Exploited Field of Study for Research," in *Languages at Crossroads: Proceedings of the 29th Annual Conference, American Translators Association,* 1988, p. 409.

40. Т.Е. Воеводина, "Устный перевод в коммуникативном аспекте и его соотношение с другими видами перевода." *Тетради переводчика*, No. 20 (1983), стр. 67.

41. Henry Van Hoof, *Théorie et pratique de l'interprétation* (Munchen: Max Hueber Verlag, 1962), p. 63.

42. Philip Vellacott, "Translating Greek Tragedy," in *The Translator's Art: Essays in Honour of Betty Radice,* ed. William Radice and Barbara Reynolds (Middlesex: Penguin, 1987), p. 200.

43. Carol S. Fixman, "The Foreign Language Needs of US-Based Corporations," Occasional Papers (NFLC at the Johns Hopkins University: Washington, 1989), p. 13.

Part I. Practical Problems

Chapter I

1. For history of simultaneous interpretation see Г.В.Чернов, *Теория и практика синхронного перевода* (Москва: Международные отношения, 1978), стр. 3-8; Е. Гофман, "К истории синхронного перевода," *Тетради переводчика*, No. 1 (1963), стр. 21-26; Jean Herbert, "How Conference Interpreting Grew," in Gerver and Sinaiko, *op. cit.*, pp. 5-10; Henry Van Hoof, *Théorie et pratique de l'interprétation, op. cit.*, pp. 9-23; Patricia E. Longley, *Conference Interpreting* (London: Pitman, 1968), pp. 1-5.

2. Quoted by Михаил Кочетков, "Без тормозов и заднего хода," *Эхо планеты,* 14 июля 1988, стр. 38.

3. Гофман, "К истории синхронного перевода," стр. 20.

4. Чернов, *Теория и практика синхронного перевода*, стр. 5, and Н.Д. Чебурашкин, *Технический перевод в школе*, изд. 4-е (Москва: Просвещение, 1983), стр. 154-155. See also Vladimir Grebenschikov, "Traductions, théories et traducteurs en URSS," *Meta,* 12, No. 1 (1967), 3-8.

5. Гофман, *op. cit.*, p. 22.

6. А.Д. Швейцер, "К вопросу о более радикальной схеме синхронного перевода," *Тетради переводчика*, 4 (1967), стр. 84: "The use of relay inevitably results in less accuracy and a less full interpretation."

7. See Чебурашкин, стр. 155.

8. П.В. Палажченко, "О предварительной обработке текста синхронным переводчиком", *Тетради переводчика*, No. 18 (1981), стр. 89.

9. *Ibid.,* стр. 90.

10. Robert V. Ekvall, *Faithful Echo* (New York: Twayne, 1960), p. 69.

11. Constantin Andronikof, "Servitudes et grandeur de l'interprète," *Babel,* 1 (1962), p. 8; and Christiane de Morawitz, "Sur l'enseignement de l'interprétation de conférence," *Babel,* 3 (1966), p. 138.

12. C. Dostert, quoted in *Proceedings of the Washington Conference in International Communications* (typescript), 4 January 1956, p. 31.

13. А.Д. Швейцер, *Перевод и лингвистика* (Москва: Воениздат, 1973), стр. 63.

14. Andronikof, p. 138.

15. А.В. Садников, "Перевод как вид социального поведения". *Тетради переводчика,* No. 18 (1981), стр. 9.

16. Ekvall, *op. cit.,* pp. 70-71.

17. Т.В. Воеводина, "Устный перевод в коммуникативном аспекте и его соотношение с другими видами перевода". *Тетради переводчика,* No. 20 (1983), стр. 69.

18. Ekvall, p. 70.

19. Davis Clyde Snelling, *Interpretation: Theory vs. Practice,* Monograph No. 16 (Trieste: Scuola superiore de lingui moderni per interpreti e traddutori, 1983), p. 32.

20. E. Weintraub, "Enseigner l'interprétation," *Etudes de linguistique appliquée,* 12 (1973), p. 113.

21. *Ibid.,* p. 110.

22. Воеводина, *op. cit.,* p. 69.

23. D. Seleskovitch, "Interpretation, a Psychological Approach to Translating," in Brislin, pp. 98-99.

24. А.Ф. Ширяев, "Специализированные речевая деятельность (психолингвистическое исследование на материале синхронного перевода)". Автореферат диссертации (Москва, 1979), стр. 27.

25. See Barik, *op. cit.;* Чернов, *Теория и практика синхронного перевода;* F. Goldman-Eisler, "Segmentation of input in simultaneous interpretation," *Journal of Psycholinguistic Research,* 1 (1972a), pp. 127-140.

26. А.Ф. Ширяев, *Синхронный перевод* (Москва: Воениздат, 1979), стр. 78-79.

27. Р.К. Миньяр-Белоручев, "О некоторых особенностях аудирования при устном переводе" в книге *Смысловое восприятие речевого сообщения* (Москва: Наука, 1976), стр. 125.

28. See Barik; Чернов, *Теория и практика синхронного перевода* and *Основы синхронного перевода;* Goldman-Eisler; P.Oléron and H. Nampon, "Recherches sur la traduction simultanée," *Journal de psychologie normale et pathologique,* 1 (1965), pp. 73-94. Lederer *(La traduction simultanée: expérience et théorie* (Paris: Lettres Modernes/Minard 1981) criticizes Van Hoof's notion (Van Hoof, p. 139) that the interpreter tries to say as much as possible during the speaker's pauses, arguing that "Le plus souvent orateur et interprète parlent ensemble." (Lederer, p. 240).

29. Barik, p. 282; Gerver, "Empirical Studies of Simultaneous Interpretation: A Review and a Model," in Brislin, 172-174; Чернов, *Основы синхронного перевода,* стр. 38-54.

30. See Ширяев, Автореферат дисс., 23.

31. See Г.В. Чернов, *Теория и практика синхронного перевода,* стр. 53-70; *Основы*

190

синхронного перевода, 129-138. See also Gerver, "Empirical Studies of Simultaneous Interpretation," in Brislin, pp. 194-196.

32. Gerver, *Ibid.,* p. 194.

33. И.А. Зимняя, Г.В. Чернов. "К вопросу о роли вероятностного прогнозирования в процессе синхронного перевода." *Вопросы теории и методики преподавания перевода. Тезисы Всесоюзной конференции 12-14 мая 1970 г., ч. 1* (Москва: МГПИИЯ им. Мориса Тореза, 1970), стр. 112-113.

34. Чернов, *Основы синхронного перевода,* стр. 187.

35. See Wolfram Wiss, "Syntactic Anticipation in German-English Simultaneous Interpreting," in Gerver and Sinaiko, pp. 343-352.

36. Henri Van Hoof, *Théorie et pratique de l'interprétation, op. cit.,* p. 66.

37. А.В. Садников, "Перевод как вид социального поведения". *Тетради переводчика,* No. 18 (1981), стр. 8.

38. А.Е. Мосьяков, "Использование фразеологии в синхронном переводе". *Вопросы теории перевода: сборник научных трудов,* вып. 127 (1978), стр. 135.

39. Henri Barik, "A description of various types of omissions, additions, and errors encountered in simultaneous interpretation," *Meta,* 16 (1971), 119-128; and Barik, diss., *op. cit.,* pp. 85-90.

40. Ekvall, p. 104.

41. See *Перевод: Средство взаимного сближения народов* (Москва: Прогресс, 1987), стр. 122.

42. See Barik, diss., p. 269.

43. П.В. Палажченко, "О предварительной обработке текста синхронным переводчиком", *Тетради переводчика,* 18 (1981), стр. 92.

44. See Danica Seleskovitch, *L'interprète dans les conférences internationales* (Paris: Lettres Modernes/Minard, 1968), pp. 50-51.

45. See B.V. Bratus et al., *Russian Word-Collocations* (Moscow: Russian Language Publishers, 1979).

46. Danica Seleskovitch, "Language and Cognition," in Gerver and Sinaiko, p. 333.

47. Danica Seleskovitch, "Interpretation, A Psychological Approach to Translating," in Brislin, p. 92.

48. Danica Seleskovitch, *Langage, langue et mémoire* (Paris: Lettres Modernes/ Minard, 1975), p. 41.

49. Н. С. Стрелкова, *Практическая стилистика английского языка и стилистическое редактирование переводов, ч. 3* (Москва: МГПИИЯ, 1982), стр. 20-21.

50. See *Ibid.,* p. 26.

51. *Ibid.,* p. 9.

52. All examples are from the English-language edition of *Moscow News,* 5 February 1989.

53. Stephanie Van Reigersberg, quoted in Kernan, "Voices in the Midst of History," *The Washington Post,* 7 December 1987, p. D 8.

54. George A. Miller, "The Magic Number 7 plus or minus 2: some limits on our capacity for processing information," *Psychological Review,* 63, No. 2 (1956), p. 95.

55. See Seleskovitch, "Interpretation: a Psychological Approach to Translating," in Brislin, p. 111; David Gerver, "Empirical Studies of Simultaneous Interpretation: A Review and a Model," in Brislin, p. 198; Г.В; Чернов, *Основы синхронного перевода*, стр. 19; В.Н. Комиссаров, "Советское переводоведение на новом этапе", *Тетради переводчика*, No. 23 (1989), стр. 18-20.

Chapter II

1. Ekvall, p. 104.

2. А.Ф. Ширяев, "О некоторых лингвистических особенностях функциональной системы синхронного перевода," *Тетради переводчика*, No. 19 (1982), стр. 79-84.

3. Sergio Viaggio, "Teaching Beginners the Blessings of Abstracting (and how to save a few lives in the process)," unpublished paper, ATA 1989 Conference, Washington, D.C.

4. А.Д. Швейцер, *Перевод и лингвистика* (Москва: Воениздат, 1973), стр. 126.

5. Т.Г. Сейдова, "Выбор эквивалента семантически неполных атрибутивных словосочетаний при переводе с английского языка на русский," *Тетради переводчика*, No. 11 (1974), стр. 59-61.

6. А.Ф. Ширяев, "О некоторых лингвистических особенностях," стр. 82.

7. Л.С. Бархударов, *Язык и перевод* (Москва: Международные отношения, 1975), стр. 222.

8. See С.Я. Шмаков, "Язык советских газет глазами англичан (по поводу учебного пособия Р. Генри и К. Янг)", *Тетради переводчика*, No. 23 (1989), стр. 172-173.

9. Н. С. Стрелкова, *Учебное пособие по практической стилистике английского языка и стилистическому редактированию перевода* (Москва: МГПИИЯ, 1984) , стр. 19-21.

10. See Р.К. Миньяр-Белоручев, *Общая теория перевода и устный перевод* (Москва: Воениздат, 1980), 105.

11. *Ibid.*, p. 106.

12. Бархударов, *Язык и перевод*, стр. 214.

13. See Я.И. Рецкер, *Теория перевода и переводческая практика* (Москва: Международные отношения, 1974), стр. 48-53; А.Д. Швейцер, *Теория перевода* (Москва: Наука, 1988), стр. 123-126; В.Н. Комиссаров, Я.И. Рецкер, В.И. Тархов, *Пособие по переводу с английского языка на русский*, ч. II (Москва: Высшая школа, 1965), Л.С. Бархударов, Я.И. Рецкер; *Курс лекций по теории перевода* (Москва: МГПИИЯ им. Мориса Тореза, 1968), стр. 55.

14. Б.Н. Климзо, "О переводе некоторых отрицательных конструкций на английский язык", *Тетради переводчика*, No. 23 (1989), стр. 101-102.

15. *Translation: Theory and Practice* (Tashkent: Ukituvchi, 1989), pp. 20-21; Комиссаров, Рецкер, Тархов, *Пособие по переводу с русского языка на английский*, стр. 34-37; G.G. Yudina, *Improve Interpreting Skills* (Москва: Международные отношения, 1976), pp. 95-96; А.Д. Швейцер, *Теория перевода*, стр. 134-35.

16. Yudina, *Improve Interpreting Skills,* pp. 74-75.

17. Швейцер, *Теория перевода*, стр. 85-86, 125-126; *Translation: Theory and Practice*, p. 29.

18. Швейцер, стр. 82-84.

19. *Ibid.*, стр. 129.

Chapter III

1. Quoted in Сергей Влахов, Сидер Флорин, *Непереводимое в переводе*, изд. 2-ое (Москва: Высшая школа, 1986), стр. 154.

2. Quoted by Roman Jakobson, "On Linguistic Aspects of Translation," in *On Translation,* ed. Reuben A. Brower (New York: Oxford University Press, 1966), p. 234.

3. *Ibid.,* pp. 235-236.

4. *Ibid.,* p. 236.

5. See J.C. Catford, *A Linguistic Theory of Translation* (Leiden, 1969), pp. 96-98.

6. Ю.М. Кацер, "К вопросу об основах методики обучения письменному переводу с русского языка на иностранный (английский) язык на переводческом факультете." *Вопросы теории и методики преподавания перевода. Тезисы Всесоюзной конференции 12-14 мая 1970 г., ч. II* (Москва, 1970), стр. 122-123; and Швейцер, *Теория перевода,* стр. 12.

7. These examples are taken from the "Donahue in Russia" (January, 1987) television shows for which the author interpreted.

8. See Влахов, Флорин, стр. 55, and *Translation: Theory and Practice* (Tashkent), pp. 6-10.

9. See Швейцер, *Теория перевода,* стр. 20, 61.

10. Richard Lourie and Aleksei Mikhailov, "Why You'll Never Have Fun in Russian," *The New York Times Book Review,* 18 June 1989, p. 38.

11. Carol E. Fixman, "The Foreign Language Needs of US-based Corporations," Occasional Papers (NFLC at the Johns Hopkins University: Washington, 1989), p. 2.

12. Швейцер, *Теория перевода,* стр. 8, 14.

13. Richard Brislin in *Translation: Applications and Research,* ed. Brislin, p. 35.

14. Helmut Morsbuch, "Words Are Not Enough: Reading through the lines in Japanese communication," *Japan Society Newsletter,* XXXVI, No. 6 (March 1989), 3.

15. Edmund S. Glenn, "Semantic Difficulties in International Communication," in *The Use and Misuse of Language,* ed. S.I. Hayakawa (Greenwich, Connecticut: Fawcett Publications, 1962), pp. 47-48.

16. *Ibid.,* p. 63.

17. See А.Д. Швейцер, "Социологические основы теории перевода", *Вопросы языкознания* No. 5 (1985), стр. 18-20.

18. See R. Bruce W. Anderson, "Perspectives on the Role of Interpreter," in Brislin, pp. 208-227, and Georganne Weller, "Bilingualism and Interpretation: An Under-Exploited Field of Study for Research," in *Languages at Crossroads: Proceedings of the 29th Annual Conference,* ATA, 1988, pp. 407-413.

19. Anderson, p. 215.

20. Н.С. Стрелкова. *Практическая стилистика английского языка и стилистическое редактирование переводов,* ч. III (Москва: МГПИИЯ, 1982), стр. 22.

21. Л.Т. Микулин, "Заметки о калькировании с русского языка на английский", *Тетради переводчика,* No. 15 (1978), стр. 63.

22. Стрелкова, *Практическая стилистика,* ч. 3, 1982, стр. 50.

23. *Ibid.,* стр. 44, and Стрелкова, *Учебное пособие по практической стилистике,* 1984, стр. 32.

24. Г.В. Чернов, "Вопросы перевода русской безэквивалентной лексики ("советских реалий") на английский язык на материалах переводов советской публицистики". Кандидатская диссертация (Москва: НГПИИЯ, 1958).

25. Стрелкова, *Практическая стилистика*, ч. 3, 1982, стр. 51.

26. Л.А. Черняховская, *Перевод и смысловая структура* (Москва: Международные отношения, 1976), стр. 241-248.

27. *Ibid.*, стр. 241-248. English translations mine.

28. Examples are from *Англо-русский и русско-английский словарь "ложных друзей переводчика"* под ред. В.В. Акуленко (Москва: Советская энциклопедия, 1969); Е.К. Попова, *Техника перевода с английского языка на русский* (Ленинград: ЛГУ, 1959); С.К. Шмаков, "Язык советских газет глазами англичан (по поводу учебного пособия Р. Генри и К. Янг)", *Тетради переводчика*, No. 23 (1989), стр. 174; and the author's personal experience.

Chapter IV

1. *Moscow News*, English-language edition, 5 February 1989.

2. А.Д. Швейцер, *Теория перевода*, стр. 198; and Стрелкова, *Учебное пособие по практической стилистике*, 1984, стр. 34.

3. Стрелкова, *Практическая стилистика английского языка*, *op. cit.*, стр. 51.

4. The author is grateful to Vadim Mil'shtein of INION of the Russian Academy of Sciences for some of these examples.

5. Many of the political terminology examples have been adapted or condensed from published UN documents and the Russian press. Changes have been made for linguistic and space reasons.

6. T. Appich, "Interlocution or Circumlocution?" *No Uncertain Terms*, FBIS, vol. 4, No. 3 (1989), 41.

7. Susan Sontag, *Illness as Metaphor and AIDS and its Metaphors* (New York: Doubleday, Anchor Books, 1989), pp. 64-65.

8. *Ibid.*, p. 97.

9. *Проблемы обучения переводу английского языка* (Москва: МГПИИЯ, 1982), вып. 203, *Сборник научных трудов*, стр. 18-19, and С.М. Шмаков, "Язык советских газет глазами англичан", *Тетради переводчика*, No. 23 (1989), стр. 170-174.

10. I am grateful to my colleague Donald Lineburgh of the United Nations for pointing this out.

11. "Neutralization" of a text should not alter its basic tone and style. The suggestions made for rendering one paragraph in Проблемы обучения переводу английского языка, *op. cit.*, in the interests of idiom—and perhaps of not ruffling too many western feathers—emasculate the text:

"В последнее время буржуазная пресса, специализирующаяся на антисоветских измышлениях подрывного характера, подняла новую шумиху с целью бросить тень на взаимоотношения братских социалистических стран".

"The Western press that makes subversive anti-Soviet propaganda its business has launched yet another campaign to put relations between Socialist countries in a bad light. (pp. 108-109)."

Condensation and neutralization of a text do not justify such radical stylistic alterations.

12. Стрелкова, *Учебное пособие по практической стилистике*, 1984, стр. 22.

13. Стрелкова, *Практическая стилистика английского языка*, ч. 3, 1982, стр. 46.

14. *Ibid.,* стр. 46.

15. Г.И. Пядусова, *Пособие по переводу для лиц, говорящих на английском языке* (Москва: Русский язык, 1988), стр. 56.

16. *Moscow News,* English-language edition, 5 February 1989.

17. Стрелкова, *Учебное пособие по практической стилистике*, 1984, стр. 24-25.

18. *Moscow News,* English-language edition, 5 February 1989.

19. *Ibid.*

20. Стрелкова, *Учебное пособие по практической стилистике*, 1984, стр. 34, 51.

21. *Moscow News, op. cit.*

22. Стрелкова, *Практическая стилистика английского языка*, ч. 3, 1982, стр. 50.

23. Стрелкова, *Учебное пособие по практической стилистике*, 1984, стр. 24.

24. *Ibid.,* стр. 24.

25. *Moscow News, op. cit.*

26. *Time,* 15 May 1989, p. 2.

27. Brand Frents, "Letter to the Editor," *No Uncertain Terms,* FBIS, vol. 4, No. 3 (1989), 44.

Chapter V

1. *Moscow News,* English-language edition, 5 February 1989, and Пядусова, *Пособие по переводу для лиц, говорящих на английском языке,* стр. 17.

2. Е. Земская, *Русская разговорная речь: Лингвистический анализ и проблемы обучения* (Москва: Русский язык, (1987), стр. 177.

3. G.G. Yudina, *Improve Interpreting Skills* (Москва: Международные отношения, 1976), p. 13.

4. On conditionals see А.М. Егорова, *Теория и практика перевода экономических текстов с английского языка на русский* (Москва: Международные отношения, 1974), стр. 107-109.

5. Земская, *Русская разговорная речь,* стр. 87-88.

6. Some of the following examples of tense translation are adapted from I. Pulkina and E. Zakhava-Nekrasova, *Russian: A Practical Grammar with Exercises,* 2nd ed. (Moscow: Russky Yazyk, 1974), pp. 359-363.

7. Земская, стр. 89.

8. Some of the examples of *чтобы* constructions have been adapted from: Л.С. Бархударов, *Язык и перевод* (Москва: Международные отношения, 1975); Pulkina, *op. cit.;* F.M. Borras and R.F. Christian, *Russian Syntax* (Oxford: Oxford University Press, 1959); and V.S. Belevitskaya-Khalizeva, *Exercises in Russian Syntax: The Compound Sentence* (Moscow: Foreign Languages Publishing House, n.d.).

9. J.C. Catford, *A Linguistic Theory of Translation* (Oxford: Oxford University Press, 1965), p. 75.

10. Charles E. Townsend, "Conative Verbs in Russian," *Russian Language Journal,* XLIII, Nos. 145-146 (1989), p. 13.

11. *Ibid.,* pp. 16-19.

12. *Ibid.,* p. 15.

13. Бархударов, стр. 198.

14. Н.М. Лариохина, *Вопросы синтаксиса научного стиля речи* (Москва: Русский язык, 1969), стр. 63.

15. The Russian examples here are from Ю. Катцер, А. Кунин, "Перевод причастий с русского языка на английский", *Тетради переводчика,* No. 1 (1963), стр. 78-83.

16. See *No Uncertain Terms,* FBIS, vol. 4, No. 2 (1989), 10.

17. *Moscow News,* English-language edition, 5 February 1989.

18. See А.Д. Швейцер, *Теория перевода,* стр. 119.

19. See А.Д. Швейцер, "К вопросу об анализе грамматических явлений при переводе", *Тетради переводчика,* No. 1 (1963), стр. 8-11.

20. See Richard Schupbach, "On Technical Russian and the Teaching Thereof," *SEEJ,* 32, No. 3 (1988), p. 450.

21. See the excellent article by Ю. Денисенко, "О некоторых проблемах выбора слова в русско-английском переводе", *Тетради переводчика* № 8 (1971), стр. 23-36. Several examples from this article are cited here.

22. *Ibid.,* стр. 35.

Chapter VI

1. Н.С. Стрелкова, *Учебное пособие по практической стилистике английского языка и стилистическому редактированию перевода,* 1984, стр. 34.

2. The author is grateful to Kibbe Fitzpatrick, a retired United Nations interpreter, for emphasizing this point.

3. Т. Левицкая, А. Фитерман, "О некоторых способах выражения эмфазы в английском языке", *Тетради переводчика,* No. 9 (1972), стр. 40.

4. F.M. Borras and R.F. Christian, *Russian Syntax* (Oxford: Oxford University Press, 1959), p. 247.

5. *Ibid.,* p. 249.

Chapter VII

1. Н.С. Стрелкова, *Учебное пособие по практической стилистике английского языка и стилистическому редактированию перевода,* 1984, стр. 49.

2. See Т. Левицкая, А. Фитерман, "О некоторых способах выражения эмфазы в английском языке", *Тетради переводчика,* No. 9 (1972), стр. 43.

3. Б.Н. Климзо, "О переводе некоторых отрицательных конструкций на английский язык", *Тетради переводчика,* No. 23 (1989), стр. 96.

Chapter VIII

1. See Andrzej Kopczynski, *Conference Interpreting: some linguistic and communication problems* (Poznan: UAM, 1980).

2. Some of the Russian examples in this chapter are taken or adapted from: Е.А. Брызгунова, *Звуки и интонация русской речи* (Москва: Русский язык, 1977); И.Л. Муханова, *Интонация в русской диалогической речи* (Москва: Русский язык, 1987); Е.А. Земская, *Русская разговорная речь: лингвистический анализ и проблемы обучения* (Москва: Русский язык, 1986).

3. Брызгунова, 214.

4. Л.А. Черняховская, *Перевод и смысловая структура* (Москва: Международные отношения, 1976), стр. 76-77.

5. F.M. Borras and R.F. Christian, *Russian Syntax* (Oxford: Oxford University Press, 1959) pp. 388-89.

6. See Л.С. Бархударов, *Язык и перевод* (Москва: Международные отношения, 1975), стр. 208-209.

7. Alan J. Cienki, *Spatial Cognition and the Semantics of Prepositions in English, Polish, and Russian,* Slavistische Beitrage, 237 (Munchen: Otto Sagner, 1989), pp. 15-18.

8. *Ibid.,* pp. 90-91.

9. *Ibid.,* p. 119.

10. For these and other examples see Frank J. Miller, *A Handbook of Russian Prepositions* (Newburyport MA, Focus/R. Pullins Company, 1989); Terence Wade, *Prepositions in Modern Russian* (South Carolina: University of Durham, 1983); and I. Pulkina and E. Zakhava-Nekrasova, *Russian: A Practical Grammar with Exercises,* 2nd ed. (Moscow: Russky Yazyk, 1974).

11. See Cienki, p. 99.

12. See Муханова, *Интонация в русской диалогической речи.*

13. The use of intonation in English and Russian with the particle -то is discussed in Joseph Lake's paper, "The Particle -то and Intonation in English and Russian," (Joseph Lake: University of Massachusetts; unpublished paper, AATSEEL National Conference, Washington, D.C., December 1989).

14. See Lake, Borras and Christian, pp. 239-246, Земская, 71-77.

15. See Брызгунова, стр. 155-156.

16. Т. Левицкая, А. Фитерман, "О некоторых способах выражения эмфазы в английском языке", *Тетради переводчика,* No. 9 (1972), стр. 36.

Chapter IX

1. А.Ф. Ширяев, "Специализированная речевая деятельность (психоаналитическое исследование на материале синхронного перевода), Автореферат дисс. (Москва, 1979), стр. 27.

2. See George A. Miller, "The Magical Number 7 plus or minus 2: some limits on our capacity for processing information," *Psychological Review,* 63, No. 2 (1956), pp. 81-97.

3. Е.Н. Филиппов. "Опыт составления лабораторных работ по устному переводу" в книге *Учебно-методические разработки к курсу теории перевода* (Москва: МГПИИЯ им. Мориса Тореза, 1972), стр. 170.

4. П.Р. Палажченко, "О предварительной обработке текста синхронным переводчиком", *Тетради переводчика*, No. 18 (1981), стр. 90.

5. Т.В. Воеводина, "Устный перевод в коммуникативном аспекте и его соотношение с другими видами перевода", *Тетради переводчика*, No. 20 (1983), стр. 74.

6. *Ibid.,* стр. 4.

7. Brian Harris, "Prolegomenon to a Study of the Differences between Teaching Translation and Teaching Interpreting," in *L'enseignement de l'interprétation et de la traduction,* Jean Delisle, ed. (Ottawa: University of Ottawa Press, 1981), p. 157.

8. For these uses of *приходится* see G.G. Yudina, *Improve Interpreting Skills* (Москва: Международные отношения, 1976), p. 13, and А.М. Егорова, *Теория и практика перевода экономических текстов с английского языка на русский* (Москва: Международные отношения, 1974), стр. 41.

9. Daniel Gile, "An Overview of Conference Interpretation Research and Theory," in *Languages at Crossroads: Proceedings of the 29th Annual Conference,* ATA, 1988, p. 367.

10. Палажченко, стр. 90.

11. Воеводина, стр. 74.

12. Г.В. Чернов. *Теория и практика синхронного перевода* (Москва: Международные отношения, 1978), стр. 184.

13. A good dictionary of abbreviations is invaluable. See *Словарь сокращений русского языка (Москва: Русский язык,* 1977). See also S. Pyatetskaia, *Introducing Russian Newspapers* (Moscow: Russky Yazyk, 1974), pp. 222-224.

Chapter X

1. John Glemet, quoted in David Gerver, "Empirical Studies of Simultaneous Interpretation: A Review and a Model," *Translation: Applications and Research,* ed. Richard W. Brislin (New York: Gardner Press, 1976), p. 168.

2. Quoted in George H. Hanna and Julius M. Katzer, "The Translation of Russian," in *МГПИИЯ им. Мориса Тореза: Конференция по вопросам и методике преподавания перевода* (Москва: МГПИИЯ им. Мориса Тореза, 1964), стр. 59.

3. Л.А. Черняховская, *Перевод и смысловая структура* (Москва: Международные отношения, 1976), стр. 5.

4. *Moscow News,* English-language edition, 5 February 1989.

5. Черняховская, 65.

6. Hanna and Katzer, p. 60.

7. T.G. Bever, "Perceptions, Thought and Language," in *Language Comprehension and the Acquisition of Knowledge,* ed. John B. Carroll and Ray O. Freedle (Washington, D.C.: V.W. Winston and Sons, 1972), p. 100.

A striking example of how syntactic differences can impede communication is provided by Japanese and English ordering of sentences and concepts:

"When Japanese read Chinese literature we need signs to change the word order, while Chinese can simply read from beginning to end and understand the sentence at once. English is like Chinese in this way. This means that the American thought processes follow a different order from ours. And so, no matter how excellent the interpreter, a Japanese will not be able to understand an American by following the order of Japanese thought processes. Regrettably, when it comes to putting our message across, the order of our thoughts puts us in a minority in the world. If we don't communicate with Westerners in an order they grasp, we cannot be understood."

Morita Akio and Ishihara Shintaro, *The Japan that Can't Say 'No': The Card for a New US-Japan Relationship.* Quoted by Ian Buruma in his review in *The New York Review of Books,* 7 December 1989, p. 20.

8. This chapter deals with practical problems of Russian syntax rather than with theory. For background material see Черняховская, *op. cit.;* И.И. Ковтунова, *Современный русский язык: Порядок слов и актуальное членение предложения* (Москва: Просвещение, 1976); O. Krylova and S. Khavronina, *Word Order in Russian,* 2nd ed., revised (Moscow: Russky Yazyk, 1988); Н.М. Лариохина, *Вопросы синтаксиса научного стиля речи,* 1979); А.Д. Швейцер, *Теория перевода* (Москва: Наука, 1988); Е.А. Земская, *Русская разговорная речь: лингвистический анализ и проблемы обучения* (Москва: Русский язык, 1987).

9. Richard Schupbach, "On Technical Russian and the Teaching Thereof," *SEEJ,* 32, No. 3 (1988), p. 448.

10. See Л.Г. Нечаев, "К проблеме вариативности актуального членения при переводе, *Тетради переводчика,* No 23 (1989), стр. 54-55.

11. See Krylova and Khavronina, p. 8.

12. *Ibid.,* pp. 41-45.

13. *Ibid.,* p. 47.

14. Г.В. Чернов, *Основы синхронного перевода* (Москва: Высшая школа, 1987), стр. 221.

15. For a detailed discussion of Russian-English functional sentence perspective see Черняховская and Krylova and Khavronina.

16. Marjorie Smith, "A Matter of Interpretation," *Newsweek,* 14 December 1987, p. 9.

17. See Krylova and Khavronina, pp. 72-80; Ковтунова, 105-107; Черняховская, 175.

18. For discussion of this type of sentence see А.Д. Швейцер, "Социологические основы теории перевода", *Вопросы языкознания,* No. 5 (1985), стр. 20-21.

19. А.Д. Швейцер, *Теория перевода,* стр. 142-144.

20. О. Мешков, "Об одном типе переводческих соответствий", *Тетради переводчика,* No. 9 (1972), стр. 48.

21. See Г. Разенко, Р. Решетилов, "Способы передачи русских односоставных предложений на английский язык", *Тетради переводчика,* No. 3 (1966), стр. 78-80; Л.С. Бархударов, Я.И. Рецкер, *Курс лекций по теории перевода* (Москва: МГПИИЯ, 1968), стр. 52-54; Ю. Катцер, А. Кунин, *Письменный перевод с русского языка на английский* (Москва: Высшая школа, 1964), стр. 25-41; А.Д. Швейцер, *Теория перевода,* стр. 118-123

22. See Разенко, Решетилов, стр. 77-78.

23. Черняховская, стр. 146.

24. See Земская, *Русская разговорная речь,* 148-160.

25. *Ibid.,* стр. 160.

26. Бархударов, Рецкер, *Курс лекций по теории перевода, стр. 52-58.*

27. See Разенко, Решетилов, стр. 80, and О. Мешков, "Об одном типе переводческих соответствий," *Тетради переводчика*, No. 9 (1972), стр. 48-49.

28. See Мешков, *Ibid.,* стр. 47-49.

29. See Черняховская, 168-69 et al.

30. Ю. Катцер, А. Кунин, *Письменный перевод с русского языка на английский*, стр. 25-26.

31. *Moscow News,* English-language edition, 5 February 1989.

32. Черняховская. 72.

33. *No Uncertain Terms,* FBIS, vol. 4, No. 2 (1989), 10.

34. See Чернов, *Основы синхронного перевода*, 218.

35. *Moscow News, op. cit.*

36. Borras and Christian, *Russian Syntax,* pp. 168-169.

37. *Ibid.,* pp. 169-172.

38. Черняховская, стр. 217, and Borras and Christian, p. 259.

Chapter XI

1. For a discussion of *функциональные стили* see Д.Е. Розенталь, *Практическая стилистика русского языка*, изд. 2-е (Москва: Высшая школа, 1968), стр. 10-19; Д.Е. Розенталь, М.А. Теленкова, *Практическая стилистика русского языка* (Москва: Прогресс, 1972), стр. 19-51; L.A. Kiseleva et al., *A Practical Handbook of Russian Style* (Moscow: Progress Publishers, n.d.), pp. 15-24; Л.С. Васильева, *Стилистический анализ художественного произведения* (Москва: МГУ, 1966).

2. А.В. Садиков, "Перевод как вид социального поведения", *Тетради переводчика* No. 18 (1981), стр. 10.

3. See Е.А. Земская, *Русская разговорная речь: лингвистический анализ и проблемы обучения* (Москва: Русский язык, 1987), стр. 17.

4. *Ibid.,* стр. 143-145, 170-176.

5. See А.В. Швейцер, *Теория перевода*, стр. 199-204; and Ю.А. Денисенко, "О некоторых приемах "обусловленной" компрессии при переводе с русского языка на английский (на материалах периодической печати)" в книге *Теория перевода и научные основы подготовки переводчиков: Материалы научной конференции*, ч. 1 (Москва: МГПИИЯ им. Мориса Тореза, 1975), стр. 141.

6. See Швейцер, 200-203. He fails to see, however, that "to scrap" is far too colloquial for the language of disarmament.

7. See Чернов, *Основы синхронного перевода*, 181-183.

8. Н.С. Стрелкова, *Ключи для пособия по практической стилистике и стилистическому редактированию перевода* (Москва: МГПИИЯ, 1980), стр. 25.

9. The author is grateful to Hans Kurr and James Karambelas of the United Nations for many of these suggestions.

10. Стрелкова, *Ключи*, 27.

11. *Ibid.,* стр. 26.

12. Much of the material in this section on proverbs was published by the author as a letter to the editor, *No Uncertain Terms,* FBIS, vol. 4, No. 1 (1989), 53-54

13. S.S. Kuzmin, *Translating Russian Idioms* (Moscow: Higher School, 1977), p. 227.

14. Корней Чуковский, *Высокое искусство* (Москва: Советский писатель, 1988), стр. 110-111.

15. *Ibid.,* стр. 110.

Chapter XII

1. O. Krylova and S. Khavronina, *Word Order in Russian* (Moscow: Russky Yazyk, 1988), p. 151.

2. See Е.А. Брызгунова, *Звуки и интонация русской речи,* изд. 3-е (Москва: Русский язык, 1977); И.Л. Муханов, *Интонация в русской диалогической речи,* изд. 2-е (Москва: Русский язык, 1987); Krylova and Khavronina, *Word Order in Russian;* Е.А. Земская, *Русская разговорная речь: лингвистический анализ и проблемы обучения.*

   While this so-called "Bryzgunova system" is not an exhaustive explanation of the entire range of Russian intonation, it provides a basic structure for analysis of intonational patterns.

   Many of the examples cited below are drawn from the above works.

3. Брызгунова, стр. 176.

4. Barik, *A Study of Simultaneous Interpretation,* Dissertation, *op.cit.,* p. 289.

5. W. Kaiser, quoted in Brian Harris, "Prolegomenon to a Study of the Differences Between Teaching Translation and Teaching Interpreting," *op. cit.,* p. 161.

6. E. Paneth, quoted in Harris, *Ibid.,* p. 161.

7. Walter Keiser, "Selection and Training of Conference Interpreters," in Gerver and Sinaiko, *Language Interpretation and Communication,* pp. 13-14.

8. Ю.М. Катцер, "К вопросу об основах методики обучения письменному переводу с русского языка на иностранный (английский) язык на переводческом факультете", *Вопросы теории и методики преподавания перевода. Тезисы Всесоюзной конференции 12-14 мая 1970 г., ч. II* (Москва, 1970), стр. 125.

9. See Henri Van Hoof, *Théorie et pratique de l'interprétation* (München: Max Hüber Verlag, 1962), p. 138.

10. Sergio Viaggio, "Teaching Interpretation to Beginners: Or, How Not to Scare Them to Death," *Languages at Crossroads: Proceedings of the 29th Annual Conference,* ATA, 1988, p. 401.

11. See Sylvie Lambert, "A Human Information Processing and Cognitive Approach to the Training of Simultaneous Interpreters," *Ibid.,* p. 383.

12. See М. Цвиллинг, "Кино на уроке перевода", *Тетради переводчика,* No. 9 (1972), стр. 110-113.

13. Viaggio, "Teaching Interpretation to Beginners," p. 401.

14. *Ibid.,* p. 401.

15. Terence, quoted by Cicero in *De Officiis,* I, 30.

Chapter XIII

1. Many of these terms are taken from accepted usage at the United Nations and from *Conference Terminology,* ed. Jean Herbert (Amsterdam-London-New York: Elsevier Publishing Company, 1962); Л.П. Ступин, А.Н. Лапицкий, *Научная конференция: Scientific Confer-*

ences, русско-английский разговорник (Москва: 1989); Gerhard Buntrock, Jean Bonnafous, Galina Kopylowa, *Konferenz-Sprache,* Deutsch, Englisch, Französisch, Russisch (Leipzig: VEB Verlag Enzyklopädie, 1989).

2. Many of the examples in this chapter are adapted from published United Nations documents.

Part II. Selected Practice Texts and Vocabulary

Escorting Delegations

1. Buntrock, Bonnafous, Kopylowa, *Konferenz-Sprache,* pp. 168-171. I have revised the English translations.

BIBLIOGRAPHY

Hundreds of library shelves are filled with dusty tomes on the theory of translation, translation of the classics, Biblical translation, etc. Works on interpretation are far fewer in number, and many of them, such as studies of the physiology of speech and the nervous system, are irrelevant to the student of interpretation. This highly selective listing includes those books and articles which have a practical slant and are of particular interest to Russian-language interpreters.

Many interesting articles and notes are contained in the journals *Babel, Language and Speech, L'interprète, Meta, and Тетради переводчика,* as well as in the US government FBIS publication *No Uncertain Terms.*

Extensive bibliographies are included in the works of Chernov, Shiriaev, Seleskovitch, and Lederer. See also the list of sources for specialized vocabulary and interpretation of conversational materials on p. 141.

Western Literature

Anderson, R. Bruce W. "Interpreter Roles and Interpretation Situations: Cross-cutting Typologies." *Language Interpretation and Communication.* Ed. D. Gerver and H. Wallace Sinaiko. New York and London: Plenum Press, 1978, pp. 217-30.

_____ . "Perspectives on the Role of Interpreter." *Translation: Application and Research.* Ed. Richard W. Brislin. New York: Gardner Press, 1976, pp. 208-28.

Andronikof, C. "Servitudes et grandeur de l'interprète." *Babel,* VIII, No. 1 (1962), 8-12.

Argenton, Elena. *The Translation of Culturebound Terms.* Trieste: Universita degli studi di Trieste, 1983.

Barik, Henri C. "A Description of Various Types of Omissions, Additions and Errors of Translation Encountered in Simultaneous Interpretation." *Meta,* 16 (1971), 119-28.

_____ . *A Study of Simultaneous Interpretation.* Diss. in Experimental Psychology. University of North Carolina at Chapel Hill, 1969.

_____ . "Interpreters Talk a Lot, among Other Things." *Babel,* XVIII, No. 1 (1972).

_____ . "Simultaneous Interpretation: Qualitative and Linguistic Data." *Language and Speech,* 18 (1975), 272-97.

_____ . "Simultaneous Interpretation: Temporal and Quantitative Data." *Language and Speech,* 16 (1973), 237-70.

Bausch, Karl Richard. *The Science of Translation: An Analytical Bibliography (1962-69)*. Tubingen: Beiträge zur Linguistik, 1970.

Belloc, Hillaire. *On Translation*. Oxford: Oxford University Press, 1931.

Bever T.G. "Perceptions, Thought and Language." *Language Comprehension and the Acquisition of Knowledge*. Ed. John B. Carroll and Roy O. Freedle. Washington, DC.: V.H. Winston and Sons, 1972, 99-112.

Brislin, Richard W., ed. *Translation: Application and Research*. New York: Gardner Press, 1976.

Brower, Reuben Arthur, ed. *On Translation*. New York: Oxford University Press, 1966.

Carroll, John B. and Freedle, Roy O., ed. *Language Comprehension and the Acquisition of Knowledge*. Washington D.C.: V.H. Winston and Sons, 1972.

Catford, J.C. *A Linguistic Theory of Translation*. Oxford: Oxford University Press, 1965.

Coughlin, Josette. "Interpreters' Training: Learning to Control the Bilingual Switch Mechanisms." *Babel*, XXXI, No. 1 (1985), 20-27.

Dejean-Le Féal, K. "Quelques aspects non linguistiques de l'interprétation et de la traduction." *Etudes de linguistique appliquée*, 12 (1973), 96-105.

Delisle, Jean, ed. *L'enseignement de l'interprétation et de la traduction*. Ottawa: University of Ottawa Press, 1981.

Doniger, Wendy O'Flaherty. "On Translating Sanscrit Myths." *The Translator's Art: Essays in Honor of Betty Radice*. Ed. William Radice and Barbara Reynolds. New York: Penguin, 1987, 121-28.

Ekvall, Robert F. *Faithful Echo*. New York: Twayne, 1960.

Fixman, Carol S. "The Foreign Language Needs of US-Based Corporations." Occasional Papers, NFLC at the Johns Hopkins University: Washington, 1989.

Fuller, Frederic. *The Translator's Handbook*. University Park: Pennsylvania University Press, 1984.

Garretson, Deborah A. "A Psychological Approach to Consecutive Interpretation." *Meta*, 26, No. 3 (1981), 244-254.

Gerver, D. "A Psychological Approach to Simultaneous Interpretation." *Meta*, 20, No. 2 (1975), 119-128.

_____ . "Empirical Studies of Simultaneous Interpretation: A Review and a Model." *Translation: Applications and Research*. Ed. R. Brislin, pp. 165-207.

_____ . "Simultaneous Listening and Speaking and Retention of Prose." *Quarterly Journal of Experimental Psychology*, 26 (1974), pp. 337-342.

_____ . "The Effects of Noise on the Performance of Simultaneous Interpreters: Accuracy of Performance." *Acta Psychologica*, 38 (1974), pp. 159-67.

_____ , Longley, P. E., Long, J., and Lambert, S.M. "Selecting Trainee Conference Interpreters: A Preliminary Study." *Journal of Occupational Psychology*, 57, No. 1 (1984), 17-31.

_____ , and Sinaiko, H. Wallace, ed. *Language Interpretation and Communication*. New York and London: Plenum Press, 1978.

Gile, Daniel. "Des difficultés de la transmission informationelle en interprétation simultanée." *Babel*, XXX, No. 1 (1984a), 18-25.

_____ . "Les termes techniques en interprétation simultanée." *Meta*, 30, No. 3 (1985), 200-09.

_____ . "L'interprétation de conférence et la connaissance des langues: quelques reflexions." *Meta*, 30, No. 4 (1985), 320-31.

203

Glenn, E.S. "Semantic Difficulties in International Communication." *The Use and Misuse of Language.* Ed. S.I. Hayakawa. Greenwich, Connecticut: Fawcett Publications, 1962, pp. 47-69.

Goldman-Eisler, F. "Segmentation of Input in Simultaneous Interpreting." *Journal of Psycholinguistic Research,* 1 (1972), 127-40.

_____ , and Cohen, M.V. "An Experimental Study of Interference between Receptive and Productive Processes Relating to Simultaneous Interpretation." *Language and Speech,* 17 (1974), pp. 1-10.

Grebenschikov, Vladimir. "La traduction en URSS." *Meta,* 12, No. 1 (1967), 3-8.

Hanna, George H. and Katzer, Julius M. "The Translation of Russian." *МГПИИЯ им. М. Тореза: Конференция по вопросам методики преподавания перевода 24-27 ноября 1974 г. Тезисы докладов* (Москва: МГПИИЯ, 1964), стр. 59-60.

Harris, Brian. "Prolegomenon to a Study of the Differences between Teaching Translation and Teaching Interpreting." *L'enseignement de l'interprétation et de la traduction.* Ed. J. Delisle, pp. 155-162.

Hendrickx, P. "Enseignement de l'interprétation simultanée." *Babel,* XV, No. 4 (1969).

_____ . "Reflexions sur l'interprétation." *Meta,* 14, No. 2 (1969).

_____ . *Simultaneous Interpreting: A Practice Book.* London: 1971.

Hendry, J.F. *Your Future in Translating and Interpreting.* New York: Richard Rosen Press, 1969.

Herbert, Jean, ed. *Conference Terminology.* 2nd ed., rev. Amsterdam: Elsevier Publishing Company, 1962.

_____ . "How Conference Interpretation Grew." *Language Interpretation and Communication.* Gerver and Sinaiko, pp. 5-10.

_____ . *The Interpreter's Handbook.* Geneva: Georg, 1952. 2nd ed. Geneva: Librairie de l'Université, 1968.

Ismailov, A. Ed. *Translation: Theory and Practice.* Tashkent: Ukituvchi, 1989.

Jakobson, R. "On Linguistic Aspects of Translation." *On Translation.* Ed. R. Brower, pp. 232-39.

Keiser, Walter. "Selection and Training of Conference Interpreters." *Language Interpretation and Communication.* Gerver and Sinaiko, pp. 11-24.

Kopczynski, Andrzej. *Conference Interpreting: some linguistic and communications problems.* Poznan: UAM, 1980.

Korchilov, Igor. *Translating History: Thirty Years on the Front Lines of Diplomacy with a Russian Interpreter.* New York: Scribner, 1997.

Kuzmin, S. *Translating Russian Idioms.* Moscow: Higher School, 1977.

Krylova, O., and Khavronina, S. *Word Order in Russian Sentences.* Moscow: Russian Language Publishers, 1976. 2nd ed., rev. Moscow: Russky Yazyk, 1988.

Lambert, Richard D. "The National Foreign Language System." Occasional Papers. NFLC at the Johns Hopkins University: Washington, 1989.

Languages at Crossroads. Proceedings of the 29th Annual Conference, American Translators Association, Seattle, Washington, October 12-16, 1988. Medford, New Jersey: Learned Information, Inc., 1988.

Lawson, E.A. "Attention and Simultaneous Translation." *Language and Speech,* 10 (1967), 29-35.

Lederer, Marianne. *La traduction simultanée: Fondements théoriques.* Diss. Université de Lille III, 1978. Lille: Services de reproduction des thèses, 1980.

———— . *La traduction simultanée. Expérience et théorie.* Paris: Lettres Modernes/Minard, 1981.

———— . "La traduction: transcoder ou réexprimer." *Etudes de linguistique appliquée,* 12 (1973), pp. 8-26.

———— . "Simultaneous Interpretation—Units of Meaning and other Features." *Language Interpretation and Communication.* Gerver and Sinaiko, pp. 323-32.

Lee, Irving J. "Why Discussions Go Astray." *The Use and Misuse of Language.* Ed. S.I. Hayakawa. Greenwich, Connecticut: Fawcett Publications, 1962, pp. 29-40.

Leontiev, A.A. "Some Problems in Learning Russian as a Foreign Language." *Soviet Psychology,* 11 (1973), pp. 1-117.

Longley, P. *Conference Interpreting.* London: Putnam, 1968.

———— . "An Integrated Programme for Training Interpreters." *Language Interpretation and Communication.* Gerver and Sinaiko, pp. 45-56.

Lubensky, Sophia. *Russian-English Dictionary of Idioms.* New York: Random House, 1995.

Marder, Stephen. *A Supplementary Russian-English Dictionary.* Columbus: Ohio, Slavica Publishers, 1992.

Miller, George A. "The Magic Number 7 Plus or Minus 2: some limits on our capacity for processing information." *Psychological Review,* 63, No. 2 (1956), pp. 81-97.

Nilski, Therese. "Translators and Interpreters—Siblings or a Breed Apart?" *Meta,* 12, No. 2 (1967), 45-49.

Palazhchenko, Pavel. *My Years with Gorbachev and Shevardnadze.* University Park, Pennsylvania: Pennsylvania State University Press, 1997.

Pinhas, R. "Les retombées scientifiques des opérations Apollo sur l'interprétation simultanée." *La linguistique,* 8, No. 1 (1972).

Sannikov, N.G. *Conference Terminology.* Moscow: Ostozh'e, 1996.

Schupbach, Richard. "On Technical Russian and the Teaching Thereof." *SEEJ,* 32, No. 3 (1988). 445-60.

Scientific Conference on Interpreting and Intercultural Barriers to Communication: Washington, 1956.

Seleskovitch D. *Colloque sur l'enseignement de l'interprétation.* Paris, 1965.

———— . "Interpretation, a Psychological Approach." *Translation: Applications and Research.* Ed. R.W. Brislin, 92-116.

———— . *Langage, langues et mémoire.* Paris: Lettres Modernes/Minard, 1975.

———— . "Language and Cognition." *Language Interpretation and Communication.* Gerver and Sinaiko, 343-52.

———— . *L'interprète dans les conférences internationales. Problèmes de langage et de communication.* Paris: Lettres Modernes/Minard, 1968.

———— . "Vision du monde et traduction." *Etudes de linguistique appliquée,* 12 (1973), 106-10.

Snelling, Daniel Clyde. *Interpretation: Theory vs. Practice.* Monograph No. 16. Trieste: Scuola superiore di lingue moderne per interpreti e traddutori, 1983.

205

Schmidt, Paul. *Hitler's Interpreter.* New York: Macmillan, 1951.

Steiner, George. *After Babel: Aspects of Language and Translation.* London and New York: Oxford University Press, 1975.

Tedlock, Dennis. *The Spoken Word and the Word of Interpretation.* Philadelphia: University of Pennsylvania Press, 1983.

Treisman, A. "The effects of redundancy and familiarity on translating and repeating back in a foreign and native language." *British Journal of Psychology,* vol. 56 (1965), 369-79.

Van Hoof, Henri. *Théorie et pratique de l'interprétation; avec application particulière à l'anglais et au français.* München: Max Hüber, 1962.

Visson, Lynn. *From Russian Into English: An Introduction to Simultaneous Interpretation.* Ann Arbor, Michigan: Ardis, 1991.

_____ . "Getting the Message Across: The Simultaneous Interpreter." *Spacebridges: Television and US-Soviet Dialogue.* Ed. Michael Brainerd. London and New York: Citizens Exchange Council and University Press of America, 1989, pp. 72-80.

_____ . "Interpreter Training: The Stepchild of Language Teaching." Ed. Kurt E. Miller. Papers of the Center for Research and Documentation on World Language Problems. Lanham, Maryland: University Press of America, 1996, pp. 91-96.

_____ . "Syntactical Problems for the Russian-English Interpreter." *No Uncertain Terms,* FBIS, vol. 4, No. 2, 1989, 2-8.

_____ . "The Interpretation of Politics: Some Problems in Russian-English Interpretation." *New Studies in Russian Language and Literature.* Ed. Anna Lisa Crone and Catherine V. Chvany. Columbus, Ohio: Slavica, 1987, pp. 271-278.

_____ . "The Interpretation of Politics: Some Problems in Russian-English Simultaneous Interpretation." *Russian Language Journal,* XL, No. 135 (1986), 195-202.

_____ . "The Perestroika of the Russian Language: From Marx to Marketing." *Language Studies in the Post-Cold-War Era,* Ed. Kurt E. Miller. Papers of the Center for Research and Documentation on World Language Problems. Lanham, Maryland: University Press of America, 1996, pp. 49-58.

Weintraub, E., Lederer, M., de Clarens, J. "Enseigner l'interprétation." *Etudes de linguistique appliquée,* 12 (1973), pp. 111-126.

Wills, Wolfram. "Syntactic Anticipation in German-English Simultaneous Interpreting." *Language Interpretation and Communication.* Gerver and Sinaiko, pp. 343-52.

Works in Russian

Акуленко В.В.. *Англо-русский и русско-английский словарь "ложных друзей переводчика".* Москва: Советская энциклопедия, 1969.

Американа. Англо-русский лингвострановедческий словарь. Под. ред. Г.В. Чернова. Москва: «Полиграмма», 1996.

Бархударов Л.С. *Язык и перевод.* Международные отношения, 1975.

Бенедиктов Б.А. "Основные вопросы психологии устного перевода". *Fremdsprachen,* 2 (1968), стр. 96-105.

Бережков, Валентин. *Как я стал переводчиком Сталина.* Москва: «ДЭМ», 1993.

Брызгунова Е.А. *Звуки и интонация русской речи,* Изд. 3-е. Москва: Русский язык, 1977.

Влахов С.И. *Непереводимое в переводе*. Москва: Международные отношения, 1980.

Воеводина Т.В. "Устный перевод в коммуникативном аспекте и его соотношение с другими видами перевода". *Тетради переводчика*, No. 20 (1983), стр. 66-77.

Вопросы теории и методики учебного перевода. Сборник статей под. ред. К.А. Ганшиной и И.В. Карпова. Москва: Изд. Академии педагогических наук РСФСР, 1950,

Гофман Е.А. "К истории синхронного перевода". *Тетради переводчика*, No. 1 (1963), стр. 20-26.

Денисенко Ю.А. "К проблеме функциональных (переиодических) соответствий в английском языке некоторым типам русских конструкций". Дисс. на соискание степени канд. фил. наук. Москва: МГПИИЯ, 1964.

_____ . "О некоторых приемах 'обусловленной' компрессии при переводе с русского языка на английский (на материалах периодической печати)". В книге *Теория перевода и научные основы подготовки переводчиков*. Материалы всесоюзной научной конференции. ч. I, Москва, МГПИИЯ им. М. Тореза, 1975.

Дубровин М.И. *Русские фразеологизмы в картинках*. Москва: Русский язык, 1977.

Егорова А.М. *Теория и практика перевода экономических текстов с английского языка на русский*. Москва: Международные отношения, 1974.

Ермолович Д.И. *Основы профессионального перевода*. Москва: "ROU," 1996.

Земская Е.А. *Русская разговорная речь. Лингвистический анализ и проблемы обучения*. Москва: Русский язык, 1987.

Зимняя И.А., Чернов Г.В. "Вероятностное прогнозирование в процессе синхронного перевода". *Предварительные материалы экспериментальных исследований по психолингвистике*. Москва, 1973, стр. 110-116.

_____ . "К вопросу о роли вероятностного прогнозирования в процессе синхронного перевода". В сб. *Вопросы теории и методики преподавания перевода. Тезисы Всесоюзной конференции 12-14 мая 1970 г., ч. I*. Москва: МГПИИЯ им. Морис Тореза, 1970, стр. 111-113.

Иванов А.О. *Английская безэквивалентная лексика и ее перевод на русский язык*. Ленинград, 1985.

Катцер Ю.М. "К вопросу об основах методики обучения письменному переводу с русского языка на иностранный (английский) язык на переводческом факультете". В сб. *Вопросы теории и методики преподавания перевода. Тезисы Всесоюзной конференции 12-14 мая 1970 г., ч. 1*. Москва, 1970, стр. 122-127.

_____ , Кунин, А.В. *Письменный перевод с русского языка на английский*. Москва: Высшая школа, 1964.

Климзо В.Н. "О переводе некоторых отрицательных конструкций на английский язык". *Тетради переводчика*, No. 23 (1989), стр. 92-102.

Ковтунова И.И. *Современный русский язык: порядок слов и актуальное членение предложения*. Москва: Просвещение, 1976.

Комиссаров В.Н. *Лингвистика перевода*. Москва: Международные отношения, 1980.

_____ , *Слово о переводе*. Москва: Международные отношения, 1973.

_____ , "Советское переводоведение на новом этапе". *Тетради переводчика*, No. 23 (1989), стр. 3-14.

_____ , Рецкер Я.И., Тархов В.И. *Пособие по переводу с английского языка на русский*. ч. I. Москва: Издательство литературы на иностранных языках, 1960. ч. II. Москва: Высшая школа, 1965.

Коммуникация и обучение иностранным языкам. Москва: Высшая школа, 1970.

Кунин А.В. "Перевод устойчивых образных совосочетаний и пословиц с русского языка на английский". *Иностранные языки в школе,* No. 5 (1960), стр. 129-33.

Лариохина Н.М. *Вопросы синтаксиса научного стиля речи.* Москва: Русский язык, 1979.

Левицкая Т.Р., Фитерман А.М. "Виды работы по переводу с английского языка на русский". *Вопросы теории и методики преподавания перевода.* Методический сборник, ч. I. Москва: Переводческий факультет МГПИИЯ, 1969.

_____ , _____. "О некоторых способах выражения эмфазы в английском языке". *Тетради переводчика,* No. 9 (1972), стр. 34-35.

_____ , _____. *Проблемы перевода на материале современного английского языка.* Москва: Международные отношения, 1976.

Ломб Като. *Как я изучаю языки.* Москва: Прогресс, 1978.

Луканин С.А. "О механизме обработки синтаксической информации при синхронном переводе". *Тетради переводчика,* No. 11 (1974), стр. 87-91.

Мешков О. "Об одном типе переводческих соответствий". *Тетради переводчика,* No. 9 (1972), стр. 46-50.

Микулин Г.Т. "Заметки о калькировании с русского языка на английский". *Тетради переводчика,* No. 15 (1978), стр. 59-64.

Миньяр-Белоручев Р.К. *Как стать переводчиком.* Москва: Стелла, 1994.

_____ . *Методика обучения переводу на слух.* Москва: Международные отношения, 1959.

_____ . *Общая теория перевода и устный перевод.* Москва: Воениздат, 1980.

_____ . *Последовательный перевод.* Москва: Воениздат, 1969.

_____ . *Пособие по устному переводу.* Москва: Высшая школа, 1969.

Мосьяков А.Е. "Использование фразеологии в устном переводе". *Вопросы теории перевода. Сборник научных трудов.* МГПИИЯ, вып. 127. Москва: Министерство высшего и среднего специального образования, 1978, стр. 133-136.

_____ . "О роли штампов в синхронном переводе". *Тетради переводчика,* No. 21 (1987), стр. 74-79.

Муханов И. Л. *Интонация в русской диалогической речи.* Москва: Русский язык, 1987.

Нечаев Л.Г. "К проблеме вариантности актуального членения при переводе". *Тетради переводчика,* No. 23 (1989), стр. 49-56.

Пазенко Г., Решетилов В. "Способы передачи русских односоставных предложений на английском языке." *Тетради переводчика,* No. 3 (1966), стр 77-81.

Палажченко П.Р. *Все познается в сравнении, или несистематический словарь трудностей, тонкостей и премудростей английского языка в сопоставлении с русским.* Москва: Валент, 1999.

_____ . "О предварительной обработке текста синхронным переводчиком". *Тетради переводчика,* No. 18 (1981), стр. 89-97.

Перевод как лингвистическая проблема. Сборник статей. Москва: МГУ, 1962.

Перевод – средство взаимного сближения народов. Москва: Прогресс, 1987.

Попова Е.К. *Техника перевода с английского языка на русский.* Ленинград: ЛГУ, 1959.

Проблемы обучения переводу английского языка. Сборник научных трудов, МГПИИЯ вып. 203. Москва: Наука, 1982.

Пумпянский А.Л. *Пособие по переводу научной и технической литературы на английский язык.* Москва: Наука, 1965.

Пьянкова Т.М. *Пособие по переводу русских полиэквивалентных терминов на английский язык.* Москва: Высшая школа, 1973.

Пядусова Г.И. *Пособие по переводу для лиц, говорящих на английском языке.* Москва: Русский язык, 1988.

Пятецкая С. *Давайте познакомимся с русскими газетами.* Москва: Русский язык, 1974.

Рецкер Я.И. *Теория перевода и переводческая практика.* Москва: Международные отношения, 1974.

Садиков А.В. "Перевод как вид социального поведения". *Тетради переводчика,* No. 18 (1981), стр. 3-12.

Сейдова Т.Г. "Выбор эквивалентов семантически неполных атрибутивных словосочетаний при переводе с английского языка на русский". *Тетради переводчика* No. 11 (1974), стр. 59-66.

Сладковская В.Н. "Прогнозирование на уровне цели высказывания". *Тетради переводчика* No. 8 (1971), стр. 61-64.

Стрелкова Н.С. *Ключи для пособия по практической стилистике и стилическому редактированию переводов.* Москва: МГПИИЯ, 1980.

_____ . *Практическая стилистика английского языка и стилистическое редактирование переводов,* ч. 3. Москва: МГПИИЯ, 1982.

_____ . *Учебное пособие по практической стилистике английского языка и стилистическому редактированию перевода.* Москва: МГПИИЯ, 1984.

Теория перевода и научные основы подготовки переводчиков. Материалы научной конференции. ч. I. Москва: МГПИИЯ, 1975.

Уваров В.Д. "О трех направлениях в переводческих исследованиях". *Тетради переводчика,* No. 15 (1978).

_____ . "Парадоксы ролевого поведения участников ситуации перевода". *Тетради переводчика,* No. 18 (1981), стр. 13-15.

Учебно-методологические разработки к курсу теории перевода. Москва: МГПИИЯ им. Тореза, 1972.

Федоров А.В. *Введеие в теорию перевода.* Москва: Изд. лит. на иностранных языках, 1953.

Федоров А.Ф. *Основы общей теории перевода.* Москва: 1983.

Филиппов Е.Н. "Опыт составления лабораторных работ по устному переводу". *Учебно-методические разработки к курсу теории перевода.* Москва: МГПИИЯ, 1972.

Цвиллинг М.Я. "Кино на уроке перевода". *Тетради переводчика,* No. 9 (1972), стр. 109-114.

Чебурашкин Н.Д. *Технический перевод в школе.* Под редакцией Б.Е. Белицкого. Изд. 4-е. Москва: Просвещение, 1983.

Чернов Г.В. "Вопросы перевода русской безэквивалентной лексики ("советских реалий") на английский язык на материалов переводов советской публицистики". Дисс. на соисикание ученой степени кандидата фил. наук. Москва: МГПИИЯ им. М. Тореза, 1958.

_____ . "Еще раз о схеме организации синхронного перевода". *Тетради переводчика*, No. 14 (1977).

_____ . "Коммуникативная ситуация синхронного перевода и избыточность." *Тетради переводчика*, No. 12 (1975).

_____ . "Многоуровневая структура вероятностного прогнозирования в синхронном переводе". *Учебно-методические разработки к курсу теории перевода.* Москва: МГПИИЯ, 1972, стр. 146-157.

_____ . *Основы синхроного перевода.* Москва: Высшая школа, 1987.

_____ . "Синхронный перевод: речевая компрессия – лингвистическая проблема." *Тетради переводчика*, No. 6 (1969).

_____ . *Теория и практика синхронного перевода.* Москва: Международные отношения, 1978.

Черняховская Л.А. "Некоторые особенности передачи сказуемого при переводе с русского языка на английский". *Тетради переводчика*, No. 10 (1973), стр. 37-40.

_____ . *Перевод и смысловая структура.* Москва: Международные отношения, 1976.

_____ . "Перестройка речевой структуры для передачи компонентов смыслового членения высказывания при переводе с русского языка на английский". Автореферат канд. дисс. Москва: МГПИИЯ им. М. Тореза, 1971.

_____ . "Смысловая структура текста и ее единицы". *Вопросы языкознания* (1983), стр. 117-126.

Чолганская В.Л. *Краткий международный терминологический справочник.* Москва: Наука, 1981.

Чуковский К.И. *Высокое искусство.* Москва: Советский писатель, 1988.

Чужакин, А. *Мир перевода -2. Practicum.* Москва: «Валент», 1997.

_____ . *Мир перевода-3. Practicum plus World of Interpreting and Translation.* Москва: Валент, 1999.

_____ , Палажченко, П. *Мир перевода, или Вечный поиск взаимопонимания.* Москва: «Валент», 1997.

Шанский Н.М., Быстрова Е.А. *700 фразеологических оборотов русского языка.* Москва: Русский язык, 1980.

Швейцер А.Д. *Глазами переводчика.* Москва: "Стелла", 1996.

_____ . "К вопросу об анализе грамматических явлений при переводе". *Тетради переводчика*, No. 1 (1963), стр. 4-12.

_____ . "К вопросу о наиболее рациональной схеме синхронного перевода". *Тетради переводчика*, No. 4 (1967), стр. 82-85.

_____ . "К проблеме лингвистического изучения процесса перевода". *Вопросы языкознания*, No. 4 (1970).

_____ . *Перевод и лингвистика.* Москва: Воениздат, 1973.

_____ . "Социологические основы теории перевода". *Вопросы языкознания*, No. 5 (1985), стр. 15-24.

_____ . *Теория перевода. Статус/проблемы/аспекты.* Москва: Наука, 1988.

Ширяев А.Ф. "О некоторых лингвистических особенностях функциональной системы синхронного перевода". *Тетради переводчика*, No. 19 (1982), стр. 73-85.

_____ . *Синхронность синхронного перевода*. ВИИЯ, Труды института иностранных языков, No. 7, Москва, 1971.

_____ . *Синхронный перевод*. Москва: Воениздат, 1979.

Шмаков С.А. "Язык советских газет глазами англичан (По поводу учебного пособия Р. Генри и К. Янг)". *Тетради переводчика*, No. 23 (1989), стр. 169-174.

Booth Behavior

by Margaret Bowen et al.
(*The Jerome Quarterly*, Vol. 12, Issue 3, p. 11)

The transition from the classroom to a real conference setting, surrounded by experienced colleagues, is seldom easy. In any competitive profession, the newcomer may be regarded with a certain amount of suspicion. In turn, he or she may be intimidated working with the great figures of the profession and in turn overcompensate with brash behavior. To help new interpreters get off on the right foot, we are listing below a few DO's and DON'Ts.

DO be at the meeting well before it is scheduled to start—at a very minimum, fifteen minutes before the time specified in your contract. If you do not know the building well, give yourself extra time to get lost.

DO find out where the nearest restroom is before the meeting starts.

DO introduce yourself to the team leader and indicate your language combinations. Also introduce yourself to the other interpreters and to the technician, as well as to any assistant in charge of the documents.

DON'T volunteer to interpret from all languages you can say "good day" in—just your working languages. DON'T let anyone persuade or browbeat you into working from or into a language that is "practically the same as..." (fill in a language you have).

DON'T pull in with your entire collection of dictionaries.

DON'T go around shaking hands with every delegate in sight. You are there to interpret, not to play the ambassador of good will.

DO come prepared. Presumably you will have received some documents beforehand. Pay attention to names and titles. Some meetings have a "chair," some have a "president."

DO have a list of pertinent terminology, culled from documents you have received, from previous meetings, from the Internet, etc.

DON'T fight over who sits where. Some people have strong preferences— the right side of the booth, near the door, or whatever. This may be simply a matter of habit, or handedness, or marking one's territory. Avoid getting set in your ways yourself and let those who have get their way.

DO make sure that you have a glass of water in the booth. Avoid ice, since it clinks terribly over the microphone. Voice coaches stress that frequent sips of water are good for your voice, while frequent throat clearings or coughs should be avoided.

DON'T engage in enthusiastic greetings or exchanges of news behind the booths or in the coffee bar. The noise can be disturbing and you may miss the beginning of your meeting.

DO determine in good time who will start. The sound of the chairperson's gavel signaling the beginning of the meeting is not the time to do an "after you, cher Gaston" enactment. Normally, the senior interpreter will start. Two beginners should not share a booth.

DON'T take seemingly simple things for granted.

DO have a note pad and pencil handy to jot down figures, names, and interesting expressions. Your colleagues may find your jottings helpful, too, but not if they are illegible.

DON'T work until you are out of breath and your boothmate has to take over in the middle of a sentence. Turn-taking should be so smooth that the audience hardly notices it.

DO stay in the booth as much as possible the first day. Although you and your boothmate will probably take turns every half-hour or, if 20 to 30 minute papers are read, will read alternate speeches, you want to get a feeling for the direction the meeting is taking by following the proceedings for most of the day. You can also learn a great deal from listening to your colleague [or from colleagues in the other booths - LV], especially if that colleague has worked for the same organization before.